Cambridge Studies in Social Anthropology

GENERAL EDITOR: JACK GOODY

31

PATRONS AND PARTISANS

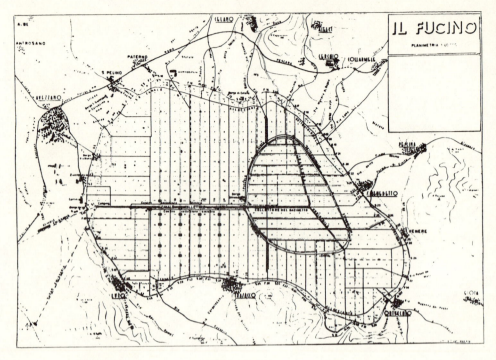

Il Fucino
(Ufficio Trasformazione Fondiaria)

Patrons and partisans

A STUDY OF POLITICS IN TWO
SOUTHERN ITALIAN *COMUNI*

CAROLINE WHITE
Research Fellow
University of Kent, Canterbury

CAMBRIDGE UNIVERSITY PRESS

Cambridge
London   New York   New Rochelle
Melbourne   Sydney

Published by the Press Syndicate of the University of Cambridge
The Pitt Building, Trumpington Street, Cambridge CB2 1RP
32 East 57th Street, New York, NY 10022, USA
296 Beaconsfield Parade, Middle Park, Melbourne 3206, Australia

First published 1980

Printed in Great Britain at the University Press, Cambridge

Library of Congress Cataloguing in Publication Data
White, Caroline, 1941–
Patrons and partisans.
(Cambridge studies in social anthropology; 31)
Bibliography: p.
Includes index.
1. Local government – Italy – Case studies.
2. Villages – Italy – Case studies. I. Title.
JS5727.W48   320.9′45   79-53406
ISBN 0 521 22872 7

*For a list of the titles
in the series see page 196*

For Simon and Kate

CONTENTS

ILLUSTRATIONS

TABLES

ACKNOWLEDGEMENTS

Beginning, as it did, as a doctoral thesis, this book bears the imprint of many encouraging hands. I would like to offer my thanks especially to: Robert Wade, who aroused my interest in Social Anthropology and urged me to resume academic work; Ann Whitehead who, in her meticulous supervision of the writing, passed on her belief that women, in particular, should always aim high; Paul Littlewood, Lucy Mair and Paul Stirling, whose constructive criticism aided the transition from thesis to book; Kay Cooper, who brought perceptiveness as well as accuracy to the typing of the manuscript; my father, who has gone well beyond the call of parental duty in compiling the index; the late Irlanda Franceschini, who, like a true *luchese*, cared for me and protected my reputation although our politics differed; Jan Beattie, Fiorella Carra, Anna Ciliberti, Sean Conlin, Stefan Heiner, John Mepham, David Moss, Desmond Ryan, Amalia Signorelli, Paola Splendore, Dennis Woodman, Stephen Yeo, and all the people of Luco and Trasacco who were unstinting in their inspiration and hospitality. Finally, there is hardly a sentence which has not benefited from discussion and argument with David Youlton. His rigour, clarity of thought and kindness have supported me when the task seemed unending. For any faults that have slipped through this close-knit web I take full responsibility.

Caroline White

x

ABBREVIATIONS

Acli   Associazione Cattolica Lavoratori Italiani (left-wing Dc leisure organisation)

Anb   Associazione Nazionale Bieticoltori (Christian Democrat beet growers' association)

Cbf   Coltivatori di Bietola Federati (Socialist/Communist beet growers' association)

Cgil   Confederazione Generale Italiana del Lavoro (Federation of Italian Trade Unions with affiliations to communist and socialist parties)

Cisl   Confederazione Italiana Sindacati Lavoratori (Confederation of Italian Trade Unions with affiliations to the Christian Democrat Party)

Dc   Democrazia Cristiana (Christian Democrat Party)

Fgci   Federazione Giovani Comunisti Italiani (Communist Youth)

Ind   Independent

Msi   Movimento Sociale Italiano (Neo-Fascist Party)

Pci   Partito Comunista Italiano (Communist Party)

Pli   Partito Liberale Italiano (Italian Liberal Party)

Pri   Partito Repubblicano Italiano (Republican Party)

Psi   Partito Socialista Italiano (Socialist Party)

Psdi   Partito Socialista Democratico Italiano (Social Democrat Party)

Psiup   Partito Socialista Italiano di Unità Proletaria (Socialist Party of Proletarian Unity)

Spiga   'Wheatsheaf' (Independent)

Udi   Unione Donne Italiane (Communist Women)

Uil   Unione Italiana dei Lavoratori (Trade union federation affiliated to Psdi)

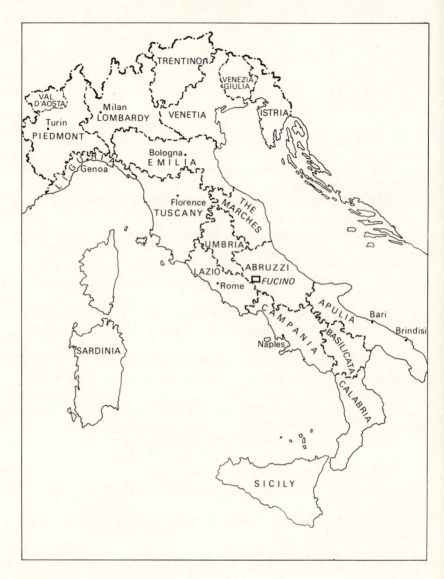

Map 1   Italy, with regional boundaries

1 Introduction

The word peasant is synonymous with land. The peasant derives his livelihood from the land which he cultivates. But he is often dependent on others for access to it or for the capital to make it produce. This book traces the evolution of the relationship between peasants of two neighbouring villages in Southern Italy and their access to the means of subsistence. The central argument is that the evolutionary path of this relationship crucially influences the way that peasants confront the world. Traces of past struggles to maintain or transform their access to basic resources are reflected in political consciousness and practice.

The two villages of Luco and Trasacco form part of a distinctive area of the central Apennines which is known as the Fucino basin. Its distinctiveness derives from the fact that, as the basin of a drained lake, its soil is particularly fertile, and that, until 1951, it was the largest privately-owned estate in the Abruzzo. In 1951 the Fucino basin was included in a land reform programme which expropriated some large estates and distributed the land to owner-cultivators.

I began the research on which the book is based with the following questions: What happens to the political activities and ideas of peasants when they are transformed from tenants or landless labourers into smallholders? Does it make any difference if the land reform was enacted as a result of peasant struggle? If there has been a struggle, does this experience create a propensity amongst peasants to take collective action in support of subsequent demands? Or do they settle down as supporters of the *status quo*? To what extent are peasant interests represented by trade unions and political parties?

It is widely accepted that land reforms, even those wrenched from resistant landowners and unwilling governments, 'deradicalise' the peasants who have struggled for them. Those radical parties around which opposition had coalesced cease to have their former appeal, and peasant membership declines. Governments as well as academics have become convinced of this tendency: United States policy in Latin America is now to encourage governments to introduce land reform programmes in the hope of reducing support for radical movements. In the Italian case land reform was forced on the government by widespread peasant unrest, backed by the organisational support of the Communist Party. However, the government was resistant to the more radical demands for collectivised farms. Individual land-holding held out some hope of reducing militancy. Collective ownership, on the other hand, threatened to institutionalise it.

It has been argued that after the reform of selected estates was complete, the traditional Southern Italian patterns of political organisation — clientelism and personalism — re-emerged as the dominant modes of recruiting political support, not only in the Christian Democrat Party (Dc), but in the Communist Party (Pci) as well.

The Communist Party of Italy has a proud history of struggle and has produced some theoreticians of international repute. Most notable of these was Antonio Gramsci (1890–1937). His overriding preoccupation was to articulate a vision of revolutionary transformation that took into account the specific history of Italy. For him the only force that could transform Italian society in a revolutionary way was a political alliance between the Northern working class and the Southern peasantry. Although it may be true that the Pci is characterised by internal tensions, I was not convinced that Gramsci's line could have been so subverted as to have permitted the party to abandon the rural areas of the South to the reactionary forces of clientelism.

The main reason why I chose to study peasant politics in Fucino rather than in some other land reform area, was that Silone's book *Fontamara* had first aroused my interest in the predicament of Italian peasants. The story tells how the peasants of Fontamara, a fictitious village in Fucino, are duped by the local bigwig, Don Carlo Magna, who claims to be the 'people's friend'. When the authorities threaten to divert the peasants' irrigation water, he offers to intercede, as he always has done. Instead he makes sure that the stream is diverted onto his own land. In the resulting uprising the peasants' leaders are killed and dispersed, and the revolt is crushed. It gives dramatic emphasis to the powerlessness of the peasants, who struggle for their living at the bottom of a hierarchy of armed guards, politicians, Prince Torlonia, the fascist government and the Pope. Their attempt to stand up for their rights is doomed to failure in the absence of outside help.

Under the guise of fiction, Silone gives a remarkably accurate picture of the ruthless exploitation of Torlonia's dominion over Fucino. A hundred years after its inception the Torlonia regime was finally brought to an end by protracted unrest between 1943 and 1950. The final assault was led by peasants and trade unions supported by the Communist Party. Fucino was expropriated in 1951 and distributed in smallholdings to the tenant-cultivators. In the early 'fifties all eleven *comuni* of Fucino had communist administrations; by 1973 all but Lecce and Luco had swung to the Dc at some time in the intervening period. Only a handful of *leccesi* own any land in Fucino, so the land reform had had little impact for them. It was a village with a communist majority that I was looking for, on the assumption that it was more likely to be different from what had been described as typical Southern villages — in short, that it would be less prone to clientelistic forms. For this reason I chose to start the research in Luco and moved to Trasacco nine months later, for reasons which I discuss below.

For anthropologists the efficacy of participant-observation as a research technique has been established by generations of ethnographers. But I had serious reservations about the premises of many of the monographs I had read. Participant-observation is a powerful tool for uncovering the pattern of social relations, and its particular value lies in the access it can give to the meanings that people attach to those relations. However, the very power of this lens has often immobilised researchers: their focus remains fixed on one small locality and their vision fails to adjust to the wider context in which it is set. To avoid this, I determined to do a comparative study, but it was some time before I decided to go to a second village in the same area rather than elsewhere.

The second problem that I had with much of the literature was that many anthropologists seemed themselves to have become enmeshed in their informants' construction of reality. For example, incidental and allusory evidence in the monographs suggests that most Mediterranean villages are highly stratified, but the authors have a tendency to accept statements that 'we are all equal here' as objectively true. Social constructions of reality are only interesting to the extent that one can measure the angle of distortion, yet many anthropologists have failed to portray the objective reality. A comprehensive breakdown of income and property distribution is a prerequisite for a good study, and I spent some time constructing this.

Two important decisions about the direction of my fieldwork led me to an expanded understanding of social relations in Luco and Trasacco, and these decisions could only have developed out of employing the techniques of participant-observation. Listening to *luchesi* talking about themselves I became aware that they kept measuring their political morality and economic judgement against those of the people of Trasacco, a village seven kilometres away, and explained their own actions and beliefs in terms of their individual and collective experiences of the past. Despite the scepticism of colleagues who assured me that what the *luchesi* said about the *trasaccani* was typical of inter-village rivalry, I decided to find out what Trasacco was like for myself. The choice had other advantages: by doing a study in the same geographic area, some of the variables were held constant. Dialect, courtship and marriage customs, the mode of implementation of the land reform, the size of holdings at the time of the land reform, land fertility and access to services, irrigation, main centres and industries could all be ruled out as explanations for any political differences between the two villages.

3

Introductory

The question with which the research started concerned the relations of smallholders to political parties in the wake of land reform. The decision to conduct fieldwork in Trasacco led inevitably to a change in focus to the question of how strikingly different forms of political participation and their associated moralities can emerge and survive within a limited geographic space.

The familiar image of peeling an onion to its heart fits the process by which the argument unfolded over the fieldwork period. My earliest assumption was that the form of political participation in villages with a Pci electoral majority would differ from that where the Dc were in control. This assumption was destroyed by the evidence of Lecce which, despite having consistently elected a Pci local administration, was dominated by a 'patron' who used clientelistic methods to gain support for the Pci and electoral office for himself. Election results could not therefore explain or even act as a reliable indicator of different forms of political practice and consciousness.

In explaining their political allegiances, *luchesi* referred back to the struggles leading up to the land reform relating their involvement to their experiences of the Torlonia regime. But records of that period, whilst confirming what *luchesi* said about their differential involvement as individuals in those struggles, could not explain contemporary differences between Luco and Trasacco. At the experiential level the dramatic events that led to the defeat of Torlonia and the land reform dominated the memory of all Fucino villages, but it found particular and unique expression in Luco. The puzzle remained. It was in the archives of Luco, L'Aquila, Naples and Rome that the residue of earlier changes that had been imposed on the recalcitrant population of Luco survived. Trasacco had no such history reaching back beyond the present generation. Luco's unique past provided the final explanation for their self-reliant and collective rejection of clientelism.

In all societies resources and the power to control them are unequally distributed. Power underlies the relations between classes in ways that are sometimes visible and often measurable. But, more commonly, power which is institutionalised can prevent conflicts of interest from becoming political issues, or even being conceived as conflictual at all. Much of the conflict latent in the unequal distribution of resources is defused by those in power and allowed mediated expression through the institutions of the political process — the political parties. In Luco and Trasacco conflicts over the distribution of resources are expressed in terms of the legitimacy of the way that parties compete for power.

One way of competing is to use the methods of clientelism. Although clientelism has historical and conceptual links with the patron—client relation between landlord and peasant that pre-dates the formation of the modern state and the development of party politics, the 'clientelism' under discussion

4

here exists within the ambit of contemporary political parties. Parties compete for votes so that they can form the government and distribute state-
controlled resources. *Within* clientelist parties individuals compete for
positions of power in order to distribute resources to their own advantage.
Clientelist parties can fruitfully be conceived of as alliances between individuals who, because they are acting within the constraints of a party system,
cannot obtain positions of power without being attached to a party which
forms the government.

The clientelistic form is prevalent throughout Southern Italy, including the
Abruzzo, the region where Luco and Trasacco are situated. Clientelism gains
legitimacy by being perceived in the idiom of exchange — *scambio di favori*
(exchange of favours) is the phrase that is used. Scarce resources such as jobs,
loans, grants, electrical and water connections, tarred roads and so forth are
distributed (or often only promised) in exchange for political support. The
'client' gives his own vote and his energy in recruiting the votes of others for
the party of his benefactor. But the exchange is not an equal one, despite the
language used to describe it. For what the 'patron' distributes (or withholds)
are the means of subsistence and an acceptable standard of living, what the
'client' exchanges is not just his vote but his freedom to associate with others
of his class in order to pursue their common interests. In short, he forgoes
the right to engage in class struggle. Only a few *trasaccani* perceive what is
forgone in such a surrender of the vote; many regard the exchange as a fair
one and indeed are grateful to pay so small a price for the favours they
receive or anticipate.

The idiom of exchange is one mode of legitimation for clientelist political
practices; that of kinship is another. The notion of political support lends
itself to being subsumed under the general obligation to support kin. Politicians who operate the clientelist form may defend it, whilst admitting that it
is *arretrato* (backward), by claiming that it is the electorate which feels the
moral weight of kinship obligations in the political sphere. Even in an electorate of 3000, kinship ties can be traced with hundreds of individuals, so
that political support can, in the last resort, often be claimed or justified on
the grounds of kinship.

Clientelism pervades village life in most of the eleven *comuni* of Fucino
and indeed the whole of the region of Abruzzo. The national Dc party relies
heavily for its support and success at both local and national elections on the
continued acceptance of clientelism. In order to operate patrons must have
some control over essential resources such as employment and credit, and so
clientelistic politics have implications in other spheres of social and economic
organisation.

In sharp contrast with this general tendency to clientelism, in Luco the
overwhelming majority explicitly condemns clientelism as backward, immoral

and degrading. For *luchesi* political conduct which is both modern and morally superior is that which is articulated in terms of Communist and Christian Democrat, of maintaining or overthrowing the existing structure. It consists in organising mass parties in order to influence the distribution of resources in favour of classes of people rather than individuals.

The most consistent advocates of this view are the Communist (Pci) and Socialist (Psi) Parties. Their spokesmen try to expose the underlying conflicts of interest between bourgeoisie and proletariat, and argue that only by organising on class lines (and forming class alliances) can workers and peasants change the system to their advantage. Only just over half the electorate of Luco actually voted Pci or Psi in recent elections, but it is remarkable that most supporters of the Dc (the only other significant contestant) in Luco also condemn clientelism. Although at one with their party's stand against communism, they reject the methods used by the Dc elsewhere to fight it. Many Dc supporters in Luco also talk about class interests and defence of the Catholic order, and see the Dc as a party which protects their class and religious interests (although in ways that they cannot always approve). These views are rarely expressed in Trasacco. The majority of *luchesi* have political attitudes very different to those of *trasaccani*: besides their abhorrence for clientelism, they distinguish between kinship and politics so that obligations and loyalties in one sphere do not influence actions in the other. For this majority the only respectable form of political activity is that based on and articulated in terms of party. It can also be articulated in terms of class, though the boundaries of class and party are by no means coterminous.

Clientelist forms are most often encountered in societies which lack industrial development. But they do not simply reflect industrial backwardness, though they are more likely to survive in a context of scarcity. Elites play an active role in maintaining or reviving clientelist forms when circumstances allow, but people's past and how they perceive it influences these circumstances. Generations of clientelist practices contribute to the political inertia of *trasaccani*. In Luco the efforts of clientelist politicians meet with resistance because of the strength of feelings of the majority. In recounting its history I show why the type of political conflict prevalent in Luco became rooted there and not elsewhere, and how it is maintained as the only morally acceptable way of conducting political and economic relations.

Trasacco closely resembles the villages of Southern Italy that are familiar in the literature. And so, after a general introduction to the history of the Fucino basin, I draw on studies which have contributed to our picture of Southern Italy, in order to establish Trasacco as the repository of similar values, attitudes and practices. It is in contrast to Trasacco, and to Pisticci, Accettura, Calimera, Montevarese and Montegrano that Luco is striking. But without an investigation of its past Luco appears simply anomalous. It is in the unfolding of its history that Luco can be seen, not as an inexplicable aberration from the pervasive pattern of clientelist politics in Southern Italy, but as exemplifying the past imminent in the present, and continually influencing morality, and political conduct and consciousness.

However, despite its singular qualities, Luco is not unique, but rather one pole of a spectrum of which Trasacco forms the other, with the remaining villages of Fucino showing varying degrees of similarity with both. Nor does it seem likely that Luco is the only such village in the whole of Southern Italy. This could only be so if one were to believe that it was a quirk of fate which took me there. On a brief visit to 'Montegrano', the 'typical' village which Banfield studied, I spent a short time in the neighbouring *comune* of Francavilla. With only a few hours at my disposal, I could not claim that what I found there proves that it is 'another Luco'. But there were some parallels which would merit further investigation. In the conclusion to this book I suggest how such *comuni* could be picked out and what indicators should be looked for to establish their character.

2 Economic history of the Fucino basin

In capo a tutti c'è Dio, padrone del cielo.
Questo ognuno lo sa.
Poi viene il Principe Torlonia, padrone della terra.
Poi vengono le guardie del Principe Torlonia.
Poi vengono i cani delle guardie del Principe Torlonia.
Poi, nulla.
Poi, ancor nulla.
Poi, ancora nulla.
Poi vengono i cafoni.
Ed è finito.

(Spoken by the peasant, Michele, in *Fontamara* by Ignazio Silone)
(Translation: At the head of everything is God, Lord of the sky. Everyone knows that. Then comes Prince Torlonia, lord of the earth. Then come Prince Torlonia's guards. Then come the dogs of the guards of Prince Torlonia. Then nothing. Then more nothing. Still more nothing. At the bottom are the peasants. And that's all.)

The mountains that ring Fucino sheltered its people from the great upheavals of the successive conquests and colonisations that marked the history of Southern Italy. After the fall of the Roman Empire the great Roman road, the Via Valeria, which connected it with Rome and the Adriatic, collapsed and disintegrated in the rigours of the Apennine winters, and left Fucino inaccessible to wheeled vehicles until the nineteenth century. With the collapse of the road the tunnel built in AD 50 by Emperor Claudius to lower the level of the lake also fell into disrepair and the lake returned to its natural level. From then until 1854 the eleven *comuni* on its shores stood undisturbed except for periodic flooding. Of glacial origin, Lake Fucino was rather shallow (about twenty metres) but it covered an area of about fourteen thousand hectares and was the third largest expanse of water in Italy. Its fish were caught by the inhabitants of three villages with feudal rights to fish which in 1806 became *usi civici* or common rights. One of these villages was Luco.

Crops grown along the lakeside and on the mountain slopes behind were typical of Apennine zones at this altitude (670 metres and over): grains and pulses. But owing to the benign influence of this large body of water on the climate, vines, olives and almonds flourished as well. A large part of the mountain slopes of each *comune* was common land available for a small fee to citizens for grazing. Sheep and goats were walked from these summer pastures to winter in the more temperate plains of Apulia, in the heel of Italy (see Map 1).

The distribution of cultivable land, which was privately owned, varied considerably between one *comune* and another. In Trasacco, for example, where more land was situated on level ground, a number of large landholdings were worked by landless labour or granted in small tenancies. In Luco, where most of the land was on rising terrain, almost every householder owned a small plot and there were no large landowners. The census of 1823 suggests that all *luchesi* supplemented their subsistence and possibly also their cash income with fishing, but not *trasaccani*, who had no rights to fish.

Having no natural outlet, the level of Lake Fucino rose and fell depending on winter snowfalls and summer evaporation. Every six years or so homes and fertile fields on its shores were flooded. The inhabitants frequently petitioned the king of Naples to reopen the old drainage tunnel, but surveys into the feasibility of this project always advised against it on the grounds of cost.

A series of dry summers and winters of light snowfalls between 1848 and 1853 exposed more land than usual of extraordinary fertility. This probably encouraged a group of businessmen led by a Roman banker, Alessandro Torlonia, to tender for and obtain a contract with the king of Naples to drain the lake completely. This was to be done in exchange for a ninety-nine-year lease on the land which was below the water. The company was dissolved a fortnight after the contract was signed when the shareholders realised how long it would be before the return on their capital would materialise. This left Torlonia as the only shareholder and later the sole owner of Fucino.

A new era for Fucino began with the arrival of engineers and equipment in 1854. The drainage works introduced wage labour on a large scale, the land base was transformed and so was the ownership and distribution of productive resources. The work took twelve years to complete and employed up to three thousand men a day, mostly from the neighbouring *comuni* of Luco and Capistrello, a village situated above the tunnel outlet into the river Liri, (see Map 2). On its completion in 1876 Torlonia was honoured by the king (of Italy, which had been unified in 1861) with the title of Prince. He was granted ownership of Fucino's fourteen thousand hectares in perpetuity. To the present day the Torlonia family has retained its powerful position based on land in Rome and the provinces. Prince Alessandro and the succeeding heads of the family rarely visited Fucino, but their unseen dominance has given to the name 'Torlonia' a potent symbolic value. Although the holders of the princely title have changed, in Fucino they are known indiscriminately as 'Torlonia'. I shall follow this practice.

In 1876, when the last canal and road were complete, Torlonia appointed

9

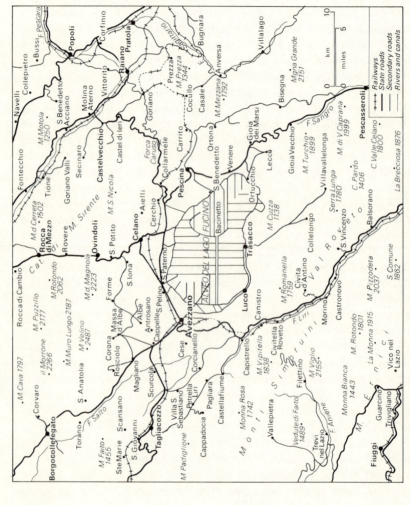

Map 2   La Marsica (from Pizzuti, *Le affittanze agrarie nel Fucino*)

10

an administrator to run the estate, and he introduced a regime that remained largely unchanged until 1952. Nine hundred of the fourteen thousand hectares were kept under the direct control of the Administration in two 'model' farms. They were worked by a small number of salaried employees with the addition of short-contract seasonal labour from neighbouring villages.

The remainder of the land was divided into *appezzamenti* (allotments) of twenty-five hectares each. Tenancies of these *appezzamenti* were granted by Torlonia to selected men in the area, some living as far as fifty kilometres away, but most of them in the eleven Fucino *comuni*. In the first ten years some land became infested with marsh weed and was returned to the Administration. A new administrator, who was a qualified agronomist, imported fifty-five families of experienced sharecroppers from the eastern coastal region of Abruzzo to restore the abandoned land. Each family was settled on a twenty-five-hectare *appezzamento* according to a *mezzadria* contract based on the Tuscan sharecropping system. The contract defines the division of rights and obligations between landowner and *mezzadro* 'on the principle of dividing the investment and the products of the enterprise theoretically half and half . . . [The cultivators] receive approximately half of the crops in kind and half of the cash income from market sales is credited to their account.' (Silverman, 1968.) The landowner advances the land, buildings, large implements and inputs for one year. The *mezzadro* and his family provide the labour. All the farming operations of the *mezzadri* were controlled by Torlonia's resident *fattori* (agents) and the relations of the *mezzadri* with the inhabitants of the surrounding villages were severely restricted. Extra labour was obtained by work exchanges amongst the *mezzadri* or by employing living-in labourers who came from outside the area.

The tenants of twenty-five-hectare *appezzamenti* (other than *mezzadri*) became known as *grandi affittuari*. They usually divided and sub-let their land and took little interest in its cultivation. This practice provided them with an income without the burden of farm management. There was no security of tenure for the sub-tenants, who were not encouraged to make improvements or to regard the land in any way as their own.

Therefore, as in other parts of Southern Italy, the tenant took as much as he could from the soil, and put nothing back. Competition for land was very fierce and the rent charged by the *grandi affittuari* increased with almost every new sub-letting. Pressure on the land had two causes: immigration and declining fertility in the land outside Fucino – *fuori-Fucino*. Draining the lake had lowered the water table and removed its ameliorating influence on the climate – olive trees disappeared completely and grapes ceased to ripen. The miraculous fertility of the Fucino land, in contrast, acted as a magnet on the inhabitants of barren areas further south, who helped to double the population in less than fifty years. Competition for land led to high rents, resulting in increasing subdivision of the land in a process known locally as *polverizzazione* (pulverisation) which reduced some plots to a few square metres.

As early as 1910 people agitated for the elimination of *grandi affittuari* and the establishment of direct cultivator status as the sole criterion of eligibility for a direct tenancy with Torlonia. Periodic unrest on this issue continued right up to the imposition of fascist local government in 1923. Tenancies were so much in demand that they came to have a cash value and were exchanged for capital as though they were freehold (see Liberale, 1956). Agitations for direct tenancies were accompanied by demands for security of tenure with the right to pass on tenancies to heirs and as dowry to daughters on marriage.

Between 1876 and the Land Reform in 1952 farming underwent substantial changes. From 1876 to about 1890, the main crop was grain for both subsistence and the market, and Indian corn, pulses, tomatoes, onions and garlic were grown for domestic consumption. Rent was payable in grain or its cash equivalent. The regime was already oppressive: with the introduction of sugar beet it became more so.

In 1892 Torlonia opened a sugar refinery near Avezzano. In order to guarantee its supply of sugar beet and increase the profitability of the estate, all subsequent tenancy contracts stipulated that the rent be paid in sugar beet by weight. Only with a special dispensation granted to a privileged few could rent be paid in grain or cash. Thus in order to guarantee his rent a tenant had to plant beet on a large proportion of his land. Beet is not a subsistence crop and the necessity to produce it threatened the tenants' ability to grow food crops. Beet was not easy to grow and harvests were often poor. When the tenant got into debt he was constrained to borrow from the only bank in the area, which was owned by Prince Torlonia. Excess beet (over and above the rent) could not be sold on the open market, but had to be sold to the factory at prices set by Torlonia's manager.

Torlonia placed other restrictions on the tenants and residents of the Fucino villages that were onerous by any standards. Where before the drainage people had been free to travel on the lake wherever they wished, they were now allowed to set foot in Fucino only to go to their own plots: this meant that a trip to the Administration or the market in Avezzano meant taking the road all round the edge of the estate. Tenants were not allowed to live on the land: they could not build even a small hut in which to keep their implements and other necessities so that these had to be carried each day the long distances from the villages where they had to live. (Only *mezzadri* and *fattori* lived on the land, in houses built for them by the Administration where they were required to live.) They were not allowed to use dead wood from the numerous poplar trees that lined the roads and canals (and sometimes grew on their handkerchiefs of land) nor to take water from the canals for irrigation.

In 1949 an old man of Luco aged 89, reflecting on the changes he had lived through, observed:

'Fucino has not changed much from when it was a lake: then the water could never belong to those who worked it, like the land today; certainly more people work there today, but they pounce on the land of Fucino as they used to pounce on its fish: one moment they had the boat here, the next over there, because the water belonged to everybody and to nobody. It is just the same with the land: this year here, the next over there, because the land also belongs to everybody and to nobody. In addition, people are not allowed to stay put on the land either, for one cannot build a house or live on the land − just like on the water. So much land without any houses: very much like a lake, no?' (Pizzutti, 1953: 30.)

The opening of the Fucino basin to agricultural production in 1876 had been heralded as a triumph of modern engineering and a boon to the population. By the end of the Second World War (and even earlier − see Silone's searing novel about the area, *Fontamara*) as a result of subdivision, over-intensive cultivation, high rents and lack of investment in the maintenance of the substructure of roads and canals, the Fucino basin had become an area of extreme deprivation in a region already noted for its poverty. Indebtedness was so prevalent and burdensome that the Administration was frequently compelled to waive payment in order to avoid mass evictions (Pizzutti, 1953; Russo, 1955; *Rinascita*, 1944). By 1951 the basin had become so divided and subdivided that there were 11 248 tenants of whom 2415 were sub-tenants; 57 per cent of the holdings were less than two hectares in size and 27 per cent were less than one hectare. Plots were not only small but widely scattered, so that the average tenant's total holding consisted of three parcels of land situated in two or more *comuni* (see Figure 3). After the initial massive investment in the drainage and setting up the *mezzadria* system, Torlonia did not reinvest any of the income from Fucino. By the 1940s, when the critics of the regime were able to publish, the roads and canals were so neglected that it was difficult to take a cart to many holdings and large areas were waterlogged or subject to flooding. The population of Fucino had the lowest literacy rate in the province of L'Aquila (Census, 1961). A social worker employed by the Ente Fucino since 1951 suggested that this was because Torlonia had actively opposed the establishment of schools there.

The end of the war brought the return of demobbed soldiers to their homes, and it was their unemployment coupled with the increasing immiserisation which provided the background to the later unrest. In 1945 the government passed the series of laws on which trade unions in Fucino based their subsequent demands: the Gullo Decrees and the Norms for the Maximum

Employment of Agricultural Labour. The Gullo Decrees forbade sub-letting. Their immediate effect was that thousands of tenants, encouraged by their unions, flooded the Administration with requests for recognition of their direct cultivator/direct tenant status. But it was not until 1950 that the *braccianti* (landless labourers), taking advantage of the law on maximum employment, began a work-in known as the *sciopero a rovescio.*

From the original participation of 2000 *braccianti* and 3000 small tenants the strike spread to involve 12 000 more sympathisers amongst the shop-keepers and larger tenants (Colapietra, 1957). It was a mass outbreak of unrest, agitation, demonstrations, meetings and occasionally violent encounters with the police, known as the *Lotta del Fucino* (Struggle for Fucino). As the struggle continued and the classes involved spread to include larger tenants, so the demands changed from 'work for the landless' and 'the repeal of manorial—feudal obligations' to a full-scale land expropriation.

Fucino was one of a number of rural areas experiencing mass protests at this time. To allay these, in 1951 the government decided to embark on an experimental land reform programme in selected areas. One of the Land Reform Boards was established to expropriate land in the Maremma and the entire Torlonia estate in Fucino (*L'Ente per la Colonizzazione della Maremma Tosco—Laziale e del Territorio del Fucino*). Following on agitations for local control in 1954 a separate board was set up to administer Fucino — the Ente Fucino.

In most areas of land reform, including the Maremma, the main benefici-aries were the landless *braccianti*. In Fucino land was allocated only to those who had been direct tenants of Torlonia. These numbered 8833 plus 273 of the former salaried employees on the Administration farms. Grants varied from four hectares to one, depending on the size of the tenant's pre-reform holding. Sixty-two per cent of the holdings were two hectares or less. Had the landless and sub-tenants been included, the average size of holding would have had to be reduced from its already exiguous 1.5 hectares. Besides dis-tributing land, the Ente employed the landless on improving canals and roads, on rehousing assignees and in constructing 'cooperative' buildings, and it assisted those who wished to emigrate. It gave technical and financial aid to assignees and built a new sugar refinery designed to break the Torlonia monopoly.

The amount of land granted to each assignee was equal to the amount previously held in tenancy and was, at least in principle, restricted to those who worked their own land. The annual repayments on the mortgage average 4000 lire (£2.80) per hectare. Even in 1952 this was only a fraction of the former rents; today it bears no relation at all to the value of the land. Pro-vision was made for land to be bought and sold, for the Ente wished to encourage the formation of large holdings and the emigration of the smaller cultivators. However, an upper limit of four hectares was imposed on all holdings and land could only be sold to other assignees, with first refusal given to neighbours with common boundaries. A great deal of land was sold clandestinely, without reporting the transactions to the Ente, both to non-assignees and to assignees whose holdings thereby exceeded the maximum. In 1964 the Ente revised the upper limit to ten hectares, and a few holdings have surpassed this level.

The assignees have now all been drawn into market relations, and subsistence crops are no longer produced. The most common crops are potatoes and beet; even the smallest farmers concentrate on them. Potatoes are marketed through local merchants. Beet prices are negotiated annually between the Anb and Cbf (Christian Democrat and Socialist/Communist beet growers' associations), the processors and the government. Trade unions representing the growers have won the right to control the weighing and testing of the sugar content as the product is consigned to the refineries. It has also become established practice for the Ente Fucino to buy up potatoes when the market price falls below the cost of production. This too has happened as a result of union pressure.

Since the land reform, agriculture, while still of prime importance, does not directly engage as many people as it used to. In 1971 the active population of the Fucino *comuni* was 23 451, or 35 per cent of the population. Of these, 36 per cent were employed in agriculture, 15 per cent in industry and the remainder (49 per cent) in the service sector including state and local government employment (Census, 1971). However, official figures show only an agglomeration of the *main* employment of individual people *when* they are employed. They mask massive under-employment and seasonal unemployment in agriculture, building, the retail and tourist sectors and among housewives and young women who would like to go out to work if there were jobs for them. There is employment in the factories of the 'Industrial Nucleus' at Avezzano for about 2000 and avid competition for these mostly unskilled jobs. The struggle to find secure employment has political repercussions, for the job market is an important context in which clientelist control operates.

In Fucino different *comuni* have been differently affected by the change in resources and resource allocation over the last one hundred and fifty years. But the overall economic situation is neatly summed up in Sidney Tarrow's succinct observation: 'The Mezzogiorno has too many people fighting too hard for too few resources.' (Tarrow, 1967: 40.)

3 Land and politics
from feudalism to land reform

From feudalism to its abolition

Like the history of peasants everywhere, that of the *trasaccani* is submerged beneath territorial conquests and political changes in the centres of power. The contours of their lives can only be inferred from these larger events and from what can be painstakingly reconstructed in the land transactions and population figures in dusty and often badly ravaged archives. The medieval development of the settlement at Trasacco can be dimly discerned through the history of the local church and its relations with the feudal overlords of the region.

The ruins of the palace which the Emperor Claudius built in the first century AD to oversee the building of a drainage tunnel for the lake were used to build a great church in Trasacco. By the eleventh century the Marsica had become part of the fief of the Burgundians. Conte Berardo of the Burgundians gave the church in Trasacco all the houses and gardens in the village and his son added to these land, chestnut trees and rights to fish in part of the lake (Di Pietro, 1869: 132). Through the marriage of the last heiress of the line, the Marsica became part of the territory of the ancient Roman family of Colonna. The Colonna usurped the rights of the church of Trasacco to fish. In recognition of this usurpation the Colonna sent all the fish caught in Holy Week to 'the parish' (Di Pietro, idem). The loss of the *trasaccani* rights to fish helped to make the economy and social relations of Trasacco significantly different from those of its neighbour, Luco. Without rights to fish the inhabitants were entirely dependent on access to land for their subsistence.

The Fucino, nominally under the dominion of whoever ruled in Naples, was little affected by the battles which raged between French and Spanish for control of Southern Italy. Aside from occasional forays against outlaws, the mountainous, remote and economically insignificant province of Abruzzo received little attention from the colonial government. The only products to reach the markets of Naples were saffron from L'Aquila and wool and cheese from the sheep grazed on the mountains in summer. With no need of highways, these sheep were taken on great migrations along the peaks of the

17

Trasacco

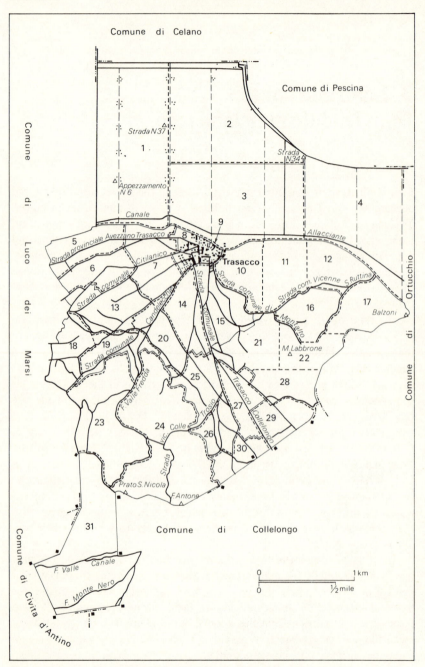

Map 3 Trasacco (from Provincia di L'Aquila, Quadro d'Unione)

18

mountains and down to the plains of Apulia for the winter and back again in the summer.

The mountain slopes provided ample summer feed. The small pockets of cultivable land in the valleys provided a bare subsistence for the local inhabitants. There was no land to compare with the grain-producing *latifundia* further south. Nobles and *signori* in Rome and Naples, only concerned with land in so far as it provided sufficient income to sustain their life in the metropoli, were not interested in acquiring property in the province of Ulterior Abruzzo.

Consequently the structure of land tenure probably changed very little between the twelfth and eighteenth centuries. The Church, as recipient of the Burgundian donations, was the effective owner of most, if not all, of the land. Some of it would have been rented in exchange for labour service, some administered directly as demesne and the rest served as commons.

It was not until 1806, when the Napoleonic army captured Southern Italy, that radical reforms were introduced. Chief among these was the abolition of feudalism which, paradoxically, was at least as much in the interests of the nobility as of the peasants. It enabled the nobility to sell off land, to the relief of many who had become impoverished and needed the capital (Procacci, 1973: 266). The Marsica was not much affected by this reform, for most land there had been donated to various churches centuries before. But in 1811, just five years later, the State expropriated Church land and put it up for auction. Later the Church repudiated this act and called on the pious to return what they had bought, but much of it remained in private hands. As Table 1 demonstrates, land was not acquired in very large amounts in those sales of Church property. This suggests that holdings were acquired by local peasants and petit bourgeois rather than by wealthy outsiders moving in.

The population of Trasacco, which had numbered about 1000 in 1595 and 350 in 1669 as a result of the plague, in 1802 had returned to about 750, a figure which was to increase slowly but steadily until the dramatic rise occasioned by the drainage of the lake.

Land distribution 1833—65

The area of the *comune* of Trasacco was then 2680.81 hectares. In the first half of the nineteenth century 1068.75 hectares was privately owned; the 1612.06 hectares of commons had passed from the Church into ownership by the commonalty. Communal lands were subject to *uso civico*: the right of every citizen to pasture animals and cut wood. The *università* (local administration) controlled access to the commons. This administration was elected by a very restricted group of the propertied and educated — in 1865 (the earliest date for which this figure is available) the electorate numbered only

44, or 3 per cent of the population. Thus the 'right' of *uso civico* was one mediated by the local elite of landowners and professionals.

Ownership of the cultivable land was distributed as shown in Table 1, which is compiled from the local *catasto* (land register). There were 292 households resident in Trasacco. This must not be confused with the total of 318 plots in the first column of Table 1. The *catasto* groups together the plots only of those holdings which total five hectares or more (holdings under five hectares were not subject to tax). Lines A to D are thus the individual holdings of 28 families in Trasacco who owned more than five hectares. Line E shows instead the total number of scattered plots (290 amounting to 229.95 ha) available to the remaining families (264), giving an average of less than one hectare per family — less than the requirement for subsistence. Thus these families would have been constrained to rent additional land or sell labour to larger landowners to supplement the family's needs. In addition, it is likely that some of these families owned no land and would have had to make permanent recourse to one or both of these expedients. At the other end of the scale 11 families (3 of them from neighbouring villages) had holdings of over twenty-five hectares each. To summarise: 10 per cent of the population together with 11 outsiders and the Church owned nearly four-fifths of the land and 90 per cent owned, on average, less than a hectare per family — a very unequal distribution (especially when compared with Luco, see pp. 85–6), though fairly typical for this area.

The landless and the smallholders were dependent on the larger land-owners in the following ways:

a. as tenants on a sharecropping or labour-service basis
b. as agricultural labourers on a day-to-day basis

Table 1 *Land distribution in Trasacco 1833–1865.*

| | Holdings owned by | | | | | | | |
| | Locals | | Church | | Outsiders | | Total | |
	No.	Area	No.	Area	No.	Area	No.	Area
A over 25 ha	8	258.04	1	44.35	3	120.44	12	422.83
B 15–25 ha	6	109.71		–	4	77.26	10	186.97
C 10–15 ha	7	84.47		–	2	22.17	9	106.64
D 5–10 ha	7	105.28		–	2	17.08	9	122.36
E under 5 ha	290	229.95		–		–	290	229.95
	318	787.45	1	44.35	11	236.95	330	1068.75
	Total families: 292							

Source: Catasto Provinciale, L'Aquila.

c. and for common rights to cut wood and pasture animals, since these were controlled by the large owners through their monopoly of elective offices.

A Tuscan interested in the problems of the South visited the Abruzzo in 1874, and commented on the conditions of its peasantry as follows:

The peasant, in order to eat, depends from one year to the next on the proprietor. And in a country where almost everything is lacking in the way of industry and commerce apart from that little exercised by artisans and shopkeepers in towns; where, in consequence, the great mass of the population is divided into two classes: owners and peasants; where the only means of escape from oppression is emigration, that dependence is a true and proper slavery. For the rest, agricultural contracts are of the most varied, not only in harshness but in the vagueness of their clauses. As for the so-called free prestation of labour, it does not exist. Almost everywhere the peasant is kept at the discretion of the owner. All the transport, all the heavy work of the proprietor is done by the peasants who present themselves periodically at shorter or longer intervals, depending on how far away they are, and for that day they eat in the owner's house. The proprietors call this system 'patriarchal' and for their part the peasants regard it in the same manner. (Franchetti, 1950: 23.)

This perceptive writer has touched on all the major features of class relations in this situation: the dependence of the peasant on the landlord, the absence of any means of upward mobility, the insecurity of tenancy contracts, the insecurity of daily wage labour, the paternalism of the proprietors and the acquiescence of the peasants. The final sentence of the quotation touches an important theme: the social and political effects of the peasants' economic dependence on locally resident landlords. Where peasants and landlords are in daily face-to-face contact, peasants are likely to act in a deferential manner (Newby, 1975); patron–clientage is more prevalent where peasantry and gentry live in close proximity (Davis, 1969a). The distribution of land in Trasacco up to the mid-nineteenth century created economic dependence, social deference and patron–clientage: the early foundations of the clientelist politics of the village today.

From the drainage to the *Lotta del Fucino*

When the new land of Fucino was brought under the plough in 1876, the land base of Trasacco was increased by 1802 hectares. This new land was not freely available to all the populace. It was rented to 'certain families of notables, carefully chosen *comune* by *comune* because they would defend the interests of the House of Torlonia in Fucino' (Liberale, 1956). In Trasacco the recipients of twenty-five-hectare *appezzamenti* in tenancy from Torlonia were chosen from those families which had, prior to the drainage, owned the larger holdings *fuori-Fucino* — the local *signori*. Although the value of that land progressively declined, the acquisition of tenants' rights on the new land enabled them to maintain their relative wealth, their leisure and their political dominance. No *appezzamenti* were farmed as single units; all were divided and sub-let (the most common way of operating land throughout the South). The increase in land thus brought little or no change in the dependence of the peasants: they were forced to be sub-tenants at inflated rents. In 1876–86 a *grande affittuario* paying 3 to 5 lire per *coppa* (one-twentieth hectare) would receive between 6 and 7 lire from the sub-tenant (Liberale, 1956).

These profits from rent were made possible by the competition for land. The population of the whole area had risen from 25 770 in 1861 to 48 588 in 1911, and this helped to drive up rents everywhere in Fucino. The population increase was particularly marked in Trasacco, where it almost trebled, compared with a rise in the whole of Fucino of only 88 per cent in the same period (see Table 2). In addition, pressure on the land was not relieved, as it was in Luco, by opportunities of employment in the sugar refinery or on the Administration farms, for these were too far away. Given these drawbacks, it is difficult to see why Trasacco rather than Luco should have attracted so many of the migrants to Fucino. A few highly speculative explanations suggest themselves: Luco is built on steeply sloping ground with the houses tightly packed together; Trasacco is on fairly level ground and the street plan even today has many spaces for new dwellings to be built. Luco is under the shadow of a mountain so that the sun sets early in the afternoon leaving it damp and chilly. Trasacco is exposed to the warming rays of the sun from morning till night. Luco, as a former fishing community was probably tightly-knit and closed to outsiders, whereas Trasacco had a social organisation more typical of the South and therefore more familiar to the Southerners who migrated there.

In addition to the effects of large-scale immigration, the sub-letting system itself played a part in driving up rents: in some cases chains of sub-letting on a single tiny plot extended through as many as five non-cultivating sub-tenants who each took their cut before paying their 'landlord' (Pizzutti, 1953: 24).

The acquisition of more land in the 1870s did not therefore herald a new era of independence from the old elite for the peasants of Trasacco. On the contrary, it increased their domination by the elite, for the distribution of land initiated by Torlonia served to bring access to the means of subsistence yet more thoroughly under the control of the *signori*. This increased dependence was enhanced by the declining fertility of the land *fuori-Fucino* where some peasants did own land. As this land became less productive due to the lowered water table and the climatic changes wrought by the drainage, so its owners were forced to seek access to more productive land in Fucino. The newcomers who helped to swell the population of Trasacco after the drainage were also competing for Fucino land. They came from further south, from the regions of Lucania, Calabria and Molise where, if anything, poverty and oppression were even worse (Lopreato, 1967: 22; Seton Watson, 1967: 23). Like all newcomers, they probably did not fit easily into the existing social framework of Trasacco, but they were used to relations of economic and political dependence and their presence is likely to have enhanced rather than diminished those already in force in Trasacco.

As we have seen, from about 1900 onwards, socialist organisations were slowly becoming established in various parts of Fucino. In Trasacco, a constant problem for these organisations was the presence of large numbers of landless labourers. One of the themes in the remainder of this chapter is that of the relations between political parties and *braccianti*.

Following on the 1915–18 war, when soldiers had been recruited with the promise of land, some *trasaccani* joined other landless ex-combatants who invaded poorly cultivated land in Fucino. There were similar incidents in many other parts of Italy. In Trasacco the invasion was led by Romolo Retico, a socialist lawyer and son of one of the largest landowners *fuori-Fucino*. In response to this invasion a commission was set up here, as in other *comuni*. It consisted of a member of the Partito Popolare (forerunner of the Dc), one of the Psi and a representative of the ex-combatants, and it distributed half a hectare to each landless ex-combatant. The land was made available by Torlonia, who terminated some large tenancies and *mezzadria* contracts.

After 1918 the socialist Peasant League attracted some *trasaccani*, though I could find no record of the numbers. In 1920 it opened a small consumer cooperative which worked well for two or three years. Then, according to its secretary, fascist harassment of the storekeeper and people's fear of being seen buying there forced it to close in 1923. During fascism and the Second World War *trasaccani* suffered the same experiences and deprivations as others in Fucino which, because of its comparatively productive agriculture, was

Table 2 *Population of Trasacco 1861–1971.*

(Base: 1861 = 100)

	1861	1911	1951	1971
Trasacco	1265	3772	5718	5311
	100	298	452	420
Fucino Total	25 770	48 588	64 540	66 705
	100	188	250	259
Provincial Total	253 783	337 610	346 567	293 066
	100	133	145	115

Source: Census 1861–1971, ISTAT, Rome.

23

important to the provincial authorities. In Trasacco there was little resistance to the fascist and German regimes, and it was not until 1948 that the communists formed a *sezione* there.

By 1948 the number of landless in Trasacco had reached about 500, swollen by the fascist interdict on emigration and by the settlement there of refugees and soldiers in disordered retreat from the northern borders at the close of the War. The membership of Federbraccianti (Federation of agricultural workers' unions, affiliated to Pci/Psi-Cgil) rose to a peak of 430. But in spite of the pleas of the Federbraccianti secretary, Antonio De Gasparis, no Pci party school was established in the village, for the local Pci did not have the personnel to provide the teaching and neither did the *federazione*, whose resources were stretched by the sudden increase in membership in the area. As a result, according to De Gasparis, this large and potentially militant body of *braccianti* could not attend night school to improve their literacy or their political understanding: they were not encouraged to read and did not have discussions guided by skilled party cadres on the situation and their role in it.

Although their poverty might suggest that the *braccianti* had 'nothing to lose but their chains', and that they would therefore be the most reliable supporters of the Communist Party, both their structural position and their lack of political education made them vulnerable to manipulation by less scrupulous politicians. Unlike tenants, they had no independent means of subsistence and had to rely for access to employment on offers of work which were often made contingent upon support for Christian Democrat politicians. Whilst they were easily inspired to take action by fiery speeches about the very real deprivation they suffered, the realities of the job market quickly forced them into submission. Furthermore, there were fewer *braccianti* than there were tenants. Thus when their interests conflicted with those of the more numerous tenants, their demands were overlooked, as happened in the allocation of land to tenants only. Because the Pci supported this decision, the membership of the Trasacco Federbraccianti disappeared overnight. Many *braccianti* emigrated, but the majority of those who remained reverted to their familiar mode of getting work – the clientele system. In Luco this mass desertion of the party did not occur. The reasons for this must be sought in the strength of party organisation, in material support given to the landless and in the advanced level of political education which was lacking in Trasacco.

The distribution of land in Trasacco on the eve of land reform was very similar to that pertaining in other *comuni*: there were few tenancies of over four hectares and the vast majority was in scattered allotments of less than a hectare. The *signori* of the village were no longer simply landowners but had diversified into the professions. The *pretura* (the lowest level of the judicial system) was housed in Trasacco, whose lawyers thrived on petty disputes over land boundaries and inheritances and cases of unauthorised pasturing and wood-cutting on communal land. The *signori* and their close associates had constituted the local *fascisti* and run the administration throughout the period from 1923 to 1944. Their political dominance was based on their control of the land, on their professional status, and on their links with the national fascist hierarchy and the state bureaucracy. Fascism was a system in which fear and deference played an important part. These characteristics were reflected in the community.

The *Lotta del Fucino* and the land reform

Although the leadership and organisation of the *sciopero a rovescio* (the work-in mentioned on page 14) came from outside the village of Trasacco, its *braccianti* were active participants and became renowned even in Luco for their militancy. Here, as elsewhere, the initiative of the *braccianti* was followed later by small and medium tenants.

In 1951 the government made known its proposals for land reform. In Fucino only the tenants, and not the landless, were to benefit. The *braccianti*, who felt that they had initiated and borne the brunt of the struggle, were extremely disappointed. The Pci accepted the proposals, pointing out that the already small plots would have to be halved if the *braccianti* were to be given land. The Federbraccianti leadership in Trasacco accused the party of electoralism — for the potential beneficiaries of the proposals far outnumbered the landless — and an open rift developed between the union and the *federazione*. A speaker from the Pci was warned not to attend a meeting in Trasacco lest violence break out. De Gasparis, the Federbraccianti secretary, appealed direct to the Central Committee in Rome to try to impress on them the explosiveness of the Fucino situation. He hoped to persuade the party to mobilise nationally on behalf of the *braccianti* of Fucino in their demand for land, but without success.

De Gasparis then appealed to the Ente Fucino to enlarge the sphere of its activities so as to increase the number of landless to be employed. A rota of men, each working on a fortnightly contract, had been organised by the Ente to carry out the maintenance and repairs of roads and canals. The Federbraccianti asked that the *fuori-Fucino* land be included in the reform area and that irrigation works be installed there. But this proposal was not accepted. The shortage of work and the competition for employment between *braccianti* and small tenants had violent repercussions in two villages in particular. In Celano two men were killed and in Trasacco fighting was frequent.

The rota system was manipulated by the Ente Fucino for political purposes, and this was particularly easily achieved in Trasacco where the proportion of landless was high and the Pci had been weakened and almost

25

destroyed by the dispute with the Federbraccianti: *braccianti* had abandoned both the party and the union in large numbers. Lacking any political support, they became an easy prey to the clientelist politics of the Ente Fucino.

This body, when recruiting labour, blatantly made places on the rota conditional on membership of the Cisl (Dc trade-union federation) or the Dc party. Later, when the selection of men for the rota was devolved from the Ente to the *comune* administrations, Trasacco had a Dc administration which was only too eager to add to its meagre store of political spoils. It continued to make sure that unrepentant communist labourers were excluded from the rota.

This Dc administration was elected in 1951 in the midst of all the ferment. It had been preceded by a Pci/Psi coalition administration dating from 1946. The then mayor, a popular anti-fascist shepherd named Di Cola, was forced to emigrate in mid-term in order to support his large family. The departure of this strong, almost charismatic leader, who built up his following in a highly personalised way, left a leadership gap at a most crucial moment. It is possible that he would have been able to contain the discontent of the *braccianti* within the party, but his successor, a schoolteacher, seems only to have antagonised them further.

Politics since the land reform

The announcement of the land reform by the government was carefully timed to precede the scheduled elections for local and provincial councils in 1951. In all the land reform areas the communist vote declined in favour of the Dc both because of what the government had actually achieved and because of the particularly coercive recruiting tactics of the land-reform officials. The *braccianti* of Trasacco seem, for the reasons outlined above, to have been especially vulnerable to political manipulation.

Chapter 5 will discuss in detail the kinds of problem faced by Dc administrations in Trasacco. A particular feature has been the difficulty of maintaining agreement between the factions making up the *giunta* (executive committee). The 1956—60 administration ended in complete breakdown, so that early elections had to be held under the jurisdiction of an official representative of the prefect.

This very obvious instability was one of the reasons for the election of a left-wing administration in 1960. But two other factors were involved. In these elections the Pci and Psi forged an alliance for the first time with the numerically stronger and more conservative Psdi (Social Democrat Party). Already more substantial as a result, this Left coalition received an unexpected influx of votes when a former Dc mayor defected from his party after a quarrel, and instructed his numerous supporters to vote for the Left.

Although this helped the Pci to obtain the mayoralty for their man, who headed the coalition list, it severely hampered his freedom of action, for he was constantly threatened with the defection of his anti-communist Psdi colleagues in the *giunta*.

To sum up, in spite of the dramatic changes in the size of the land base as a result of the drainage, land distribution in Trasacco did not change in any way that altered significantly the social and political relations of dependence between landowners, tenants and landless labourers. From being dependent, for the large part, on those who owned land *fuori-Fucino*, the tenants and landless became dependent on Torlonia's *grandi affittuari* who were chosen from amongst the earlier landowners. Although Torlonia was the 'real' owner of the Fucino land, access to it was mediated through the local elite. As 'direct' tenancies between the cultivator and the Torlonia Administration became more common over the period from 1910 to 1923, members of the elite diversified their interests out of land and into the liberal professions and state sinecures. This meant that they had less direct control over access to land. Land was diminishing in importance however, and other means of control were taking its place. During the same period the importance of the State increased, and political parties came to have influence on the distribution of resources at all levels. Crispi described the way in which parliamentary alliances worked in the governments which he headed between 1887 and 1896 as follows:

In parliament a kind of bilateral contract is often made: the minister gives the local population into the hands of the deputy on condition that the latter promises the ministry his vote. The prefect and the chief of the police are nominated in the interests of the deputy in order to keep local interests in his favour ... There is pandemonium in parliament when an important vote comes along as government agents run through the rooms and down corridors collecting votes and promising subsidies, decorations, canals and bridges. (Quoted by Mack Smith, 1959: 199.)

Thus it was to the political parties that the local elite turned to retain their power and status.

The *braccianti*, with no property of their own, had to sell their labour on the market. In Trasacco there was no single large estate on which they were employed, nor did they work consistently for the same employer but on short-term contracts for a variety of employers. Therefore social relations at work, both with employers and fellow workers, were of a fragmented and transitory nature. Because there were always more labourers than employers who needed them, *braccianti* competed for work and for the attention of employers. Thus political relations were vertical, individualised and clientelistic — exchanging votes for employment — and the horizontal form of class solidarity was tenuous and short-lived. Though class solidarity was forged during the post-war campaign for work — the *sciopero a rovescio* — urgent economic needs, which surfaced again once the campaign was over, led to the re-establishment of vertical ties with Ente Fucino officials, with the local administration and with anyone else who could find them work.

The *braccianti* of Trasacco are a category whose economic circumstances make them most obviously vulnerable to clientelist pressures. During the Torlonia period the same pressure can be seen acting on those who did have land but had too little to provide all their subsistence needs. They were therefore forced into the labour market along with the *braccianti*. The land reform, which gave the majority of assignees no more than one hectare, did little to alter these relations of dependence on local politicians, and the actions of Ente Fucino officials themselves make it clear that it was never their intention to encourage the independence of the assignees.

4 The village and its economy

Village and countryside

Trasacco does not, like many Southern towns, dominate its territory like a medieval fortification from a ridge or hilltop. Its houses sprawl at the foot of Monte Labrone, a rocky spur stripped bare of vegetation, and topped by a monstrous neon-lit cross. Edward Lear's dismissive words of 1830 are, sadly, still true today: 'Whatever may have been the former state of Trasacco, its present condition is sufficiently forlorn; though its church . . . [is] well worth some attention.' (Edward Lear, 1846: 32.)

The church, whose Imperial Roman origins are retold with gusto by every native, is a fine Romanesque building. To the disgust of the parishioners, its gaudy baroque stucco has recently been stripped by the provincial authorities for the arts to reveal the original mellowed stone simplicity.

The church is flanked by a small piazza, the venue for pre-election meetings but not, as in towns all over Italy, for the pacing tête-à-têtes of the town's important men as the evening's cool begins. Instead the politicians walk between this little piazza and a much larger open space, the *Aia*, along the narrow main street, constantly being forced onto the pavement by cars passing through the town. Occasionally they halt beneath the trees on the piazza's edge or retreat into the dark seclusion of the Sport Bar, but they do not lounge conspicuously – there are no seats and tables outside the bars – nor show off their long fingernails as they smoke and drink (cf. Colclough, 1969; Moss & Cappannari, 1962).

Round the piazza are the gracious stone houses with carved front doors, brass knobs and wrought-iron balconies of the old landowning families. Only one of them is still occupied as a family residence by the *medico condotto* (GP employed by the *comune*), who married into it. The others are empty, their street fronts converted into shops and bars, odd floors rented out to the Dc party and the '*Circolo*', an exclusive men's club.

From the centre, streets radiate out, lined with the old terraced housing of the peasants. South towards Fucino is a series of a dozen short streets of two-storey 'semis' built by the Ente Fucino for assignees of the land reform. Along the road to Candelecchie are six two-storey blocks of low-cost Gescal

29

apartments (built by a para-state institution using employees' contributions) and going towards Luco is a section of barrack-like bungalows such as can be found in all Fucino *comuni*, a reminder of the 1915 earthquake. The rest of the housing, more than 50 per cent of all the occupied dwellings, is in private ownership and has been built since 1945. These houses with their angular concrete construction are easily distinguished from the crumbling stone of the older dwellings. They have been built according to no town-planning logic, but simply wherever their owners could lay their hands on a piece of land with road frontage. Many of them have pumped water and are without main drainage, and the untarred roads leading to them become quagmires in the heavy winter rains. Because there has always been plenty of space in Trasacco, houses have their gardens around them rather than grouped on the fringes of the built-up area. This adds to the village's rather unusual dispersed and sprawling air: houses huddled along narrow cobbled streets and staircased alleyways are more characteristic of Italian villages and towns.

The *comune* has been recently divided into two parishes. No rivalry has developed between them and seems unlikely, as even the existing 'quarters' of the town are little more than named geographical areas. Neighbourhoods are not bound together by the links of female kin as one finds in Pisticci (Davis, 1973) or Accettura (Colclough, 1969). Houses are transmitted at marriage not to daughters but to sons, and no attempt is made to house sons or daughters near at hand. People often did not seem to know even close neighbours and certainly were not always able, like *pisticcesi*, 'by consulting with their neighbours [to] identify anyone they saw in the ordinary course of events within a matter of minutes (Davis, 1973: 67). This dispersed housing pattern, whilst uncommon for Southern Italy, is how all the Fucino villages except Luco and one other are arranged.

As in most of the South, nobody lives in the countryside aside from the thirty families of former *mezzadri* who received houses as part of their share-cropping agreement with the Torlonia Administration. Attitudes to the former *mezzadri* are indicative of a more general aversion to country-dwelling. They are known as *marchigiani* because it is thought — mistakenly — that they came originally from the Marche. The term *marchigiano* is used in Trasacco and Luco as a byword for stupidity.

Amongst the reasons put forward by Davis for town-dwelling in Southern Italian rural areas is that in town women's chastity can be protected by watchful neighbours and their honour thus maintained unquestioned. Those who live in the country, lacking this stringent control, are assumed to be lascivious. In Trasacco this insinuation was never made about the *marchigiane*. The natural configuration of Fucino, which is very flat, and the large number of people always working there might account for the fact that it is thought perfectly safe for women to work in the fields and even to live in the country.

Nevertheless, no one other than a *marchigiano* would dream of living outside the village in the countryside. The land which each *trasaccano* cultivates is not scattered around the village as it is in Pisticci, and was in Fucino before the land reform. Living in the village is not therefore a means of cutting down on the time spent travelling between parcels of land as it is in Pisticci and elsewhere (Davis, 1969b; Rossi-Doria, 1958). But like other town centres in the South, it is the best place to be seen as available for work by potential employers. Since 1952 scattered plots have been amalgamated, and the farmer no longer has to cover any distance to reach outlying plots. The land reform situated holdings within the assignee's *comune* of residence. In any case, most farmers go to their land by car or tractor. Although not identical with those suggested by other writers, there are sound economic reasons why *trasaccani* (and *fucinesi* generally) do not live on their farmland. It is because the holdings are mostly rather small and too precious to build on. Land in Fucino was fetching between £7000 and £10 000 per hectare in 1974—5. It is more sensible, if one must build a house, to sell a piece of land in Fucino and buy a building plot in town which, together with the cost of building, would require about £7000—£10 000. This is indeed how many *trasaccani* have acquired new houses since the land reform. To live in town has other advantages, even in this motorised era. Trasacco has nursery, primary and middle schools and a bus link with Avezzano where there is a choice of high schools. There is a cinema showing films every night in winter and twice a week in summer. There are bars and the *passeggiata* for meeting friends and greeting acquaintances. All these provide meeting places. For men with any political ambitions town-dwelling is essential. How else would it be possible to maintain contact with colleagues, rivals and voters? A man who needs things done, a job, a transfer, help with an application for credit or pension, has to be in town, to contact the right person at the right moment. Again, although for fashionable clothes and furniture some people go to Rome, the daily necessities, food-buying, car and electrical repairs and business with the *comune* are all easier for town-dwellers.

Earning a living

The *comune*, of which the village is the main settlement, covers an area of 51 square kilometres and had, in 1971, a resident population of 5311. The census for that year shows that 32.1 per cent of the population were active, the majority (17.2 per cent) in the agricultural sector (in industry 7.9 per cent, and other 7.0 per cent). Official figures such as these, however, are unreliable. For all kinds of reasons people do not fill their census returns correctly. As an example, a pension is payable to housewives and another, rather higher, to direct cultivators. If the husband has any occupation in addition to farming, with a pension higher than that for a direct cultivator, he will record his own occupation in that sector and his wife's as 'direct cultivator', regardless of whether she actually makes any contribution to the farm, or whether his second occupation actually takes up more of his time than farming. Entries are also distorted for fear that the authorities will uncover anomalies and lodge claims for income tax. These are distortions which citizens make deliberately.

The official figures are also questionable for quite other reasons. It is extremely common for an individual to have more than one occupation. Often a man cannot make a living in one or even two areas, and he diversifies his skills as much as possible to make up a particular *combinazione*, as a viable combination of jobs is called. For example, a man may combine working on his own land, hiring out his tractor with himself as driver and doing some bricklaying or tractor repairs. Small cultivators all over Southern Italy are constantly trying to find additional sources of income in a reliable *combinazione*:

the cultivator typically combines a variety of different means of sustenance – from different pieces of land owned, rented and share-cropped, from wage labour, sporadic non-agricultural pursuits and anything else he can improvise. (Silverman, 1971.)

The struggle for a working *combinazione* is not confined to the rural cultivator. In Italy a diploma or a degree has long ceased to be a passport to a well-paid position. For every primary-school teaching post in the province of L'Aquila there are 200 applications, and the same is true of all advertised posts requiring a diploma. Most teachers, even those with degrees, spend their first year or two giving private lessons, then as part-time *supplenti*, filling in temporarily, then a year or two in some remote and uncongenial part of the country, before they are promoted to within commuting distance of home. The same is true of the Post Office and most government departments. It applies equally to the holders of degrees as to *diplomati*. Not even doctors can be sure of a practice. There is a lot of truth in Davis's suggestion that:

In some sense all Pisticcesi [all Southerners?] are peasants. With very few exceptions all are trying to create and maintain successful *combinazioni* of separately inadequate, undercapitalised and peasant-like enterprises. (Davis, 1973: 91.)

In the remainder of this chapter I shall examine the occupational structure with this problem of the *figura mista* (Rossi-Doria's famous term for the man with more than one occupation) in mind. The pervasiveness of this phenomenon makes any analysis in class terms difficult.

A rigorous class analysis would have to start with a house-to-house census of the population in which the contribution of each individual to each of his occupations would be strictly assessed according to his labour input. Even an adequate sample census on these lines would have required more time than I could give. My discussion in terms of occupational categories is based on a random sample of families. Each individual's major occupation in terms of man-hours was assessed by a panel of two informants. These occupational categories should not be confused with 'class', and where this term has been used, and others related to it such as 'elite', and 'lower orders', these are used impressionistically to convey a position in the composite hierarchy of occupation, status, influence and power. The categories which are used in Trasacco are *bracciante* (labourer in agriculture), *manovale* (labourer in building, etc.), *operaio* (factory worker), *contadino* (peasant, farmer), *impiegato* (office worker) and *professionale* (professional). The last two categories are broken down into more specific titles, but the generic terms are frequently used. The basic division for *trasaccani* (and *luchesi* too) is that between *impiegati* and *professionali*, who constitute the elite, and the rest. A few wealthy *contadini* might be counted as 'elite' but that designation would be hedged about with doubts and questions.

The discussion of how *trasaccani* earn their living has slipped into one on how *trasaccani* relate status and class. This is no coincidence, since occupations always carry with them evaluative connotations that are difficult to disentangle. In the following sections of this chapter what people do, how they find work and the implications of the occupational order for social and political relations will be made more explicit. Table 3 shows the distribution of the male electorate by occupation and landholding. For purposes of comparison see Table 11.

Agriculture and landholding

Land is no longer the only source of subsistence for *trasaccani*, and its significance as the basis of power has long since declined. Nevertheless, it provides the main source of their income for 36 per cent of the population, and its ownership by members of the elite is one component of their status.

There are two categories of land in each *comune*, 'Fucino' and *'fuori-Fucino'* (32 per cent and 68 per cent respectively of the total Trasacco land area). Of the latter, 84 per cent is owned by the *comune* and is mountain pasture and woods. Some of it is land that was cultivated in the nineteenth and even in the early twentieth century, but with its declining fertility and the increase in other job opportunities the owners have not bothered to maintain their title. Citizens have *usi civici* rights of grazing and wood cutting which are controlled by the *comune* administration and granted on payment of a small annual fee. Only 12 shepherds graze a total of about 300 sheep

Table 3 *Trasacco: distribution of occupations and land.*

Occupational category	1975 Males over 21			
	Number who own land	Percentage who own land	Total in category	Percentage of total
Owner cultivators	400	100.0	400	22.2
Workers in permanent employment	20	17.4	115	6.4
Casual labourers	80	31.7	252	14.0
Agricultural labourers	70	30.4	230	12.8
Artisans	12	17.9	67	3.7
Traders	25	33.3	75	4.2
Teachers	6	23.1	26	1.4
Office workers	15	15.8	95	5.3
Professionals	8	44.4	18	1.0
Landowners (non-cultivating)	12	100.0	12	0.7
Business owners	0	0	10	0.6
Students	0	0	110	6.1
Pensioners	174	45.8	380	21.1
Herders	5	41.7	12	0.7
Total	827	45.9	1802	100.0

Sources: Electoral Roll, Trasacco, and Census 1971, ISTAT, Rome.

there today, though the number was greater before the land reform, and in the 1880s there were about 1000 head of sheep and goats plus cattle and horses. A few people, generally only when they are unemployed, claim rights to cut wood, and spend a few days a year cutting enough firewood for their homes. Again, before the land reform, this was much more common: firewood could be sold to the bakers in exchange for bread. So necessary was this to many budgets, that people without permits would risk prosecution and fines to gather wood. In 1949, 103 successful cases were brought by the *comune* against men and women who had cut wood illegally in Trasacco. When people tell you today that they had to go and cut wood in the past they mean to indicate that they were very poor. Anyone who cuts wood these days is regarded as rather eccentric even though it saves money.

Another 685 hectares of *fuori-Fucino* land is registered in the name of private owners. (Of what was privately registered in the nineteenth century, 383 hectares has reverted to commons.) Not all this land is actually being cultivated, as some of its owners point out. Its productivity is about 10 per cent of that of Fucino for potatoes and beet and about 30 per cent for grain. It is mostly planted with vines and wheat for domestic consumption. A new and potentially profitable initiative has been taken by Dr Ciofani, the *medico condotto*. Using government grants he has built a cattle stall on an extension of about forty hectares, where he will produce forage crops for forty head of beef cattle to be fattened in the stall. Another fifty farmers have a few cattle, but on the whole keeping animals is regarded as a *sacrificio* because they have to be fed and milked twice a day through weekends and holidays which interrupts family and social life, and a *fatica* because it is hard and dirty work. So far only Dr Ciofani and the area veterinary surgeon have taken up the government grants to increase meat production, and both of these employ stockmen.

As a result of inheritance most of the *fuori-Fucino* plots are too small and have too many owners to be viable. Only with some kind of cooperative organisation would stockraising, for which the land is well suited, become possible.

Land in Fucino is all arable, and it is amongst the most fertile in Italy. Average yields for sugar beet of 600 quintals (1 quintal = 1000 kilos) per hectare compare very favourably with the British average of 508 quintals. One hectare planted half with potatoes and half beet gave an average net profit of £800–1000 in 1974–5. Most plots are easy to irrigate using a tractor pump to siphon water from the canals which, being one kilometre apart, are never more than 500 metres away.

Holdings vary in size. Legally, no one may own more than ten hectares, a figure which was increased from a ceiling of four hectares in 1964. Land may only be sold to another assignee and only one heir may inherit. In practice all these rules are frequently broken. Consequently few transactions are registered with the Ente Fucino. Such reticence is very common: it is felt always to be safer to tell officials as little as possible.

In 1969 the number of assignees resident in Trasacco was officially recorded as 1022, a fall of 408 from 1430 in 1952. No later figures were available, but Ente Fucino officials now estimate that the 1571 hectares allocated to *trasaccani* assignees in 1952 have been reduced by sales to farmers in Luco and San Benedetto to between 800 and 900 hectares. In addition a considerable area is rented, although renting is illegal. The area affected is obviously impossible to assess, but renting seemed to be a fairly common and certainly normal practice, particularly for assignees who had other employment and less time to cultivate it.

The opportunity to rent land in Fucino was being eagerly grasped. In 1974–5, for example, a Venetian vegetable exporter was using rented land to build up a highly speculative business producing carrots for foreign markets. Carrots can be left in the ground all through the winter without spoiling and can be harvested at short notice when the market price is high. The Venetian employed a local man to find land to rent. He would plant it and employ workers on piece rates to harvest when the merchant phoned to give the go-ahead from Venice. His example was being followed by a *marchigiano* who had built a carrot-washing station where the workers could be employed if it rained (he was offering a daily, not a piece, rate); and by a farmer from San Benedetto. Whilst the *marchigiano* was operating on two of his own four assigned hectares, the two outsiders were having little difficulty in obtaining land to rent from *trasaccani* and were planning to expand in the following year.

These carrot enterprises were new departures in Trasacco. The normal Fucino crops are beet and potatoes and some grain. However, all these crops deplete the soil: without rotation, fallowing or fodder crops, very large quantities of fertiliser and anti-parasite products have to be used.

Ploughing is completely mechanised, and costs could be vastly reduced if neighbouring farmers arranged to have their land ploughed collectively. Although farmers often observed that it would be an excellent idea, they insisted that they were *troppo egoisti* (too self-centred) to do so. Two *marchigiani* have highly sophisticated harvesters for potatoes, which take the crop out of the ground and put it into bags right in the field; others use a tractor to turn the potatoes to the surface whilst labourers follow collecting them into baskets. The big harvesters are not sufficiently used and without joint ownership such heavy mechanisation tends to drive up costs without increasing the profit margin. Both farmers and Ente Fucino experts are far from optimistic about the prospects for cooperatives.

Land is widely distributed amongst the population (see Table 3) so that many whose main income is derived from another occupation also have an interest in land. The soil is fertile, but broken down into small plots and often worked by cultivators who are not full-time farmers, it is not being used to its best advantage. The system has neither the technical efficiency of the large capitalist farm nor the intensive labour input of the peasant family farm. Every Fucino smallholder is producing entirely for the market, but because the majority of landholdings assigned in 1952 were only one hectare in size, too small for family subsistence, many smallholders were forced to look for subsidiary employment. When this becomes full time, the cultivator employs others to do the work or treats it like a Sunday allotment. He does not saturate it with his labour as he would if he drew his livelihood from it and the land is consequently less productive than it might be. One clerk in the Trasacco *comune* offices planted his hectare with potatoes saved from the previous season, a practice which he knew to be risky. Instead of a normal yield he barely got back what he had sown. Alternatively and more rationally, in that it moves towards the reduction in the number of cultivators suggested by the Mansholt Plan, the man who finds other work rents or sells his land to a full-time cultivator, but this is not happening at great speed because of the scarcity of alternative employment.

Emigration

The traditional solution to the problem of earning a living from an insufficiently productive agriculture has been emigration. The picture in Trasacco is not clear cut. The region of Abruzzo—Molise suffered a net loss of 43 per cent of its inhabitants between 1906 and 1915, years of peak emigration rates. This was the highest in the whole of Italy (Lopreato, 1967: 43). But within that same period, the Fucino basin was an area of net population increase, and this has continued to the present day. The increase is actually concentrated in Avezzano, with a decline in other *comuni*.

Since 1951 the population of Trasacco has fallen by 3 per cent. This is much lower than the average decline of 18 per cent in the rural *comuni* of Fucino (and a 41 per cent increase in the population of Avezzano). It is not clear how much of the 3 per cent decline is due to emigration, and how many people have simply moved to Avezzano. It is possible that the figures do not reflect the real emigration rate at all. Migrants often emigrate and return many times before settling finally at home or abroad. Very often they do not inform the authorities of their change of residence; they keep up their citizenship in the *comune* and return there to vote. From talking to informants it was clear that *trasaccani* had emigrated to many parts of the world, before the First World War, at the time of the land reform and also more recently.

Early migrants went to the States. In the 1950s the countries that attracted them were Australia, Latin America and Canada. The most recent magnet for migrants had been West Germany, but the oil crisis of 1973 and the cutbacks at Volkswagen made it likely that many would soon be returning home. These contemporary migrants are unlikely to come back, as earlier returned migrants to the States used to do, with large savings and the intention of buying land (cf. Lopreato, 1967). Nowadays it is common for a migrant to take his family with him to northern Europe and for both husband and wife to work. This makes it impossible for him to live as cheaply as his earlier counterpart did, in all-male, barrack-like lodgings, with multi-occupation of the beds (cf. Covello, 1967). Migration is not, as it was in Lopreato's Franza, a means of rapid and dramatic social mobility (Lopreato, 1967), nor does it appear ever to have been so. In Fucino returned migrants have bought shops or bars and built houses, but many migrants and their families now return without any savings, hoping to enter wage employment. Failure to do so usually leads to re-emigration.

Industrial employment in the Marsica

The possibility of *trasaccani* finding work in the area is much better now than twenty-five years ago, but, as shown in Chapter 2, employment prospects as a whole are not very good. The land reform rationalised the system of land tenure, and in implementing that and subsequent measures it created employment for 300 office workers, 300 'cooperative' employees (i.e. employed in local offices of the Ente)[1] and a fluctuating workforce of 400 to 600 labourers employed on short-term contracts. The reform stimulated the building industry directly with the construction of local offices, houses for assignees and a whole new village of 800 people round the old Administration buildings. In addition, as many people have sold their holdings and constructed new dwellings, this has provided more employment in building. Large numbers of men find in building one element of their particular *combinazione* of the jobs that together provide them with an income. It is only for skilled workers that the building sector can provide a secure and sufficient full-time income. Contractors are loth to pay salaries and the overheads for workers who all too frequently have to be laid off in bad weather or a market slump. Employers' contributions to insurance, unemployment and redundancy schemes can easily equal the worker's wage.

The land reform rationalised land tenure. In 1964 Avezzano was nominated as the site for an Industrial Nucleus, to stimulate industrial development. As part of its general policy for the development of the South, the Cassa per il Mezzogiorno designated a number of 'nuclei' where the infrastructure and services for industry would be provided and within which investors would be given special credit and tax incentives to build factories. The first to take advantage of the concessions, with the construction of a paper mill, was the present Prince Alessandro Torlonia. The family had continued to have financial interests in the area after the expropriation of their land – the water in the canals, the outlet into the River Liri and the electricity it produced were theirs; the power ran the turbines at the Torlonia sugar refinery which the family still owns outright, and the excess electricity was sold to the national grid. The hydro-electric station easily coped with the new demands of the paper mill for current.

The paper mill was completed in 1964, and with 515 employees it is the largest employer of men in the Fucino basin. Following this, a small firm making steel-framed industrial buildings began operations and now employs 70 male workers. The four other factories which followed employ mainly women: three making garments have a total of 290 workers, and a branch of ITT producing telephone components employs 536. In terms of the employment of *trasaccani*, the most important characteristic is that women far out-

1 As part of the land reform programme the Ente Fucino had to provide a 'cooperative' in each *comune*. They have elective councils, but the president of each is an Ente Fucino official. This causes a great deal of cynicism about the real extent of their control by assignees. It gave to the word 'cooperative' a rather particular meaning in Fucino. Today they are run by Ente Fucino clerks. They sell fertiliser, anti-parasite products, seed, etc., and organise the irrigation rota.

number men. Only 32 men but 176 women work at the Nucleus. Another dozen men travel daily to the outskirts of L'Aquila where they work in a branch of the Siemens electronics group.

This disparity between the numbers of men and women factory employees may seem surprising in the light of the literature on Southern Italy. Heavy restrictions purportedly surround women in villages where a man's honour and hence his power and influence are derived from his performance of familial roles as father, husband and provider and also from his ability to control the sexuality of his womenfolk (cf. Blok, 1969; Cronin, 1970; Davis 1969a and 1969b). The Industrial Nucleus is seen by some *trasaccani* as a den of iniquity where women are easily seduced by powerful managers and their male colleagues. Many families refuse to have their women or young girls work there.

The fact that many women do so nonetheless indicates that values differ, or can be overruled by the need to earn money. Marital status is not a determining factor: both married and unmarried women work in the factories. The disparity in the numbers of men and women does not reflect a great difference in the number of jobs available for each sex, for there are approximately 790 places for men and 880 for women in the Nucleus. The explanation has to be sought in the relationship between modes of recruitment and political processes. Trasacco's clientelist politicians have connections with the factories that employ women. Trade unions in the factories with a predominantly male workforce resist clientelist intervention in the area of personnel recruitment.

The clientele system and factory employment

Various people in Trasacco, either directly or through more powerful individuals like Natali, leader of the major Dc faction in Abruzzo, can influence managers of factories in the Industrial Nucleus. Mignini is the mayor of Trasacco. He is also the *comune* employment officer and in that capacity he is informed when the ITT subsidiary, CEME is recruiting labour. Women who want to work there can, by approaching Mignini, get *raccomandazioni* from Natali, a man whom the personnel manager cannot afford to offend. Ninety women in a workforce of 500 at CEME come from Trasacco. Don Pasquale, the parish priest, helps women who apply for work at Albatros, a shirt factory where 41 *trasaccane* are employed in a workforce of 178. In CEME and Albatros they are the largest contingent from any one *comune*, outside of Avezzano itself.

Recruitment to the sugar refinery and the paper mill, which employ mainly men, is not organised through the clientele system. When these employers require workers they inform the local employment office in Avezzano. Men registered there and in other local offices are awarded points according to their circumstances. The points system establishes a hierarchy of need and the jobs go to the most needy. This format is laid down by the national industrial code, but it is only adhered to where trade unions insist on its application. The Cgil claims membership of about 75 per cent of the workforce in the paper mill and the sugar refinery. With such strong support it is able actually to prevent management, should it wish to do so, from adopting clientelist methods in recruiting new workers.

There is no trade-union presence at all in Albatros, and at CEME the Cgil only gained admittance in 1973, a full five years after the factory opened. Thus most of the workforce had been recruited when the union had no means of compelling management to conform to the law and refrain from clientelistic practices.

Trade-union action does not fully explain why so few men from Trasacco work in factories (there are rather more from Luco for example). The idea of economic security is one reason for this. *Trasaccani* prefer to work for the State, where employment is secure, even when the wages they can earn in factories are the same or higher. This attitude is common in South Italy: 'In a survey of Italian youth in the 1950s, over 55 per cent of the Southerners preferred public employment to working for a private firm, mainly for the security it represented. In contrast a majority of those who expressed a preference in the North (38 per cent of the total sample) preferred to work in a private firm.' (La Palombara & Waters, quoted by Tarrow, 1967: 57.)

The Ente Fucino, for example, employs labourers on short-term contracts of 179 days, to avoid paying full insurance contributions. It keeps its workers politically in line: '*ti sguardano* (they look at you askance) if you don't have a Cisl (Christian Democrat trade union) card', said one employee. Yet this is still regarded as 'safer' employment than the factories 'which could close in a crisis'. The Forestry Commission restricts its employees in similar ways, but many *trasaccani* still hope to work there. Most of the menial state positions are very secure indeed, and they often require little physical or mental effort. The positions of cleaners, messengers, and above all *bidelli* (caretakers) are much envied. Hence the enormous competition for these posts and the crucial role they play as counters in political bargaining.

The *braccianti*, *figure miste* and unemployment

The people referred to in Table 3 as agricultural labourers (*braccianti*) and casual labourers are frequently unemployed. Their jobs are usually seasonal and contractual. At the end of each contract they must look for work once more. In winter most of them are unemployed. Their numbers are swollen each summer by young school leavers in search of their first job. There is great anxiety about getting work, given the high unemployment levels in the area. Unemployment pay is derisory, being worth the equivalent of two packs of cigarettes a day. Those who have never been employed are not entitled to any benefit, and there is no equivalent to the British system of supplementary benefits.

Short-term employment and chronic unemployment are not new problems to the South. Their acute significance for social organisation is not so much the poverty and anxiety they induce but the way in which they feed into the political structure. As Tarrow puts it:

an individual seeking employment in a fragmented economic system must be available on all sides ... Forced to seek various forms of employment, constantly in a context of over-population and scarce resources, [he] becomes a negotiator. In this sense, all his social relations are 'political'. (Tarrow, 1967: 75.)

Diplomati and *professionali*

It is the possession of a high-school diploma or a university degree which qualifies an individual for entry into the better-paid non-manual occupations. The only requirement that must be fulfilled in order to continue to high school is possession of the Terza Media certificate, which most pupils obtain at the age of fourteen or fifteen. Thereafter, anyone who passes through the high-school exams may go on to university. The vocational high schools provide their graduates with a *diploma*: in land surveying, teaching, commerce. A certificate from the *licei* (grammar schools) is an entry to university but is not in itself a qualification like the diploma. All *diplomati* and *liceo* graduates may continue to university without further selection procedures.

The Italian education system produces far more *diplomati* and university graduates than its economy can absorb. Even though the qualifications for many menial posts in the bureaucracy have been raised to the Terza Media, applications still far outnumber the posts. Only in engineering and agriculture is the output of the universities insufficient: even doctors have difficulty finding a practice.

There are three doctors, two priests and a veterinary surgeon in Trasacco and numerous graduate teachers, many of whom are employed in other *comuni*. *Diplomati* are employed by the *comune* and in the *pretura* (law court) in Trasacco and in many different offices of the state in Avezzano. Once they have found employment they earn salaries ranging from £140 to £500 or £600 a month (in 1975). A farmer must own at least two and a half hectares of land to earn an income equivalent to that of a school teacher or *comune* office employee and much more land is necessary to reach the income level of a functionary in the Ente Fucino or a doctor.

There is no entrepreneurial middle class. The jobbing builders are essentially

41

self-employed people who take on labour on a casual basis as their needs dictate. A small cement-brick factory has been in existence for twenty years and has never employed more than four workers. Apart from these there are self-employed bar, shop and hotel keepers, none of whose businesses are expanding and none of whom can be seen as risk-taking, investing, incipient capitalists.

The occupational hierarchy and politics

Traditionally it was the ownership of land that conferred power and status. This is no longer the case in Fucino. The land reform abolished large holdings and very few farmers have been able to reconstitute holdings so large as to require or permit the maintenance of a permanent or even a semi-permanent labour force. In Trasacco there are no landholdings which can be used as a springboard into politics. Indeed most farmers in Trasacco are trying to move out of agriculture, and if they cannot do this for themselves, this is their ambition for their children, whom they educate as highly as possible so that they can find other employment. Factory work is not seen as an improvement on farming, for manual work in any form is associated with low status, here as throughout the South.

Artisans, bartenders and shopkeepers, even though they work for themselves and may earn as much as a clerk, fall on the 'manual' side of that great divide. Because their work necessitates long hours at the bench or behind the counter, they cannot take part in that 'meaningful social activity . . . the consumption of conspicuous leisure' (Colclough, 1969: 17). The pettiest clerk in the *comune* office has more prestige − he can take long coffee breaks at the café and wear *borghese* (suit and tie) to work. More significantly, he has the rudiments of power. He has passed the Terza Media, so he can read and write and fill in forms: his knowledge can be used to help or hinder those who cannot. In Italy that kind of help from a clerk is not expected as a matter of course. It is not part of his job and he expects to be paid for it. He may also be in a position to facilitate or delay the processing of various applications; he may, if he chooses, wave aside a proffered payment and suggest instead political support either for himself or a man to whom he is indebted.

It is difficult to reach these positions: education is expensive and competition for employment almost as fierce as it is for the manual worker. But the holder of a degree or diploma is crucially different from a manual worker or a peasant: he has social prestige. He has a title which in Trasacco and the South generally is very often used both in writing and in speech: *geometra* (surveyor), *maestro* (teacher), *ingegnere* (engineer), as well as *dottore* (anyone with a degree). In Trasacco membership of the prestigious men's *Circolo* is restricted to *diplomati* and graduates.

Even at the level of professional occupations the manual/non-manual divide is maintained. Southern universities are notorious for training very few students in technical and scientific fields, and there is no undergraduate course in agricultural economics in any Southern university. Table 4 shows university enrolment by region and major field of study. It demonstrates quite clearly the evaluation of technical qualifications as compared to the liberal arts and professions. Of the 42 graduates in Trasacco in 1975, none had a degree in science or engineering. Only the veterinary surgeon was qualified in a subject related to the major productive sector of the area: agriculture. According to Tarrow this happens because in the South 'strategic social roles . . . are removed from the productive process [so that] many individuals choose fields of study with less practical and more prestige value' (Tarrow, 1967: 63).

In other words, a man's success in this society does not come from engaging in the productive sector of the economy but from the manipulation of the political process; or again, as Barnes & Sani put it, 'Values are realised more through connections that involve political relationships than by means of economic entrepreneurship, hard work or frugality.' (Barnes & Sani, 1974.)

Table 4 *University enrolment by faculty.*

	Science	Engineering	Economics	Law	Literature & Philosophy	Total
1963						
North	18 634	16 286	39 202	18 646	26 833	119 601
	15.6	13.6	32.8	15.6	22.4	100%
South	7 383	4205	17 016	14 677	21 444	64 725
	11.4	6.5	26.3	22.7	33.1	100%
1973						
North	61 087	61 566	38 656	52 395	57 437	271 141
	22.2	22.7	14.6	19.3	21.2	100%
South	37 005	21 509	19 996	47 972	35 220	161 702
	22.9	13.3	12.4	29.7	21.8	100%

Sources: Annuario Statistico Italiano, 1964 p. 109 (Tarrow, p. 62); Annuario Statistico Italiano dell'Istruzione, 1974 p. 338.

5 Politics in Trasacco

The context

Italians normally go to the polling booths twice in every five years. In the series 1950, 1955, 1960, 1965 they voted in what are called *le amministrative* for councils to run the *comuni* and provinces. From 1970 onwards *le amministrative* included elections to the newly constituted regional councils. In the series 1963, 1968, 1972, 1976 they voted in *le politiche* for the two houses of parliament, 'la Camera dei Deputati' and 'il Senato'. The electoral system is one of proportional representation at all levels except for the councils of *comuni* with under 5000 inhabitants. Here only two lists may be presented and, in order to guarantee both administrative stability and the presence of an opposition, the winning list takes 16 seats and the losing one 4, no matter what their proportion of the vote.

Only at local elections do alliances between parties take the form of presenting a common list to the electorate. Occasionally alliances are made to fight elections at other levels, as when the Pci and Psi formed the Popular Front in 1948. But generally at national, regional and provincial elections each party fights its own election campaign. Only then, if there is no overall majority, are alliances formed between the elected parliamentary or conciliar parties in order to carry on the business of government or administration.

When political scientists talk about the instability of governments in Italy, they do not mean that the government loses the support of the people. On the contrary, the support base of each party is very stable. The percentage swing at elections of around 2 per cent is very much lower than in Great Britain, for example, where a 7 per cent swing is by no means uncommon. 'Unstable government' in the Italian context means that the party or parties in power cannot maintain the alliances which enable parliamentary business to be carried on. The most common cause of governmental collapse is a breakdown in the alliance between factions within a single party, the Dc, which necessitates the resignation of all ministers. In the interim between governments, a new round of bargaining takes place over which faction will get what ministry, at what price in terms of political support (see Zuckerman, 1974, for a clear exposition of the factions and bargains in the Dc). Similar

44

proceedings happen on a smaller and less publicised scale in regional and provincial councils and, above all, in local councils, especially those with a Dc majority and especially in the South.

Political divisions between and within parties

In the 1970 elections in Trasacco the Dc gained an absolute majority of the votes for the council. As a *comune* of over 5000 inhabitants, it has 21 councillors. The Dc took 12 of the seats, the remainder being divided as follows: 5 to the Psi and Pci (who had presented a joint list), 2 to the social democrat Psdi and 2 to the neo-fascist Msi.

The opposition was divided into three mutually antagonistic groups, each confronting the Dc administration from fundamentally different positions. The Pci/Psi, led by Aristotele D'Amato, made its attack from the Left with accusations of favouritism to the clients and kin of the Dc councillors, 'immobility' on social questions like housing, water supply and drains, and lack of support for the struggles of *contadini* and workers. The local Psdi found itself in an equivocal position. At regional and national levels it is allied with the Dc. It could not ally with the Left in Trasacco for ideological reasons — one of its *raisons d'être* is anti-communism. Its two councillors, led by Teofilo Courier, tended to express opposition rarely and then only on limited and specific issues. The Msi, on the other hand, was free to attack the administration since it had no ties with the Dc, but it had to differentiate itself from the left-wing opposition. It could not simply reinforce attacks already launched from the Left and so it too remained largely silent. In addition a schism developed between the Pci and Psi. The Psi accused the Pci of not keeping to the agreement on which their pre-electoral alliance had been based. As a result, in 1975 Pci and Psi presented separate lists. Throughout the period 1970—5 the opposition were unable to launch any concerted attack on the administration.

The Dc party in Trasacco is divided into two institutionalised factions which compete between themselves for office. This local factionalism reflects on a small scale the national structure of the Dc party. The national party is divided into seven recognised factions which have their own leaders, offices and organisations. These national level factions rely on segmentary alliances that stretch down to their bases in the 8056 *comuni*. At each electoral level there are intermediate leaders who guarantee support to those above them and, in turn, to the national leaders of their faction (see Figure 1).

In the Abruzzo the two major political personalities are Natali, a deputy and former minister of agriculture, and Gaspari, a deputy and recent minister of posts and telegraphs. In terms of the national factions, Natali is a *Fanfaniano*, a support of Fanfani, while Gaspari is a *Doroteo*, a follower of

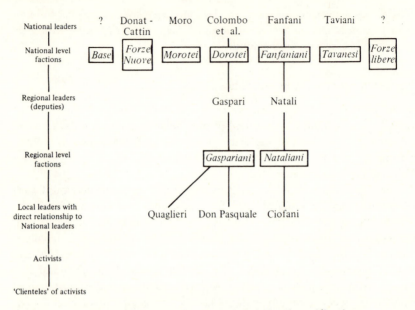

Figure 1   National factions of the Dc and their local ramifications

Colombo. Both are 'right of centre'. In Trasacco Dc activists are all supporters of either Gaspari or Natali. The electorate is, on the whole, only dimly aware of these differences. They know of the split in the local *sezione*, but see it in purely local and personal terms: Don Pasquale and Dr Ciofani 'non si possono vedè – they cannot stand the sight of one another.'

They are not aware of the import of this antagonism beyond the fortunes of the *comune* administrations. The loyalty of party members – who are not the same as activists (see below) – is to particular personalities (*politicanti*) within the *sezione*.

From 1970 to 1975 the *Nataliani* were led by Dr Ciofani. He is one of the two doctors employed and paid in part by the *comune*. Dr Ciofani was a local councillor until 1968, when he had to resign owing to his appointment as *medico condotto*, for as a *comune* employee he could not also be a councillor. From 1970 to 1975 he was a provincial councillor for the constituency of Trasacco, Ortucchio and San Benedetto. The leader of the *Gaspariani* in Trasacco is Don Pasquale – the parish priest of the main church. As an ordained and practising priest he may not be a councillor. Neither faction leader is thus in a position to be elected councillor or mayor, and the struggle for these offices goes on between their respective protégés. The *Nataliani* are in the majority in Trasacco. In the elections for the committee of the Dc

46

sezione they regularly receive two-thirds of the vote and the *Gaspariani* one-third. This signifies that when negotiations take place for the formation of the party list for the *comune* elections, the two factions are represented in the list of twenty names in the proportion of two to one. The leader of the *Nataliani* heads the list. Every vote for the list which does not stipulate a preference is automatically awarded as a preference for the list leader, so this guarantees him the most preference votes and therefore the office of mayor. In the 1970 Dc electoral list there were 13 *Nataliani* and 7 *Gaspariani*.

The Dc, with a solid majority and a hopelessly divided opposition, should have had an easy run through the five-year administration. It was not external attack but internal dissension between its own factions that caused administrative collapse in 1974.

In the formation of the *giunta* (the executive committee) hard bargaining produced 2 *Gaspariani* and 3 *Nataliani*, one of whom was the mayor, Mignini. He had been a *Gaspariano* until 1968 when Ciofani helped him to appointment as local employment officer. His defection caused difficulties with his former co-factionists almost from the beginning of the administration, and in May 1974 the *Gaspariani* in the *giunta* voted against him on a major issue. Mignini had to resign. Negotiations began immediately to find a new mayor and a *giunta* who would support him. Such was the extent of factional discord that no basis could be found for cooperation. After two months the prefect threatened to dissolve the council and replace it with a prefectorial commissioner. This would have made the Dc administration appear even more incompetent to the electorate than it already did. It would also have deprived the Dc of the opportunity to carry out vote-catching projects in the run-up to the 1975 elections. These considerations helped the factions to come to an eventual agreement. The man selected was a *Nataliano*, Del Boccio, a functionary in the Post Office. Because of his selection as mayor, the Post Office had to give him a position within easy distance of his *comune*. The *Gaspariani* were able to drive a hard bargain in exchange for their support for Del Boccio, who had thus obtained a personal benefit as well, for transfers nearer home are very difficult to obtain.

The downfall of the *giunta* in Trasacco was caused by personal animosity. Mignini apparently wanted to carry out some public works that would benefit his supporters. The *Gaspariani* were unsatisfied with the *quid pro quo* they were offered. Instead of trying to strike a new bargain in some informal setting, they chose to make it a public issue by allowing the question to come to the vote. This kind of administrative failure is very common in Southern *comuni*. Colclough reports that in Accettura, because of factional and personal ruptures, only three out of six administrations have run their course (Colclough, 1969: 191–201).

Schisms in the Dc

In cases of administrative breakdown it is in the discretion of the prefect either to hold special elections or to send a commissioner. In Trasacco the Dc usually manages to resolve internal disputes during a term of office and so avoids the intervention of the prefect. It is in the run-up to elections that quarrels often threaten to sunder the party and they sometimes do. During 1959–60 successive blows to party unity resulted in victory for the Pci.

In 1959 special elections had to be held in Trasacco because of a breakdown in the administration that had been elected in 1955. In spite of their earlier incapacity, the Dc managed to obtain 58.4 per cent of the vote. Francesco Ippoliti headed the list and returned to his former position as mayor. During the year between these elections and those scheduled for June 1960, the rivalry between the incumbent mayor and the aspiring mayor, Dr Ciofani, came to a head. When it became apparent that Ciofani could win, Ippoliti, rather than see his rival in office, instructed his supporters to vote for the list headed by the Pci. The Pci-led list won 61 per cent of the total vote. This apparent victory was not at all a measure of support for the Pci, but a measure of Ippoliti's personal following. Ippoliti left soon after to live in Rome, but he continued to have influence in Trasacco. He figures again in a recent event which illustrates once more the weight of personal against party support.

A group of young activists were formed under the leadership of a hospital doctor, Quaglieri. All were *Gaspariani* who were critical of their co-factionists' behaviour in breaking up the 1970–5 administration by voting against the mayor, Mignini. The '*Gaspariani* dissidents' suddenly emerged as a serious force five months before the *comune* elections. In January 1975 elections were held for the Dc *sezione* committee, and these 'dissidents' wrested the minority representation from Don Pasquale's 'official' *Gaspariani*. The former mayor, Ippoliti, helped the dissidents by adding his personal supporters to theirs, for he too had broken with Don Pasquale. A month before the June elections the *Nataliani* and official *Gaspariani* joined forces to exclude Dr Quaglieri and his group from the party's electoral list, and voted to include Don Pasquale's supporters instead. Dr Quaglieri's group countered by drawing up an opposing list under the symbol of the *campanile* (bell-tower, a common symbol for civic groups).

Whilst Ippoliti's break with the party seemed to have been based on personal rivalry, Dr Quaglieri's was presented, publicly at least, as based on real and important issues about maladministration and favouritism. Doubts were cast on the purity of his motives, however, when he eventually allied with the neo-fascist Msi and presented a joint electoral list with them. He had earlier criticised the Msi in personal and ideological terms whenever it had been suggested that he might have to seek their support. In the end he had to ally with them because they were competing for the same floating votes and neither group on its own had sufficient guaranteed votes to ensure even a single seat on the council.

In the same pre-election period the *Nataliani* had problems of a similar nature to sort out. A rift had developed between Ciofani and Mignini, who had always been his protégé. Eighteen years before, Ciofani had cemented his political relationship with Natali by having the deputy become godfather to his first son. This established Natali and Ciofani as *compari* (the implications of this will be discussed in the following chapter). Mignini's relations with Natali had always been mediated by Ciofani. However, on the night of his election address in Trasacco in March, Natali dined alone with Mignini. This was a symbolic confirmation of the fact that Mignini had established a relation with Natali independent of Ciofani. It was also a slight to Ciofani from his own faction leader. Ciofani suffered a second blow when he was not chosen as the party's provincial candidate. The reason given for his omission was that a man of Ciofani's clientelistic reputation would not stand a chance with Luco's voters, who were now included in the constituency. It became quite possible that Ciofani would defect and throw his considerable bloc of votes behind the Pci. To placate him the Dc regional leadership promised him the much sought-after nomination for deputy in 1977 (elections which were actually brought forward to 1976), and he stayed in the party.

An important Dc activist did leave the party at this time. His case shows how minor parties figure in the system. Apart from the Pci, which is a special case, none of the parties have any existence between elections. Just before elections they spring to life with speakers and posters. They jostle for alliances and voters. Above all they are convenient to individual Dc politicians as alternatives to which dissidents can retreat (or threaten to) together with their supporters. Romolo Salvi was a Dc councillor from 1970 to 1975. He had once been a leading member of the Pci until offered a post with the Ente Fucino as secretary of the Trasacco 'cooperative'. This position was an influential one from which he had been able to build up a personal following. At a pre-election meeting of the Dc he suggested that all the old councillors be replaced by new young men, so as to disassociate the party from its old, corrupt image. Instead of following his advice, all the old guard except Salvi had their candidatures confirmed. He resigned from the party and joined the Pri (Republican Party), who put him at the head of their list. This honour can only have been accorded him because of the votes he guaranteed to bring with him. From 3.1 per cent of the vote in 1970 the Pri doubled its share in 1975 to 6.2 per cent. From no seats in 1970 it took one seat, which went to Romolo Salvi.

The question raised by these and other machinations over candidatures, alliances, pay-offs and so on, is how individuals can come to constitute a threat to the party. Why was Ciofani's possible defection the cause of agitated discussion reaching to the regional level where nominations for the Camera are decided? Why was there endless negotiation with Dr Quaglieri to stop him forming a separate list? Individuals do not seem to be afraid of losing the backing of the party; it is the party that fears losing the support of influential individuals. The Dc fears for its overall majority when these key individuals threaten to desert it. Such individuals carry a significant number of votes which they can place at will with whichever party they decide to support.

How the clientele networks operate

The activists of the Dc explain how the system functions in terms of kinship networks. The secretary, Beppino Ippoliti (a distant relative of ex-mayor Francesco Ippoliti), took a Machiavellian pleasure in explaining it with the aid of diagrams and figures. The Dc, he told me, has 1200 paid-up members. This is equivalent to 85 per cent of the vote that it received in the 1975 regional elections: only 15 per cent of its electorate is not accounted for in the membership. I was not allowed to examine the list in detail, but I saw that there were at least two pages covered with names ending in Mignini, two pages of Ippolitis and so on. It was clear that a large number of the members were kinsmen of one another and of activists. According to Ippoliti, every year each *politicante* goes from house to house collecting dues and renewing his ties with his kin and other supporters.

Having paid their dues, party members have the right to vote in the election to the *sezione* committee. This is the limit of most ordinary members' contribution to the party. The *sezione* committee elections are held every two years. Each activist with ambitions to become a candidate, or with an obligation to help someone else, makes sure that 'his' members turn out to vote. This election is a trial of strength between the factions to determine the number of candidates each can present on the party's electoral list. It is also an occasion for the demonstration of personal followings. Any man who can muster 220 votes (the minimum vote required to ensure the election of an individual to the *comune* council) in the *sezione* election has a very strong claim to be included in the Dc electoral list for the *comune*. The man with the most *sezione* votes has a right to be placed at the head of the list, where he automatically becomes mayor. A man's showing at the *sezione* elections is taken to be a demonstration of the number of votes that he can guarantee the party in an election. Some men have additional support outside the party membership. Dr Ciofani, for example, has great influence in the party because of his personal support, measured in the number of preference votes that he gets at elections. These far outnumber the votes he gets from members in *sezione* elections, and a proportion of them – his 'vote bank' to use F.G. Bailey's term – is consistent over a number of elections.

When someone like Ciofani (or any other activist with a secure support base) does not stand himself, he promises his following to a protégé (like Mignini) or to a superior (like Natali), always, of course, within the same faction. Or it may be offered to a man of equal status who is an ally.

Kinship plays a part, but only a part, in the formation of vote banks. Where the kin networks of two *politicanti* overlap, one may stand down so as not to compete for the same votes. For example, the former deputy mayor gave his support to the Quaglieri group and did not stand for it himself. He did this, he said, because he and Quaglieri were first cousins, the sons of sisters. His abstention meant that another candidate could be chosen who would bring support for the list from his own, different, group of kin.

It is interesting in this context that, while the Quaglieri group had originally coalesced on the basis of criticism of the administration, when asked what alternative policies they were presenting to the electorate as '*Gaspariani* reformists', the same ex-deputy-mayor replied: 'Here in Trasacco it is not a matter of arguments or policies, but of the number of kin that your candidates can rely on for votes. The "real communists" are the only ones who vote on ideological grounds. Anyone from the Psi rightwards will vote for his kin.'

Although it is in terms of kin networks that these activists explain the composition and success of their electoral lists, links into the networks of job distribution are at least as important. Mignini, the mayor, is the employment officer of Trasacco, a key position for the acquisition of information about jobs and for influencing who gets them. Don Pasquale is a parish priest, and as such his *raccomandazione* is an essential accompaniment to some job applications. Ciofani and Quaglieri are doctors. As Colclough points out, doctors often occupy key positions in the political systems of Southern villages: they are educated, they know everyone's secrets, they are often creditors, and they can sometimes influence marriage alliances (Colclough, 1969: 169–70). In addition, it is said, Dr Ciofani can influence appointments to CEME and the state hospital in Avezzano.

An example which demonstrates, among other things, the significance of being a doctor, is that of Dr Dalla Montà. In 1958 he stood as a candidate for the Camera dei Deputati, under the emblem of the Msi (neo-fascist party). He took 44.7 per cent of the Trasacco vote, although he conducted no election campaign. He had no kin, but he was a trusted and popular doctor. Dr Ciofani is neither; on the contrary, many people go to Dalla Montà for treatment although they are registered as patients of Dr Ciofani.

People register with Dr Ciofani because they want to keep on the right side of him but they believe Dalla Montà to be a more competent doctor. Ciofani is one of a number of key individuals who can do a person a *favore*, or are at least believed to have that power. The electoral success of such people depends on a mixture of kinship obligation and the judicious distribution of *favori*. One elector becomes obligated to vote for someone who does him a *favore*. Another tries to extract a *favore* from an influential man by promising him political support. Each relationship is a unique and separate one. It may last only a short time if the client gets impatient with waiting for a promised *favore* that never materialises, but it may become a long-term one for a variety of reasons. Where kinship and economic dependence coincide, the relation comes closest to being the kind of life-long bond that constituted the traditional landlord—peasant, patron—client tie. Dr Ciofani, for example, had a number of kinsmen who were *braccianti*. They seemed to be totally committed to him, never thinking of voting against him and always hopeful that one day he would get them a secure job.

The following example shows how various obligations and commitments are weighed up in arriving at a decision to vote one way rather than another. One evening Beppina D'Amato (sister of the secretary of the Pci *sezione*), her son, Michele, and I were sitting at supper. Michele had graduated in economics six months before and was still unemployed. The Dc secretary, Beppino Ippoliti, who is a cousin of Beppina's deceased husband, dropped in for coffee. She immediately asked him if he had heard of any openings for Michele. Ippoliti said that a branch of the Banca Del Santo Spirito (Vatican bank) was opening shortly in Avezzano, and there might be a job there he could lay his hands on. Beppina began to thank him profusely, promising that if he was successful he would get her vote. Indeed she would vote for anyone who fixed Michele up with a job, she said. Beppino protested that he would *never* ask for her vote; it belonged to her brother, 'who is unique'. 'Unique in what sense?', I asked, imagining that he might have opinions about the vital role of opposition in a democracy. But no, he meant 'unique in being her only brother'. Kinship ties obliged her to vote for him. He had no doubt that where kinship and any other obligation conflict, the obligation to the closest kinsman is paramount. This showed a measure of altruism in Ippoliti − or sensitivity to my presence. I was a foreigner likely to disapprove of the *favore* system and, besides, it was he who had earlier explained the support for the Dc to me in terms of kinship. However, he could easily have glossed over that kinship tie and claimed her vote on the grounds of their relationship by marriage. Besides, she was only too eager to give it to him. She even had other kin who voted for her brother because he was a kinsman. She could probably have persuaded them to vote for Ippoliti too, out of gratitude for Michele's job.

Michele himself was highly embarrassed by this discussion. He votes Pci because he would like the party to form a national government and realise a socialist programme. He said nothing, even though to have accepted Ippoliti's offer would have violated all his principles: it meant working for a Vatican bank, getting the job through a clientele network and 'selling' his and his kinsmen's votes. Michele needed the job very badly and had become disillusioned by the rejections that had so far been the only result of all his direct and un-supported applications.

I asked twenty electors in Trasacco how they would choose to vote in the forthcoming elections if they were presented with three lists:[1] one containing a close kinsman, one including a man who had done them a *favore* and one consisting of people whose party they supported. Two people said that they would have liked a list of good, honest administrators, but that was an alternative that never presented itself. One said she would vote Pci no matter who was on the list (she was the daughter of Beppino Di Cola, at one time leader of the Pci). All the rest said that they would vote for a kinsman *unless* someone had done them a *favore* and they had promised their vote in exchange. Some added that this was a very good way of repaying a *favore* because it cost the voter very little and was of value to the candidate, just as the *favore* was often of low cost to the giver and great value to the recipient. In any case, having promised the political support, which is often the price exacted for a *favore*, the respondent could not 'in conscience' vote against a benefactor even if the latter could never discover the betrayal.[2]

In contrast to Banfield's epithet 'amoral', there is no lack of morality in this personalistic style of politics. Colclough also argues that obligations are strongly felt and honoured to the letter. In Accettura one man refused a drink from a Dc candidate lest this oblige him to vote for him (Colclough, 1969: 154). That does not mean that the system is endorsed by the electorate. Many observers have commented on the cynicism of the Southern electorate (e.g. Tarrow, 1967: 7), on the suspicion that everyone is simply out to further their own interests (e.g. Banfield, 1958: 38), on the dis-affection and alienation of Southerners from the political process (Almond & Verba, 1963; Sartori, 1966: 152). The following story shows how such attitudes might develop.

As I sat having my hair washed one day, Gigina, the hairdresser, began to complain how unfair life was being to her family. Her husband, Cesidio, had been with the Post Office for six years. First he had been posted to the

---

1 I do not suggest that this is a statistically significant sample. It was merely a numerical check on the more haphazardly obtained information which follows.
2 Some people believed that it was possible for their votes to be recognised. In the past voters had sometimes been given unusual combinations of preference votes so that their forms could be checked. It is possible that such practices were still being pursued (see also p. 107).

province of Friuli in the north-east, an area regarded as very backward. Then, four years before, he had been moved to the Valle Roveto. He could live at home, but that meant travelling for four hours each day. His many applications for transfer closer to home had been refused, though he had seen others, such as Del Boccio, who were lower down on the *graduatorio*, moved and promoted. Although he did not himself approve of gift-giving to stimulate the granting of *favori*, his mother had taken many hams and chickens on his behalf to Don Pasquale, who has '*una certa amicizia*' (a particular friendship) with Gaspari, who was, of course, once minister of posts and telegraphs (and heads the Doroteo faction in Abruzzo). Rather than make gifts, Cesidio offered political support, and in the 1972 elections he distributed pamphlets, pasted posters, erected platforms, wired sound systems, and promised the votes of his family to the *Gaspariani* candidates. Three years later he was still working in the same Post Office. Thinking that Cesidio might be a known communist, I suggested that maybe he was in the wrong party so that all his present efforts could not erase his past. But, I was assured, 'Cesidio is a *piacione* (he likes to get on with everybody). If a communist does him a *favore*, he will vote for him, if a Christian Democrat he will vote Dc. Up to now no one has done him the *favore* he really needs, and this election we are all going to spoil our votes.' The other women present murmured their agreement.

Relations between voters and *politicanti*

This story raises important questions about the power of clients: their ability to influence *politicanti* in their favour. Resources *are* limited; not everyone who asks for a transfer can be satisfied. Some selection must be made, and it is likely that one of the criteria that *politicanti* use is the number of votes that can be given in exchange. In Cesidio's case he could influence the voting only of his wife and mother.

On the other hand, the *politicanti* need votes both to make their way inside the party and to be elected to office. As another woman observed: 'Now that it is election time everybody is offering you coffees and ice creams and promising you the earth.'

A third woman who had recently returned home to Trasacco was having difficulty getting her children accepted into the right grades at school. 'I can't walk two paces down the street without some *politicante* stopping me and promising to fix up the children', she said. Whilst these women felt there was no harm in giving their votes — it was a cheap exchange if something really got done — they were sceptical and cynical on two grounds. Once the elections were over, they said, the *politicanti* would neglect even to greet them. On the other hand, maybe what the *politicanti* did was not so much actively to help prospective voters, but to make things difficult for them if they withheld their support. 'As a result', one woman said, 'some of us simply assure everyone who asks that we will vote for them and, unless there is a specific reason not to, we vote as we feel best'.

One man, Teofilo Courier, was singled out by a number of informants as a man who had built up a *clientela* on the basis of promises alone. He was a *bidello* in the middle school. Although the position of *bidello* is menial and low-paid the income and job are secure. As a *bidello* he could join the public service branch of the Uil (Social Democratic trade union) and he had plenty of time (schools close at 1.0 p.m.) to pursue other business. His wife said that the house was always full of people asking for his help. In less than an hour I saw three people in whispered conclave with him. His wife said proudly that he did not take money but asked people to vote for him. It was said that the increase in the Psdi vote in Trasacco (from 9.5 per cent in 1965 to 17.6 per cent in 1975) was an index of his increasing influence in the village.

The source of his power was reputed to be his relationship with a functionary in the pensions office in L'Aquila. This man apparently kept him informed of the receipt of claims from *trasaccani*. Courier would then call on these people, saying that he had been in L'Aquila and had happened to notice their claims gathering dust in a corner. He would offer to get his friend to speed things up. Then in the fullness of time the pensions or what have you would arrive, the claimant would come to his house to express gratitude, perhaps with the first month's pension payment, which is regarded as a reasonable exchange for help, and Courier would graciously waive payment and ask for political support instead. In fact, it was suggested to me that all he did was to allow matters to take their usual course. Courier was proud of the help he was giving to the *povera gente* (poor unfortunates). Through his membership of Uil and connections with important people in the Psdi, he had been able to help a lot of people, he said. Since he had started this work 'politics in Trasacco had taken on a different aspect as people began to realise that they were not dependent on the doctor and the priest for everything'. Rather than representing change, however, he was simply a new element in the system. He had used neither land nor profession, in the strict sense, to build up his clientele, but rather the resources of a political party combined with personal connections. He is an example of what Weingrod has called a 'modern patron'.

Courier's case raises some important questions about the clientele system. A number of people expressed doubts as to whether Courier made any difference to the speed with which they received their pensions, but they continued to go to him, they said, because they were afraid that if they refused his help he might slow the process down, or have their file lost altogether.

Some *trasaccani* at least continue to function within the clientele system because they are afraid of the consequences if they do not. Dr Ciofani is the most prestigious man in Trasacco. He is widely thought of as medically incompetent: stories abound of how patients in his care died or were rushed in the nick of time to hospital or to Dr Dalla Montà. Ciofani's surgery is almost always empty, not because people are not sick, but because they prefer to attend Dalla Montà's surgery even if they have to queue from 7.0 a.m. to see him by noon. Fortunately Dalla Montà is near retirement and does not insist on payment. He cannot claim his fee from the insurance institutes because these patients have lodged their *libretti* (insurance cards) with Dr Ciofani. Time and again when asked why they did not register with Dalla Montà people replied that Dr Ciofani *'ti sguarderà'* (would look askance at you). 'One has to keep in his good books because he controls so many things: jobs in the factories, beds in the hospital, places in the football team, you name it . . . ' The *libretti* Ciofani keeps in his surgery are not insurance against illness but insurance against his indifference when their owners require help that Ciofani can provide through his many contacts.

Fear of Ciofani and his informants is extremely pervasive. Two very bright medical students who were involved in ultra-left politics at university always talked Dc politics in Trasacco, because Ciofani controls the entry of young doctors to the hospital at Avezzano. A student complained that because he was known in Trasacco as a communist, a fellow student, his closest friend in Rome, would not give him so much as a flicker of recognition in Trasacco. A boy was offered a place in the football team at Ortucchio, a neighbouring village. His mother begged him, with tears in her eyes, to clear it with Ciofani first (he is president of Trasacco's football club, in the junior division of which the boy was playing). The boy objected, but she insisted: 'You never know when we might need him, you can't risk alienating him.' Another woman who had been away for five years in Milan was met by her father-in-law at the station in Avezzano. The family knew that she and her husband were now members of the Pci. The father-in-law's 'first words' to her were 'for God's sake don't go around offending people with your ideas and endangering the welfare of the family'.

Clientelism and the Pci

Parties other than the Dc, Psdi and Pci have a somewhat ephemeral presence in Trasacco. We have seen the Pri being used by a dissident from the Dc to wreak revenge on his colleagues by transferring his vote bank. This can happen to the Psi and Msi as well. The Msi is led by Don Pasquale's assistant, Don Evaristo. He actually stood for election in 1970 knowing that, as a priest, he would have to resign his seat. The Msi has a fairly steady share of about 1 per cent of the vote, except when a locally popular figure such as Dalla Montà stands for election, or it joins an alliance with Dc dissidents as happened in 1975.

The Pci has also had internal problems, the nature of which it proved impossible to uncover. In 1965 its present secretary, D'Amato, resigned and joined the Psiup (Socialist Party of Proletarian Unity). He stood as a candidate of this party in 1965, 1968, 1970 and 1972 for various offices, winning only between a hundred and 200 votes each time. Then in 1973 he resumed leadership of the Pci in Trasacco. In 1975 the Pci collected 1548 preference votes for the various people on its list in the *comune* elections, only 300 fewer than those for the Psdi. Nationally the party discourages the casting of preference votes, but D'Amato was rather proud of the 800 or so that he personally collected. He is said to derive many of these from family connections rather than devotees of the party, and some of the people who went with him to the Psiup were related to him. Other Psiup voters were people who admired him personally and would vote for him no matter to what party he belonged. But most of those who now give him preference votes never abandoned the Pci for Psiup. He is one of only two men in Trasacco who have strong links with the regional Pci organisation. The other is Taricone. He is a trade unionist in the Alleanza Contadina and a very serious young man. D'Amato and Taricone always attended meetings in Avezzano and often in Luco as well. They were rather despondent about the prospects of building up a strong party in Trasacco itself, where in 1975 they had only 26 paid-up members.

It was impossible to discover whether there were connections of a clientelistic nature within the Pci. This party makes clientelism a major issue in its attacks on the government parties, and its own supporters are unlikely to divulge information of that nature to outsiders. Nor could I find anything out from its opponents. A casual comment, however, suggested that at least the post-war leader of the Pci in Trasacco, Beppino Di Cola, had had, if not a real clientele, a strong personal following. In answer to a question about the decline of the Pci after the land reform, an informant said: 'It was because Beppino went to Venezuela [from whence he returned in 1965]. What can the sheep do without the shepherd?' Subsequently I saw Beppino off to Rome with a young lad he was going to help with his military service posting. Beppino's son, whilst serving in the army, had pleased his commanding officer with his guitar playing. The officer had since been promoted to take charge of the postings of national servicemen. Di Cola said that he would not help everyone, and I never heard it said that he did it for money. He refused to tell me the criteria by which he accepted or rejected requests for help, but a common factor was that they were for sons of comrades.

The question that this raises is precisely what we mean by 'clientelism'. Di Cola was certainly using both individual and political criteria in choosing whom to help. It is very likely that those whom he helped would vote for him and his son (who stood in 1975 for the *comune*) out of a sense of obligation.

But it was my impression that communists did not *ask* people for their vote nor make help conditional on a vote. Help was given rather to people who were already 'comrades', to party members and sympathisers and to members of the communist trade unions.

The Pci's lack of support was not due so much to its having no *favori* to disburse (though these were seldom more than advice and help with filling in forms) but that many *trasaccani* were afraid of being associated with it. As we have seen, politics in Trasacco tend to breed cynicism, suspicion, distrust and fear. Southerners, says Tarrow:

may be very conscious of politics but they do not discuss them as freely as does the 'ideal' citizen . . . The Almond and Verba data show that almost 60 per cent of the Southern respondents will discuss politics with no one or with very few people, as compared to 46 per cent of Northerners. Clearly *all* Italians are suspicious of discussing politics openly but greater suspicion marks the Southern sample. (Tarrow, 1967: 79–80.)

Commonly, *trasaccani* claimed to be 'not interested in politics', to have no political preferences, to be neutral. Colclough remarks on a similar finding in Accettura (Colclough 1969: 202). It was very difficult to discover, except in the cases of the few who were *politicanti* or politically active, what most people's party sympathies were. Even at electoral meetings, where one might have expected to see support manifested, the behaviour of the public was extremely guarded and unrevealing.

Meetings were held in the piazza in the evening, beginning at twilight. The only spectators actually visible to the speakers were the activists of the party holding the meeting, and they stood in a group immediately in front of the platform. The rest of the public stood among the trees and cars on the other side of the streets running round the square. Apart from the little group of activists who were already known to everyone as supporters of the party, it was impossible to tell, even from the applause, who sympathised with whom, for the only people who clapped and cheered were the claque by the platform. The impression was that *trasaccani* wanted to hear what was going on but were anxious not to be identified with any party at all (see Figure 2).

The effects on administration

When local councils achieve power by the methods and tactics common in the South, the path of smooth and ordered administration is severely hampered. As Colclough points out, when factionalism threatens the survival of adminis-trations even between elections, long-term planning is impossible. Elections are won not by detailed plans and programmes but by promises to individuals, some at least of which must be fulfilled. Any 'programme' that is put out at

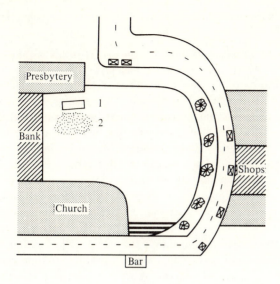

1 - platform   ✿ - trees

2 - party activists   ▨ - parked cars

Figure 2 The main piazza, Trasacco

election time is couched in the vaguest terms: 'improvement of social amenities' or 'attraction of investment'. Administrators of the type we find in
Trasacco rarely even have an ideology that might inform their policy making.
Administrative decisions are subject to pressures from both inside and outside
the administrating group. As Maraspini bluntly puts it:

The abuse of *raccomandazioni* causes the actions of the municipality to be
erratic and arbitrary, since, whatever the merits of any individual case, it is
not decided according to its merits and the regulations governing it, but
according to how strongly it is 'recommended'. (Maraspini, 1968: 113.)

The strength of the *raccomandazione* depends on who has given it: because
of the faction/clientele system, it is quite possible for an ordinary citizen to
have a member of parliament recommend his suit:

One 'reaches' the structure of authority, not by merging one's demands with
the parallel demands of others, but by linking oneself to a hierarchical chain

of personal acquaintance that reaches power holders at the higher level. (Tarrow, 1967: 75.)

Courier, for example, received many letters in answer to his requests for help for his clients, in which deputies and others highly placed in the Psdi hierarchy addressed him with the pronoun 'tu' which denotes considerable familiarity. A surprising number of *trasaccani* made claims to personal acquaintance, which there was no reason to doubt, with leading political figures, and a farmer arranged an interview for me with one of the most exclusive of Italian personalities, Prince Colonna. Anyone who can get a deputy to put in a word for him, or who can mobilise a body of votes, has considerable leverage on the administration: to find a job for a cousin's child, turn a blind eye to a home improvement that violates building regulations, have public utilities laid on to houses, and so on; the list can be expanded at great length.

Waiving building regulations only makes a town look rather untidy; but many of these concessions and personalised expenditures have serious consequences for the municipal budget. According to recent writers, 'Southern communes (compared to Northern ones) incur the largest debts both in absolute terms and as a percentage of total expenditure' (Acquiviva & Santuccio, 1976: 145), and in a comparison of forty large *comuni* Fried discovered that the budgets of Dc-run *comuni* were less often balanced than those controlled by the Pci. He observed also that:

Southern cities are heavily in debt, not from capital investment, but from borrowing to cover inefficient administration and heavy spending. *Clientelism is undoubtedly an important cause of this.* (Fried, 1971. My italics.)

On the financial side, Trasacco runs true to Southern and Dc form: its budget has been balanced only twice since the war, on the only two occasions when the mayor was Pci.

Because the *comune* is always in debt, little is spent on civic amenities. What money there is, is spent not on drains and water supply or roads in residential areas, but on grandiose projects like the giant neon cross or the huge paved *Aia* — where nobody walks, but which makes an impression of lavish spaciousness on the tourist. One is reminded of Maraspini's bitter observation that 'In Calimera the public garden is built for passers-by to Lecce, not the inhabitants.' (Maraspini, 1968: 112.) Meanwhile, all through the winter housewives must wear Wellington boots to go shopping because the roads are ankle-deep in mud.

When I asked the mayor why so few roads inside the town were tarred, he replied that it was not like Luco (a village with much greater housing density) where the council could afford to tar all the roads. Trasacco is spread out, and tarring would cost far too much. But the reason why Trasacco is spread out is because it has not got a building plan, and it has not got a building plan because when you have a building plan you annoy too many people who want to build outside its limits. Meanwhile, the council is tarring six kilometres of winding mountain road to Candelecchia 'because the people like to picnic there at Easter'. *'Who* likes to picnic there?' 'Actually, Franco Ippoliti and his friends' — they go almost every weekend by car, whereas a lot of *trasaccani* go on foot and are not bothered about the stones. Colclough's pessimistic conclusion must have struck many students of the South:

Indeed there is nothing . . . to suggest that politicians will be able to solve any of Accettura's major problems, or to challenge the villagers' assumption that its leaders are only interested in deriving the greatest possible advantage from their offices for themselves, their protectors and their clients. (Colclough, 1969: 202.)

For Accettura one may substitute Trasacco, Pisticci (Davis, 1973), Franza (Lopreato, 1967), Calimera (Maraspini, 1968), Montevarese (Brögger, 1971), Surughu (Weingrod, 1968) and even Montegrano (Banfield, 1958), although in the last case the ethnographer lays the blame for the insolubility of that village's problems at the door of the villagers and their inability to form 'corporate organisations' to improve their conditions.

Summing up, the contours of the political process outlined in this chapter will be familiar to anyone who knows Italy. National newspapers periodically recount the scandalous dealings of the Land Reform Boards, the Cassa per il Mezzogiorno and other state bodies. Local ones report the fall of yet another *giunta* amidst cries of corruption, favouritism and misappropriation of public funds. Just as national alliances crack under the pressure of factional disputes, so local ones can be sundered by dissatisfaction with the way resources are apportioned and by personal animosities between men who command vote banks of kin and clients.

Familiar too to the student of the South is the way that election results can vary from one election to another. This happens because people will follow instructions to switch their votes at the whim of an affronted patron. Loyalties to individuals such as Franco Ippoliti can override loyalties to parties even when the parties are as ideologically divergent as the Dc and the Pci.

Besides involving a swing to the neo-fascist Msi, the case of Dalla Montà demonstrates another aspect of the phenomenon of 'personalism'. It shows that when presented with a popular candidate who is considered a good and honest man, a considerable percentage of the electorate will vote for him without the added incentive of kinship ties or claims for political support in settlement of debts incurred. Of course some people voted for Dalla Montà in gratitude for his medical care, but this is not like the practice of building up a vote bank on the basis of promised benefits.

In the discussion of the political tactics of Courier and Ciofani, some important questions emerge concerning the exact nature of the benefits distributed. There are serious doubts as to whether either man does much more than threaten to exacerbate problems if the client does not actively seek his help and generally keep in his favour as an *insurance* against future need. Keeping *libretti* with Dr Ciofani, keeping a low political profile, not greeting radical friends, is not confined to the poor and ill-educated. Even well-to-do university students are very careful not to jeopardise their cordial relations with those who can influence their employment opportunities. Fear of unemployment is a powerful incentive to conform to the norms of clientelism even for those who, like Michele, have strong moral and ideological objections to it.

The public apologetic for the system is an explanation couched in terms of kinship ties, and many voting choices are indeed based on notions of kinship obligation. A significant proportion of votes are, however, placed in the hope of receiving tangible benefits. Many of these expectations cannot be fulfilled, for resources are indeed in short supply. To keep the system going the *politicanti* husband limited resources such as jobs, and are liberal with the *raccomandazioni*, form-filling, letter-writing and phone calls which require only the expenditure of time. In this way benefits can be distributed in just sufficient quantity to sustain confidence in the system as a whole.

On the one hand, political success derives ostensibly from a judicious combination of ties of kinship and obligation; on the other, there is no doubt that it depends on fear: the fear of clients that their needs will be ignored or even obstructed by the *politicanti*.

Aside from the doubtful morality of such a system, one is forced to question its efficiency. Personalised and political criteria in the selection of personnel bring in an element of uncertainty about the competence of employees, managers and civil servants. This is reduced in systems that employ the universalistic criteria of merit and qualifications. When clientelism dominates the political process, administrative efficiency and budgetary control are sacrificed to the squabbling of factions and their leaders.

6 Social relations

For the purpose of analysis I have so far separated 'Economics' and 'Politics' in Trasacco. In this chapter I wish to re-embed them in the other social processes, organisations and values from which they cannot, in reality, be sundered. The composite 'thing' which we call the social system has a multiplicity of elements, including the Political and the Economic, which both sustain and contradict each other; indeed without antagonisms and contradictions there would be no social change.

The clientelistic form particularly needs to be seen in its setting so that it is not perceived as an exotic aberration from 'normal' forms of social organisation. Clientelism is a relation of dominance and subordination. Much in this society can be seen as mitigating the harshness of the conditions in which those who are subordinate struggle to live and work, and tempering the acerbity of the competition between them. Clientele relations are played out in contexts other than the strictly political, and are often expressed in terms derived from egalitarian or familial relationships. Both context and language often mask the real conflict of interests, and avert any open confrontation between patrons and clients.

Voluntary associations

Organisations which are not strictly political, but where relations of dominance often emerge very clearly, are associations which are formed to pursue common interests, be they local history clubs, football clubs, or trade unions. Students of Southern Italy generally accept Banfield's observation that there is a paucity of voluntary associations in comparison with Britain or the United States. Many have rejected his conclusion that 'amoral familism' is the reason (see for example Cancian, 1961; Davis, 1970; Pizzorno, 1966; Tarrow, 1967: 72–3).

One study of the relation between the structure of land distribution, organisations and emigration distinguishes usefully between, on the one hand, the 'feudal-style class stratification of Apulia and the interior of Sicily' (where latifundia predominate) and, on the other hand, the 'mixed system of property distribution' (large and small farms) of the 'typical South'. This

63

study by McDonald (1956) concludes that, historically, it was in the latter, the 'typical' South, that the incidence of voluntary associations was lowest. The link between the formation of organisations having political goals, such as peasants' unions, and the incidence of other organisations of all kinds is clearly made. McDonald points out that in latifundist Apulia it was associations to fight for the rights of peasants that were widespread during the last half of the nineteenth century, and it was here that emigration rates were lowest. Where there was a deep, clear-cut division between classes, class-based associations developed to fight for higher wages and better conditions of work for the landless labourers. The suggestion is implicitly rather than explicitly made that these organisations provided *braccianti* with the incentive to stay and fight *collectively* rather than to emigrate, which is an *individual* solution to economic and social subordination.

In the 'typical South', which includes Abruzzo, the only formally constituted voluntary associations during the years of heaviest overseas migration (1890–1920) were 'clubs for little rentiers and white collar workers, but they functioned as informal rendezvous, without purpose or formal constitution' (McDonald, 1956).

The purpose of such clubs is not to pursue common interests, but to demarcate social barriers in a society where gross social differences that derive from gross differences in land ownership do not in fact exist. Where there is a mixture of small and medium farms, and therefore relatively little income disparity, class differences have to be justified and expressed in other terms, such as *civiltà* (civility) and education. Such a distribution of land does not facilitate the emergence of clear-cut class divisions and conscious class formation. Rather is each minor difference between individuals in land-ownership, educational qualifications, income and family history accentuated and endlessly discussed to provide the criteria by which each *individual* can be placed on a finely graded status hierarchy (see also Davis, 1969a).

A club which limits its membership according to such criteria provides a cut-off point between classes which would not otherwise exist. It justifies the superiority of its members by appearing to endow them with the trappings of *civiltà*. The Circolo Culturale of the 'typical South', and of Trasacco today, serves this purpose. In the words of the president of Trasacco's *circolo*, Dr Ciofani, it provides a rendezvous for its members, selected from among the *diplomati* and *laureati*, to meet 'away from the riff-raff in the bars'. To sustain its image of exclusiveness and refinement, the *circolo* rented rooms in an old *casa signorile*, and defined its purpose as 'raising the level of cultural life in the village'. Its record of fulfilling its aims is not good: between 1970 and 1975 it held one 'debate' on divorce (with all four main speakers supporters of the Vatican view) and one exhibition of the work of local painters. It was in reality little more than an exclusive bar where members could play cards and discuss politics undisturbed.

Ostensibly to combat the exclusiveness of the Circolo Culturale, a new Circolo Febonio was initiated in 1974. It was to be 'classless and apolitical', and 'stimulate real discussion about the village and its problems' with open debates, outside speakers, organised visits and exhibitions. Its instigator was Dr Quaglieri, who was at that time forming a group of *politicanti* within the Dc party to challenge the official internal opposition of the *Gaspariani*. The initiative collapsed after only a few meetings, amidst accusations against would-be office holders of power seeking, confusion about its objectives, and suspicion that its sole purpose had been to get funds for Quaglieri's election campaign from the Ministry of Tourism, which disburses money for local voluntary associations, particularly those concerned with civic amenities. As one member observed, 'Who does he think he's kidding? He's no different from Ciofani, just out for himself'. This cynical observation reveals an underlying truth: that the *circoli* not only serve to mark off their membership from the rest of the population, but can also be used to provide some of the status and personal following necessary for a political career.

The *circoli*'s cultural aims alone would have served to guarantee their exclusiveness. The Football Club has, on the contrary, great popular appeal. Yet although it had a large membership, an annual general meeting, and weekly matches which gave it the illusion of participation, it was again Dr Ciofani, its president, and a small clique of his friends who made all the effective decisions. In 1975 the football ground was being improved with a large grant from the Cassa per il Mezzogiorno. The contractor was a member of the committee and apparently a loyal henchman of Dr Ciofani. Employment on the project was rumoured to be conditional on political support for Ciofani and his faction.

Whereas Don Pasquale and Dr Ciofani had established a kind of *modus vivendi* or armed peace, Quaglieri's opposition took a more active form. Having failed with the *circolo*, Quaglieri opened a second front in the football arena. He started a junior team which was to be run by a 'non-sectarian, classless' association. When Quaglieri applied for permission to use the football ground (which is the property of the *comune*), the mayor, Del Boccio, a *Nataliano*, refused. He said that the semi-professional league team had acquired exclusive rights to it. In the ensuing court case the judge ruled that the ground was public property and ordered it to be made available to the junior team in the mornings. This effectively prevented the new team from playing, since its members were students and workers who were not free to play in the mornings, a point made to the judge, but not acted upon.

Whatever Quaglieri's motives were, and again he was suspected of pursuing his own political ambitions, the club aroused a good deal of interest. The forces which Ciofani commanded were far more powerful than those which opposed him, however, and an initiative which might have provided a measure of participation in the organisation of a favourite sport was crushed. .

'Cynicism and disaffection', it has been said, 'pervade Southern society'. The explanation offered for this social pathology is 'the juxtaposition of modern institutions and organisations with a society imbued with traditional values and loyalties' (Tarrow, 1967: 54). A simpler explanation lies on the surface of people's experience in Trasacco: they know that in any clash with Dr Ciofani it is Ciofani who is likely to win. As Tarrow has pointed out, there is a tendency for people, even those who join associations, to reject them as 'illegitimate or corrupt'. It is curious that Tarrow should leave this statement as an unsolved and apparently insoluble problem. For anyone who has experienced Southern Italy, the 'perception' that organisations are illegitimate and corrupt is strikingly akin to reality; they very often are. Local associations are used in Trasacco as arenas for the playing out of political rivalries. None have been started and run by people who did not have the objective of promoting private interests and political ambitions.

Trasaccani do nevertheless join local clubs, but they do so to a greater extent when they are branches of national organisations, particularly parties and trade unions. According to Don Pasquale, until the late 'sixties there had been a 'flourishing' branch of Azione Cattolica, but by 1974 it had inexplicably declined to a dozen pious women. Although they join them the prevailing attitudes of members towards their trade unions were again cynical and suspicious. In Campania Pitkin discovered that trade unionists (of Cisl – the Dc federation) insisted on payment for help with the form-filling, which was supposed to be part of their job and free to members. I am convinced that in Fucino the trade unionists did not behave incorrectly. Those of the Cgil (Pci/Psi) in particular were indefatigable defenders of their members' rights and considered it their most important task to educate members in those rights. Yet many farmers in Trasacco doubted whether their rights were being protected. Members of the Cbf (Federation of Beet Cultivators), an organisation for beet producers, affiliated to the Cgil (Pci/Psi) said to me: 'trade unionists are all bought by the factory. They stand at the factory gates, weighing in your crop and checking its sugar content, but they are creatures of the factory manager; there is no one to protect our interests.' Instead of going to their local representative, Taricone, who gave people free help and advice, many of the members would go instead to Courier, pay him a little something and vote for him. 'You don't get something for nothing' was their attitude. The communists, they suspected, must gain some advantage by giving help free – just as it had not been pure altruism that inspired Quaglieri's cultural and football initiatives.

However, it is not enough to say that people are highly suspicious of organisations because officials really are corrupt. Nor have we explained much when we say that cynicism learned in some organisations is inappropriately transferred to organisations where officials are not corrupt. We have still to ask why corruption is present and why voluntary associations are few.

Schneider (1972), instead of relying on an explanation in terms of the cynicism and suspicion that are 'prevalent' or 'predominant' among Southern Italians, situates the problem materially and in its historical context. He is concerned with a specific area — western Sicily — and with the absence of joint-stock companies, but what he has to say is relevant to the problem of voluntary associations as well.

Like western Sicily (and other mountainous inland areas of the South) the central Abruzzo has been subject to repeated foreign invasion and domination by colonial powers; its rural communities have been linked directly to the outside world rather than by means of a hierarchically organised division of labour between villages and market towns; until the late nineteenth century there were no carriageable roads to the capital cities; the region was penetrated by the market before the establishment of effective legal and bureaucratic institutions and before the State had gained the monopoly over the use of violence.

Such conditions, Schneider argues, are not favourable to the formation of joint-stock companies; nor, I believe, are they conducive to the growth of voluntary associations, which need a similar legal—bureaucratic context in which to grow and develop. The constitutional rules of both joint-stock and voluntary associations enable legal action to be taken against those who pursue private interests to the detriment of the association, but they depend on the assumption that litigation will be effective. These conditions are largely absent in Trasacco.

Friendship

Friendship among men was clearly important in Trasacco, though the all-male dinners at which friendship was celebrated (as in western Sicily — Schneider, 1972) were not open to me for personal observation. Schneider sees the celebration of friendship as necessary to the development of trust, vital to the kind of business transaction that the friendship coalitions engage in. In Trasacco, however, it seemed to me that friendship was a form of 'pure sociability' — men enjoyed each other's company and found perhaps in friendship a freedom from the tension which marks some other relationships. Men who spent much time in the company of their friends were the subject of adverse comment from their wives. One woman observed ruefully, 'You know why men around here are so fat? They eat two dinners every day. I cook my husband a meal when he gets home in the evening, then he rushes out and before midnight he's had another.'

Men express themselves quite often on the subject of friendship, on the differences between a friend and an acquaintance, between the friendships of men and of women and so on. They are clearly an important source of social cohesion and a relationship in which emotions can be legitimately expressed. But friendships are not a latent form of class cohesion, for relations between members of different classes are also expressed in terms of friendship. This is particularly true of clientship. A client never refers to himself by the self-deprecating word *cliente*, but says that he is an *amico* of, for example, Dr Ciofani. People would say of Don Pasquale's relationship to Gaspari: 'Ha una certa amicizia con lui' (he has a particular friendship with him). The employment of the language of friendship with its tones of social equality, serves to mask the inequalities of the patron–client relationship.

Comparaggio

This word, which means co-godparenthood, signifies a continuous life-long relation between the parents of a child being baptised and its godparents. It is used for the sponsors at a wedding as well, but the former is the most common and enduring bond.

The relationship has been dealt with extensively in the literature on peasant societies of the Mediterranean and Latin America, most notably by Gudeman (1971). I have nothing to add to the discussion of its structure, for the pattern in Trasacco differs little from what has been described elsewhere. The bond has a social significance which goes well beyond its doctrinal specifications. A major component is the mutual observation of 'respect': 'Briefly, respect . . . is exhibited through various forms of "proper" behaviour such as greetings, farewells and general demeanour.' (Gudeman, 1971.)

In the Fucino area people often observed that whilst expectations of respectful behaviour continue to be fulfilled, the components of respect are less rigorous than they once were. Only very old men now, for example, doff their hats as they pass the house of a *comare* or *compare*. But other forms continue to be observed such as the form of address (*comà, compà*), a flurry of attention if a *comare* calls, and meticulous observation of the duty to invite *compari* to all important family occasions.

The choice of *compari* is often made when the future parents are adolescents, but many choices are of course made later, often during the mother's pregnancy. My impression was that the relationship was often used to strengthen an existing tie between workmates, friends and kinsmen (see also Colclough, 1969: 41). Most frequently it was a tie between social equals creating a generalised sense of strong mutual obligation. This suggests that in a society where social equals are frequently in competition for employment, promotion, votes, influence and so on, *comparaggio* creates a tie of special trust and obligation lacking in other relations.

Because the bond is culturally freighted with obligation, a person, by choosing well, can increase the likelihood of getting help from an equal with such work as ploughing and harvesting, or from a *compare* in a more powerful economic or bureaucratic position. Doctors, middle- and upper-range state employees, employment officers and politicians, tend to have more god-children than others.

Invitations to be godparent can be useful to an aspiring politician, but the obligation is sometimes felt to be onerous, particularly because of the expenditure involved. A child must be given a gold chain at the baptism and birthday presents as it gets older. One man told me that he had been rather relieved when the Church forbade communists to be godparents because he had been approached rather too often. As a teacher with no children, people had felt that he would have money to spare from his secure employment.

Considerations of financial and political influence seemed to be much less important today in the choice of godparents than they had been in the past. With increasing affluence the desperate need which had prompted the choice of superiors as godparents was no longer so compelling. In Trasacco the best-known case of *comparaggio* between unequals was that of Ciofani and Natali, leader of the Fanfani faction in Abruzzo. I was told that this relationship had been much more common between patrons and clients right up to the end of the war. Containing as it does notions of equality and mutuality one can see its importance as a legitimating ideology for traditional patron—client relations.

The bond does not provide an inviolable guarantee: most people have more kin and *compari* than they can keep up with. Therefore they must choose which relations they will activate. The powerful and influential have many more demands on their 'obligations' than they can possibly fulfil. For example, in March 1975 Natali was ignoring Ciofani, who looked as though he was falling out of favour. But by the time I left the field, Ciofani had persuaded the party to make him a parliamentary candidate. Obviously his influence had not diminished as much as had been thought (or hoped). It would have been surprising if Natali had continued to ignore him, for Ciofani still controlled the largest vote bank in Trasacco.

Kinship

Banfield has suggested that in Montegrano ties beyond the nuclear family are very weak. This may have been peculiar to Montegrano, and it may need further investigation. My own information accords with other studies which suggest that close kin are expected to cooperate, and do feel a mutual obligation to help in crises (for example, Colclough, 1969).

In a society where welfare benefits are non-existent or insufficient, the kin network remains an important source of economic support in times of illness or unemployment. It is in the interests of the less-advantaged, who are at greater risk of loss of income, to emphasise obligations to support kinsmen. Pressure to fulfil such obligations is particularly strong on those who have managed to attain professional employment, and therefore a more secure income and entitlement to welfare benefits. That these obligations are still respected is clear from the fact that people in Trasacco attach great importance to having kinsmen who are well placed. It is my impression that the level of interaction between small farmers and workers in rural areas and their kinsmen with city employment is far higher in Italy than it is in Britain. Rural cousins carry baskets of country produce on visits to the city, and insist on filling the boots of the cars of visiting kin when they come to the country. In return they expect their city kin to provide accommodation for student children and make strenuous efforts to find work for these children in the city.

In Trasacco informants who were asked about kinship ties all spontaneously mentioned the obligation to invite kin and affines to *rites de passage* (see also Colclough, 1969). The web of relatives who would be offended if excluded from these occasions often extends to the cousins of grandparents. In the case of a death I was told that if there was any suggestion of a link either by blood or by marriage people would drop what they were doing to call on the bereaved. Failure to do so gives rise to gossip and *critica* (criticism).

Kinship obligations can be felt as onerous, as the popular saying indicates: 'I parenti sono come le scarpe; piu sono stretti, piu ti fanno male.' (Relatives are like shoes, the tighter (closer) they are, the more they hurt.)

Beyond the absolute obligation of inclusion in *rites de passage*, there is continual discussion as to what *parenti* are or are not expected to do, and complaints against the high expectations of some and the low performance of others are frequent.

On one other matter, however, there is little disagreement. This is the obligation to vote for *parenti* if they stand for election, or have a particular reason (like their own indebtedness for a *favore*) to ask that your vote be placed as they indicate. Beyond the immediate *famigliari* (nuclear family plus uncles, aunts and cousins) the obligation to vote is not absolute, but claims to kinship ties are constantly made by politicians, in the hope of outweighing other allegiances which the voter might feel obliged to honour.

Dc politicians also explained their support in terms of the kinship networks of *politicanti*. Clientelistic forms are under heavy attack in Italy, and from time to time the leaders of the Dc disclaim clientelistic practices. Local politicians, who could trace extremely extensive, if sometimes tenuous, links, prefer to mask their activities in the ideology of kinship rather than talk openly about *favori*.

The cases of Dalla Montà and Di Cola raise questions about the importance of kinship for political success. Neither had many kin in Trasacco at the time of their candidatures, but both were very popular with the electorate nonetheless. Kinship is clearly a useful ideology for recruitment, but in exceptional circumstances both kinship and *favori* obligations can be overridden.

The Church and religion

It has already been noted that Don Pasquale, the parish priest, has considerable political influence in Trasacco. Such involvement of the clergy is not at all uncommon, especially in the South. Following Unification and the enforced incorporation of Rome into united Italy, the Church instructed its followers not to participate in the State, and above all to abstain from voting. However, there was a gradual *rapprochement* between Church and State, which was formalised in the Lateran Treaty of 1929 between Mussolini and the Pope.

During the fascist period this concordat allowed for the increasing political involvement of the Church — in education, in the armed forces and in local organisations for women and children. After the fall of fascism and liberation from German occupation (north of Monte Cassino) the Church was virtually the only operative organisation outside the Liberation Movement. The reviving Partito Popolare, renamed Democrazia Cristiana, found in the parish priests a ready-made network of influence, the usefulness of which even the most radical elements in the party found it difficult to ignore. Although Fanfani's organisational reforms of the Dc, which began in 1954, were aimed at disassociating it both from the old land-based clienteles and from the Church, individual priests and the Church hierarchy as a whole continue to have a powerful influence on the party. Apart from any direct pressure which the Vatican may put on the party leadership over matters like abortion (see, for example, *L'Espresso* magazine April 1974, which reported telephone calls from the Vatican to national Dc leaders), even local priests cannot be ignored, since they can mobilise voters. Davis sees priests as closely identified with the Dc politicians. He describes them as equally concerned to control new resources which enter the community with industrialisation. In Pisticci one of the priests managed to obtain information from the new factory about employees and 'walked up and down the main street giving advance information to any workers or their parents that he happened to see' (Davis, 1973: 153).

Priests are as likely as lay political leaders of the Dc to be in dispute with one another over resources (Davis, 1973: 154) or on personal grounds

(Banfield, 1958: 87). In Trasacco Don Pasquale was the acknowledged head of the Gaspari faction. His young assistant Don Evaristo was a leading light of the Msi. In 1970 Don Evaristo headed his party's electoral list, giving it the aura of clerical support and thus a certain legitimacy, even though, as a priest, he had to resign immediately following his election. The party managed to win two seats.

The priest enjoys advantages that accrue to his profession, whether or not he wishes to mobilise them for political purposes. The priest's letter accompanying an application for a job is regarded as a minimum requirement. It is believed that priests are asked for references for all kinds of positions, and that through the Church hierarchy they can obtain benefits for their parishioners. Therefore people not only try to keep on the right side of the clergy, but in times of particular need the priest will be one of the influential people whom they will automatically approach for help. There is a great deal of traditional anti-clerical feeling amongst men. Some women also think that priests are too much involved in politics: 'non è prete quello' (he's no priest), as one woman informant commented of Don Pasquale. People are nonetheless extremely wary of the kind of influence priests might have, and take care not to offend them.

A priest who wishes to make use of his position can very easily do so. As Davis points out, they are free to devote themselves to many interests, including politics (Davis, 1973: 57); they can and often do give highly political sermons, particularly near elections; they can influence parishioners very directly in the Confessional and elsewhere, and through the children who attend crèches and schools. For example, a young woman going to ask for her wedding banns to be announced was asked by Don Pasquale for details of her fiancé. On hearing that he was a worker and a *luchese* he asked her if she was aware that 'all *luchesi* are communists. Did she really want to marry one?' Even more directly, I was told, Don Pasquale asked mothers who were enrolling their children for a summer camp in 1975 to be sure to vote for the *Gaspariani* preferences in the May elections. The Church as a body encourages the devout to vote Dc (Galli & Prandi, 1970: 164), both by admonition and via the control of recommendations, references and resources.

Besides the work done on its behalf by the clerisy, the Dc has a much more subtle grasp over electors through their religious beliefs. Anyone who has studied politics in the South will have heard electors, especially elderly women, say that they cannot, when it comes to the point, restrain themselves from 'putting a cross on the Cross' —the symbol of the Dc is a Christian Cross on a shield, a highly potent symbol.

In addition Catholicism offers a philosophy that accords particularly well with the experience of the peasant and small farmer. This has been brought out most clearly in a paper by Guizzardi aptly subtitled 'Structure of an

"Ideology for Consent" '. He suggests that the Catholic Church in Italy is

the organic intellectual[1] of the rural people. In fact it is the only intellectual agency which can offer them a global interpretation of their daily life and is able to offer some historical and unitarian meaning to these social strata and place them inside a frame of reference in which their experience acquires a meaning above the mere phenomena of circumstance (Guizzardi, 1976.)

The global interpretation offered by the Church to the small peasant farmer is that of the 'rural civilisation'. The sanctity of the rural life is derived from man's special relationship with God; this places him above all other animals and establishes his absolute domination over nature. From this is derived the right to private property. Because of the fundamental link between man and his family and his duty to provide for it, the small family farm is, for the Church, man's ideal setting for his work and his duties. The small family property is thus given a sanctified value through

the deductive chain, God—man, nature—property, family—work, and has as its inductive counterpart the chain, property — family — work — man — nature — God, which is attached to the former by a very delicate thread: pseudo-empiric observations on the 'real' rural life. (Guizzardi, 1976.)

The weight of papal authority is given to the Church's pronouncements on the value of the rural life and small peasant farm. The Coldiretti (Dc-linked organisation for direct cultivators) and its subsidiary organisations for women and children enjoy papal audiences two or three times a year.

The sanctity of the small peasant farm signifies that the 'rural civilisation' construct is impregnated with both a God-given rectitude and

with anti-communism, right from its roots, and this is one of the pivots of the relationship between church and Dc. The fight against Communism equals defence of the Church and its religion but at the same time it equals support too of the Catholic Party. (Guizzardi, 1976.)

The Church thus plays a contradictory role in the political life and consciousness of the peasant. On the one hand it gives the small farmer self-esteem and a sense of his own significance in relation to other men and to God. On the other, by supporting the Dc, which is a clientelist party, and by itself practising clientelist methods, it gives to both party and practices an authority which drains away the peasant's capacity to recognise and take action to improve his situation. There is another contradiction between the 'rights of property' and the notion that 'all men share a substantial equality of rights in the social and economic fields' (a notion derived from the equality of man in the sight of God: Guizzardi). As increasing numbers of

1 Reference to a Gramscian concept, cf. the Prison Notebooks, pp. 6 and 330.

peasants are extruded onto the labour market, a few young priests are finding themselves unable any longer to support the notion of the 'rural civilisation' and are turning for enlightenment to Marxism and the Christian Socialist movement. They are, however, a tiny minority, mostly confined to the industrial areas and the big cities of Rome and Naples. In rural parishes the old-style priest, closely tied to the dominant strata, continues to hold sway and preach support for the Dc and destruction of the anti-Christ, communism. The only 'Marxist' priest in Fucino had been refused a parish, and in the summer of 1975 the bishop of the Marsica was threatening to remove him from his teaching post. Although a great deal of criticism is levelled at parish priests — outspoken doubts as to their celibacy, attacks on their involvement in politics, accusations of nepotism, suspicion that they overcharge for masses and accumulate private fortunes, and simple resentment at their nosiness — their political influence continues.

Values and attitudes

To conclude the discussion of the context of clientelist relations in Trasacco I shall focus on what can loosely be termed values and attitudes. I shall be concerned with the evaluation of work and land, the components of social status and people's aspirations for themselves and their children.

The economy of Southern Italy has always lagged behind that of the North in its continuing dependence on agriculture. Figures for 1960 show that industry contributed only 14.6 per cent of the net national product, services 23 per cent and agriculture 34 per cent whilst the South accounted for 38 per cent of the national population. Until as late as 1950 over half the active population in the South was engaged in agricultural pursuits, as against a third in the North. Today this proportion has dropped to 30 per cent. However, those areas of the South which are industrialised are concentrated into the triangle Bari — Taranto — Brindisi, leaving the remainder of the Southern *comuni* still heavily dependent on agriculture.

In spite of the importance of agriculture and the number of people involved in it, there is overwhelming evidence (almost every author mentions it) that, as Pitt-Rivers has remarked of Andalusia: 'they go out to cultivate the earth but they do not love it' (Pitt-Rivers, 1954: 47). Cancian (1961) observes that peasants in South Italy are alienated from the land, they have no hope of progress in agriculture, casual conversations do not include the discussion of farming techniques, they seem to deny that there is any system involved in efficient farming and are not interested in classes that are held to improve agricultural methods.

As long ago as 1886 a visitor to Trasacco wrote as follows:

The *trasaccani* cultivate their land very little and badly ... filth overflows onto the streets and huge deposits of rubbish infect the air. A young cultivator whom I met, but who is not from the village, said that he had settled there exactly for that reason, that is to profit from those great piles of organic substance and undertake at little cost a rational and useful system of cultivation ... That filth, on the fields, is as valuable as, in the middle of the village, it is the cause of degradation and death. (Marcone, 1886: 49—50.)

An old *mezzadro* interviewed in 1975 said that his family had also used to take advantage of the *trasaccano*'s dislike for handling manure. In the 1920s and 30s they had had an arrangement with a number of farmers who kept sheep in the village to take the manure away, a service for which the *trasaccani* paid them! Even today *trasaccani* are judged by Ente officials and by *luchesi* to be, with few exceptions, rather incompetent and tradition-bound farmers.

Allied to the dislike of farming is the fact that people live predominantly in towns rather than on their farms. Davis (1969b) and Rossi-Doria (1958) have argued that the basis for this preference is economic. It stems from the scattered nature of land-holding: it is better for a peasant to live in the village where he is likely to be midway between his plots than to have his dwelling on any one of them. Davis points out that town-dwelling is important for other reasons too — for control over women and for the effective playing of political roles. Colclough (1969) comments that all facilities such as shops, *comune* officials and schools are concentrated in the urban centres, making town-dwelling a more sensible choice. Pitkin further suggests that the Southerner equates 'being civilised' with 'being urbanised' (Pitkin, 1963). For historical reasons urban values predominate in the South, and the first essential of *civiltà* is to live in town. Cronin says that in Sicily people live in the town because they do not want to be isolated in the countryside. They farm out of necessity, not because they have chosen a rural way of life (Cronin, 1970: 40—1).

Such negative attitudes towards the land derive not from the land itself, which has been the traditional source of prestige, but from the fact of having to perform manual labour on it. 'Manual work is associated with low status', Colclough tells us. 'The basic social division is between those who work with their hands and those who do not.' (Colclough, 1969: 117.) His observation is repeated by Banfield, 'manual labour is degrading' (Banfield, 1958: 51), and by Pitkin, 'manual labour is everywhere deprecated' (Pitkin, 1963). Tarrow points out that it is important to own land but not to work it oneself, hence 'the vast number of middle class individuals who live on their scanty incomes from the land' (Tarrow, 1967: 61).

The deprecation of manual labour imbues all attitudes to work. Davis says that in Pisticci work is not valued for its own sake. 'I never heard any *pistic-*

cese say anything that could possibly mean "work has an intrinsic value" '
(Davis, 1973: 93). McDonald observes that 'typical' Southerners (i.e. from
the smallholding areas) 'strive to disassociate themselves from work of any
kind' (McDonald, 1964: 4). To quote Davis again, 'the scale of evaluation is
clear: farmwork is a hard lot; infinitely preferable is to work as a clerk or professional *or to do no work at all*' (Davis, 1973: 94, my italics).

The deprecation of manual work is reproduced in the evaluation of different kinds of professional specialisation: 'The "typical" South produced
lawyers, doctors and accountants when the Centre and North were producing
agricultural engineers' (McDonald, ibid). The Southern rural bourgeoisie
failed to diversify into business and technology and remains for the most part
concentrated in the traditional professions. It is a bourgeoisie 'more inter-
mediary than producer, more lawyer than engineer, more philosopher than
inventor, more notary than agronomist, and more functionary than expert'
(Sereni quoted by Tarrow, 1967: 49). Gramsci noted a similar tendency: in
comparison with the North which produces technicians, '(It is) the South
which produces functionaries and professional men' (Gramsci, 1971: 12).

The state bureaucracy is manned overwhelmingly by Southerners, both in
the 1920s when three-fifths of its employees came from the South (Gramsci,
1957: 42) and today (Tarrow, 1967: 51).

What Gramsci said of the aspirations of Southerners still holds; the traditional goals of the Southern bourgeoisie and the middle peasants are the
professions and the state bureaucracy rather than industry or entrepreneurship; the man with money to invest has always chosen to use part of it at
least for educating his sons:

The peasant always thinks that at least one of his sons could become an intellectual (especially a priest), thus becoming a gentleman and raising the social
level of his family by facilitating its survival through the connections he is
bound to acquire with the rest of the gentry. (Gramsci, 1971: 14.)

Families struggle to put children through university, not in 'technical'
(manually-oriented) subjects however, but in the traditional faculties of law,
literature, philosophy and medicine. Once the son has embarked upon his
career, even whilst still a student, he is not allowed to help on the family land
(Cancian, 1961) for now he is the embodiment of the family's prestige: a
sign that it is emerging from the squalor and drudgery of manual labour, that
it can begin to claim some importance in the eyes of the community.

The people of Trasacco are predominantly dependent on land: few alternative sources of income are available and men in particular have not been
successful in obtaining factory employment. The number of artisans, shops
and bars is not high in comparison with Luco, for example, where there are
both more factory workers and more self-employed in proportion to the

population. Nonetheless, attitudes to land, as evinced in what people say, are very similar to those dealt with in the literature on Southern Italy. There is a widespread desire to get out of farming and into non-manual occupations, and particularly to enable one's children to do so. There is evidence that people are managing this: the land-holding figures from the Ente Fucino show that between 1958 and 1975 the number of assignees in Trasacco fell by one-fifth (1075 to 865). In view of the under-recording of sales it is possible that this number is even lower, my own survey suggesting that it has fallen by a further 38. Figures on tractor-ownership show that investment in agriculture is lower than in some other *comuni* of Fucino and diversification into crops other than beet and potatoes is not very common — crops such as salads are more labour-intensive and require new skills and markets. This would suggest that people do not want to remain in agricultural pursuits and acquire the relevant skills. Children too, in a survey that I conducted in the middle school, showed a marked distaste for farming as a future career and preferred non-manual work, as one would expect given parental ambitions (see below, p. 115).

What, one may ask, induces people to sell land if alternative sources of income are so scarce? Firstly, of course, some of the sales are accounted for by 'natural wastage' — farmers selling land as they reach pensionable age. Older men often sell land to provide the house which a son is customarily given on marriage. Others sell land on acquiring an alternative employment in construction or industry — very few workers in permanent employment had land (20 out of 115, see Table 3). Very often the money raised is spent on building a new house. (As mentioned earlier, more than half the housing stock of Trasacco has been built since the land reform.) I was told of a number of people who had bought apartments in Rome from which income was obtained without the labour or risks of agriculture. Sometimes only a portion of the land owned is sold off, perhaps to meet a sudden demand such as the expenses of a daughter's marriage.

Emigrants who decide to settle away from Trasacco usually sell after an initial period of renting. Migrants who return with savings never, as far as I was able to ascertain, buy land. Unlike that in the town of Franza, described by Lopreato, land here has no prestige value and cannot be used by emigrants to raise their social status. This may be changing however. During 1974 Dr Ciofani, with the aid of government grants, set up a beef-raising stall on his wife's land *fuori-Fucino* under the care of a manager. A migrant planning to return from Venezuela, where he had made a lot of money in construction, told me that he was thinking of buying up disused *fuori-Fucino* land and starting a similar enterprise. But he had no intention of working it himself — he was going into politics.

As far as the duplication of the manual/non-manual divide at the professional level is concerned, Trasacco runs true to the Southern type. It has about forty university graduates but these, with one exception, the area veterinary surgeon, are all qualified in medicine, law, literature, philosophy and pedagogy. Similarly those with diplomas are most commonly qualified in teaching, accountancy and rather fewer in land surveying.

Peasant families with children at university try to avoid having them work on the land, even during the long summer vacations when harvesting is in progress. To avoid a farmer's life can become almost an obsession. Michele Morisi and his mother illustrate this. He has been mentioned (see above pp. 52–3) in connection with his mother's willingness to vote for anyone who found him a job. Michele's father had been a *contadino* with three hectares of land. He and his brother had bought complementary agricultural machines which they shared. On his death in 1972 the land was rented to the brother. When Michele graduated in economics in 1974 he was unemployed for a year. The question of taking back and farming the land was never considered. Michele argued, when I raised it, that he knew nothing about farming. His uncle would have helped him, but he resolutely continued to write letters of application and attend interviews until finally he got a job in Bologna. Some of his relatives criticised him for his superior airs, but most people accepted that 'his family had not made sacrifices so that he could go and toil on the land'. These attitudes, that manual labour is degrading and that to do no work denotes superiority, are important in a society where a small elite lives in luxury on the productive labour of a much more numerous majority. The attitude of Michele and other young graduates is not an anachronism, for the division between the wealthy and the poor still correlates closely with those who do no manual work and those who do.

Michele's mother was deeply unhappy at his departure for Bologna. With his sister already settled as a teacher and married in Sardinia she was going to be very lonely. But her pain was offset by her pride and satisfaction that she had done her best for her son. Family honour had been upheld.

This brings me to the complex of values that surround the notion of 'honour', which Davis has skilfully dissected and analysed in the context of Pisticci, an 'agro-town' above the Metaponto plain in Lucania. 'Honour', he tells us,

is a way of ranking people. Potentially it is an absolute ranking system: each individual has a unique position: shared positions, equality, indicate not solidarity but a struggle for dominance, an attempt to become superior and unequal. (Davis, 1969a.)

It was my impression that the struggle among near equals for a unique position in a finely-graded hierarchy was not characteristic of the whole society. It seemed to be confined to the *politicanti* in Trasacco, to those who were involved in local politics, who had some chance of becoming councillors, if not immediately, then at some later date. It was my impression that labourers did not participate in this struggle, but accepted an undifferentiated *social* position among the *nullatenenti* (have-nothings). A man had to have surpassed a certain minimum status 'bar' before he had any 'honour' at all in the sense of being either himself concerned with the hierarchy or, more importantly, considered by others as a candidate for it. This is not to say that there was no competition between the *nullatenenti*. On the contrary, competition was fierce, but it was for work.

For those on short-term or daily contracts the struggle for employment was a constant concern. Success in getting a job did not influence a man's social status, however, for in the long run everyone got about the same amount of work over the year.

Even where there was competition for dominance, among the *politicanti*, it was not couched in the idiom of honour. The impression that one gains from the literature on the South is that honour is the predominant form in which competition and hierarchy are expressed. In Fucino the concept was regarded as something of a historic curiosity. It may well be that 'honour' is related to a particular pattern of inheritance, for in this respect Fucino and Pisticci are different, at least as regards the inheritance of houses.

Davis tells us that what honour is 'for' is to provide a crucial control on people's behaviour at home, in the neighbourhood and, indirectly, in the all-Pisticci political arena; and that it is found in communities which are relatively isolated, where resources are scarce and where other generally accepted ways of distinguishing between individuals are absent.

A man's honour is a set of expectations about how he will behave in most of the social encounters of his life: it is his ticket of entry into the trust-based field of politics. (Davis: ibid.)

In other words, it is used as a general predictor of behaviour: a man's honour will reveal the risks one takes in doing business or making a political alliance with him, or giving him one's daughter in marriage. A man's honour is tied into that of his family: it is based on economic standing and 'additionally on the way he controls his women'. A man whose wife commits adultery or whose daughter is not a virgin is a man who cannot be trusted with other responsibilities. If he cannot maintain his women in such a way that they are immune from the suspicion of sexual laxity, if because of economic exigency they have to work in the fields where their sexuality cannot be overseen and controlled by other women, then the man is deprived of his honour. Consequently, social control over women is important to men and it is for this reason that women should remain in town under the watchful eyes of neighbours, rather than work in the countryside where, out of sight of the neighbours, they are at risk of seduction.

In Pisticci female neighbours were very often kinswomen because of the pattern of inheritance of houses. In Fucino it is not girls but boys who inherit or are given houses at marriage, and it may be this that makes the tie between honour and control over women's sexuality less stringent.

Nonetheless, Trasacco farmers' wives did work rather less in the fields than wives from the neighbouring village of Luco, where attitudes to work (and to some extent to women) are rather different. I was told that it was not necessary for wives to work in the fields because most farmers could afford to pay labour. Some of the labourers were of course women, the wives of *braccianti* and the poorest in the village. When I suggested that it might be for reasons of honour – that it might cause the chastity of the wives to be called in question, men assured me that they were more modern than that and left women to take care of themselves.

However, there was still very strict control over girls, who had to be home by 7.0 p.m. Any gathering would suddenly become bereft of girls at about 6.30 p.m., 'the curfew', as one young man called it. Men were very concerned about their daughters and could be acutely embarrassed if they drew attention to themselves by wearing a short skirt or talking with boys. 'I don't want to hear my daughter's name on my friends' lips', one father said. In another discussion a group of men talked about the difference between a *donna* and a *femmina* (both words meaning woman, the second commonly used in dialect speech). It was clear that a desirable spouse was *una femmina*, a woman who had a sense of *vergogna* (shame). As one put it: 'Men buy their smart clothes and fast cars to attract women, and yet the woman they wish to marry would never turn her head at your outfit or get into your car'. Students involved in this discussion were outraged. 'Is a woman nothing to you but a table ornament?' one of them demanded angrily. Attitudes to women were certainly changing amongst the educated young, but there was a weight of 'traditional' responses to combat both amongst the fathers and the women themselves.

It is worth noting, however, that all men who held political offices were married, which is in line with what Davis has said, that 'people are fully responsible for their actions when they are adults – and adult status and married status are coterminous'. A man's probity cannot be judged until he is married and his performance as provider and protector of his women becomes the subject of scrutiny. There was plenty of gossip – amongst women – about the infidelity of politically active men, but their control of their wives was a subject never alluded to. When confronted openly with the question men agreed that a man whose wife was unfaithful was unlikely to be entrusted with a public role, and that unmarried men had not ever been successful in local politics.

This chapter examined the ways in which political processes affect and are affected by other social relations; both the consistencies and contradictions between them. These can be seen in various contexts.

The stated objectives of Trasacco's voluntary associations are to improve cultural life or provide good football. Ostensibly, the men who run these clubs are elected as office-holders because they will further those aims and be efficient administrators. In fact voluntary associations are used to build up vote banks and to create the prestige which office-holders will use in the political arena. There is here a confusion between the idea that people are selected to run clubs because they are good at it and the idea that a person who runs a club is important. At the same time, the blatant use of voluntary associations to further personal political ambitions does not pass unnoticed. The cynicism that this engenders spills over into people's dealings with other organisations such as trade unions, even when these are trying to offer a real alternative to clientelism.

The client is no longer the servant or employee of the patron, and this can be seen in the changing language used to describe him. A client no longer calls his patron *padrone* (master, boss) but *amico* (friend), or refers to him as a member of his kin group. Whilst, however, the client perceives (or explains) his own relationship in the language of friendship or kinship, which have positive connotations, he condemns similar relations that others have as 'fear' ('tutti hanno paura di Ciofani' (everyone's afraid of Ciofani)). The client perceives clientele relations in general as bad, but perceives (or explains) his own as special and worthwhile. It is not surprising to find this detachment of the self from the common weal in a hierarchical social system which encourages deference to superiors, aspirations to join them and competition with one's fellows to do so. It is not a situation conducive to the development of solidarity among clients.

Ties of kinship and friendship are used by participants in clientele relationships, but the extent to which they are manipulated to mask clientelism and political favouritism should not be exaggerated. On the one hand, kinship obligations are real and are honoured. On the other hand, people constantly complain that the *comune* administration is corrupt and inefficient because of kinship ties. When somebody such as Dalla Montà with a sound reputation stands for election, the support he receives cannot be explained in terms of kinship or the exchange of *favori*. Those who vote for him do so in the expectation that he will behave differently from the usual run of *politicanti*.

The political obligations of kinship and the insurance mechanism of clientelism can, it seems, be overthrown.

In dealing with the role of the Church and priests in Trasacco, a clear contradiction emerged between the Church's celebration of the peasant as especially close to God and the provider of food for mankind, and its support of the Dc party and the actions of its own priests, both of which undermine the independence of the peasant. Clientelism, as practised by the Dc party and by priests, prevents the peasant from realising the 'dignity' with which ideas in the theology endow him.

Trasaccani do not value manual labour, and the labour involved in agriculture is regarded as particularly degrading. Prestige accrues to men who do no manual labour, who earn high incomes and work relatively short hours. We find therefore a tendency for people to sell or rent their land rather than work it themselves. The proceeds are spent on consumption items (such as conspicuous houses) and on the education of children so that they can find highly-paid, non-manual employment, preferably in the state bureaucracy. Investment, in other words, is not in the productive sector but in 'prestige' which, as the foundation of a political career, can lead to influence over the distribution of resources. People who aspire to high status generally move out of land ownership. Ciofani, the most prestigious man in Trasacco, is moving back into land, using government grants to increase its productivity, but characteristically, employing others to do the work.

7 Some themes in the history of Luco

Luco, like Trasacco, has its own history, but it has been involved closely in events that affected Fucino in its entirety. Some of these will be elaborated here because of their particular salience for *luchesi*. The *Lotta del Fucino*, for example, involved many people in the whole area, especially the *braccianti*, and the land reform wrought fundamental changes in the pattern of land-holding, but these events are not referred to constantly in other villages as they are by *luchesi*, to explain how things are now. The *Lotta* and the land reform are present now in the lives of *luchesi* at a conscious level in the sense that they frequently explain why they behave and think as they do by referring to those events.

The early settlement of Luco

Like the history of Trasacco, that of Luco is obscure right up to modern times. It has never attracted the attention of local historians, no local enthusiast has undertaken the task of researching it, and even the local archive contains very little. The same nineteenth-century source which revealed the gift of land to the church of Trasacco and the usurpation of the fishing rights there tells that the land around Luco was given to the Benedictine monks at Monte Cassino to colonise.

The monks settled the area by engaging sharecroppers to clear and cultivate the mountainside and the flatland bordering on the lake. The monks exacted an annual payment from the sharecroppers and took one-tenth of the value of any property sold. The colonisers of Luco were entitled to fish in the lake – a right which they shared with the *comuni* of Celano and San Benedetto – on payment of one-sixth of their catch to the Benedictines (Don Andrea di Pietro, 1869: 136–7).

This early distribution of land and fishing rights meant that even until the mid nineteenth century Luco was strikingly different from other *comuni* in Fucino, as statistics drawn from the Bourbon archive show (see Table 5).

Land and occupations in the early nineteenth century

In this same period land in Trasacco was rather unequally distributed. Eleven

83

Luco dei Marsi

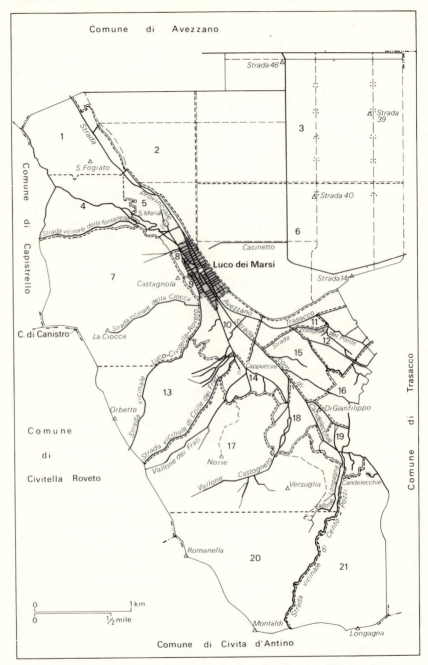

Map 4 Luco dei Marsi (from Provincia di L'Aquila, Quadro d'Unione)

families and the Church owned 40 per cent of the arable land, and a similar
amount was divided amongst another 28 families, in holdings of 5 to 25
hectares. The remaining 90 per cent of the population owned only 20 per
cent of the land in tiny smallholdings, or had no land at all (see Table 1, p. 20).

The table for Luco (Table 5) shows a remarkably different distribution.
There were 580 families in Luco with access to a total of 831.25 hectares of
arable land. This means that there were twice as many families as there were
in Trasacco, and the quantity of land available was 237 hectares less than that
of Trasacco. The owner of the largest landholding in Luco was a man called
Colonna who lived in L'Aquila and had properties scattered all over the
region. This property was only 16.36 hectares in extent. The eight biggest
landowners (including Colonna) and the Church together controlled only 9
per cent of the land. The remainder was divided amongst all the rest of the
households, giving an average of about 1.3 hectares each. Whilst some holdings were more than 2 hectares in size and others under 1 hectare, there were
very few families (and possibly none) who were landless. With this widespread
ownership of small holdings and no concentration of land in the hands of a
small elite, the population of Luco was economically much more homogen-
eous than that of Trasacco and there was correspondingly less economic and
social dependence of the poor on landowners.

In addition, *luchesi* had free access to the products of the lake. The last
available census of the Kingdom of Naples, taken in 1823, shows the number
of people in each occupational category (Table 6). Because the categories are
not defined in the census, one has to make a number of logical assumptions
about these figures. The 'Total' for each *comune* is the sum of the figures in
each occupational category; it is also the total population of the *comune*

Table 5 *Land distribution in Luco 1833–1865.*

	Locals		Church		Outsiders		Total	
	No.*	Area	No.*	Area	No.*	Area	No.*	Area
A over 25 ha	—		—		—		—	
B 15–25 ha	—		—		1	16.36	1	16.36
C 10–15 ha	1	10.79	—		—		1	10.79
D 5–10 ha	6	41.55	1	9.02	—		7	50.57
E under 5 ha	642	753.53	—		—		642	753.53
							651	831.25

Total families: 580

*Refers to number of *holdings* not individuals.
Source: Catasto Municipale, Luco dei Marsi.

Table 6 *Distribution of occupations in Fucino 1823.*

Category	Avezzano		Luco		Trasacco		Pescina		Celano		San Benedetto	
	No.	%	No.	%	No.	%	No.	%	No.	%	No.	%
Possedienti (landowners)	1431	50	322	24	172	18	389	15	524	16	79	15
Impiegati e arti liberi (officials and professionals)	80	3	2	–	1	–	88	3	16	–	7	1
Preti e frati (priests and monks)	29	1	12	1	7	1	23	1	41	2	4	1
Monache (nuns)	25	1	–	–	–	–	30	1	–	–	–	–
Artisti e domestici (artisans and servants)	72	3	26	2	4	1	106	4	174	5	–	–
Mendici (mendicants)	12	–	44	3	–	–	120	5	171	5	39	8
Pescatori (fishermen)	30	1	453	34	–	–	–	–	–	–	108	21
Contadini (peasants)	1167	41	490	36	760	80	1853	71	2396	72	276	54
Total	2846	100	1349	100	944	100	2609	100	3322	100	513	100

Source: Census 1823; Archivio di Stato, Naples.

(Giustiniani, 1802) and therefore one must assume that the dependants of the person active in each occupation have been included in the figure for each category. Further, there are two categories for agricultural occupations: *possedienti* (landowners), which must indicate that the family head owns sufficient land to live off, and *contadini* (peasants), which surely includes both landless and smallholders who sell their labour. Since we know that every family in Luco owned some land, it seems probable that most families both cultivated and fished and the designation *pescatore* (fisherman) indicates the main occupation of the family head. It is unfortunate that this is the only information available on the number of fishermen since it is rather inadequate and speculative. Meagre as the information is, it does demonstrate the striking difference between Luco and other villages. San Benedetto was the only other Fucino *comune* having any significant number of fishermen.

Popular tradition in Luco supports the view that fishing was a vital part of the local economy and that the catch was marketed outside the area. The elderly recall their grandparents' accounts of fishing from groups of boats, and of the women gutting and packing the fish into large baskets ready to be carried by porters on their heads. This is what Edward Lear had to say in 1846:

The present town of Luco contains about sixteen hundred inhabitants (Giustiniani), nearly the whole of whom are supported by fishing in the lake; the result of which they carry by Capistrello and Canistro to Subiaco and even to Rome. (Lear, 1846: 21.)

The journey that Lear describes is across mountainous country and was accomplished 'by a series of runners who managed to get [the catch] to its destination within 15−18 hours' (Brisse & De Rotrou, 1882: II).

Avezzano was not connected with Naples by a carriageable road until 1854 and not with Rome until 1870. By this time *luchesi*, through the marketing of their catch, already had contact with the outside world and were no strangers to the marketplace. Just as in western Sicily (Schneider, 1972) the product was exported direct to the regional market, not collected and distributed from a market town close by. Thus the local people had direct connections with the metropolis. Since lake fishing required only rather simple equipment, capital for fishing was probably widely distributed. Since the method used required the concerted operation of several boats, joint ownership and fairly permanent cooperative fishing groups were probably important.

Thus, by the time that the Torlonia company started to construct the tunnel to drain the lake in 1854, Luco was unusual among the Fucino villages in a number of ways which derived from their fishing and from their more equal access to the means of production. This was true even though the resources of land were limited and a tax of one-sixth of the catch was payable (after the abolition of feudalism in 1806) to the *comune* administration.

It is difficult to avoid seeing a connection between the particular friendliness and industry of the *luchesi*, repeatedly referred to by nineteenth-century writers, and this relatively equal distribution of productive resources. They created a favourable impression on Lear:

We passed through Luco, a lively little town . . . its inhabitants are considered by the Marsicans generally as being the finest race among them, strong and healthy, though not handsome . . . We remarked at every step the courtesy and pleasing cordiality of the peasants, nearly every individual saluting us, both while passing through the town, and afterwards from the vineyards by the roadside: most of them added a benediction 'V'accompagna Maria!' or 'Vi benedica Gesù!' or 'Faccia felice viaggio!' at the least. (Lear, 1846: 21−2.)

They also impressed the chief engineers on the drainage project as being 'certainly the most industrious of the workmen' (Brisse & De Rotrou, 1882: II). Another writer in a eulogy of Torlonia's massive undertaking refers thus to the *luchesi*: '(Luco's) population gave the major contingent of expert and robust labourers to the drainage of Fucino.' (De Felippis, 1893: 64.)

In another reference to the *luchesi*, the engineers suggest that the drainage works were of particular benefit to the *luchesi* who, with insufficient land and only seasonal fishing, had been forced to emigrate for a period each year

to the unhealthy neighbourhood of Rome or to the province of Puglie. No sooner had draining operations commenced than this mode of life was forsaken and among the workmen employed in the construction of the emissary they were always reckoned the most industrious. (Brisse & De Rotrou, 1882: II.)

De Felippis states that they were particularly adept at working under water, a skill in demand at the lake end of the tunnel. All these writers single out for comment the industry, independence and cheerfulness of the *luchesi* as well as the peculiarities of their economy.

The drainage project

The following account depends heavily on the three volumes of a presentation book, *Il prosciugamento del Lago Fucino* (The Drainage of Lake Fucino), written by the two French engineers, Brisse and De Rotrou, who brought the project to completion. They recount in detail the construction of the first tunnel built by the Emperor Claudius to control flooding, the successive surveys of the viability of reopening it by the chief engineer of the Kingdom of Naples in the first half of the nineteenth century, the formation of the company headed by Alessandro Torlonia, the decision to build a new tunnel that would drain the lake completely, and the reasons why the other shareholders withdrew, leaving Torlonia determined to continue the undertaking alone.

According to his obituary in *The Times* he was

The youngest and most enterprising of the sons of Giovanni Torlonia, who was originally a small shopkeeper in Siena but eventually became a banker of great wealth and influence and Duke of Bracciano. Alessandro was born in Rome in 1800. He inherited a large patrimony which he largely increased by taking long leases on the salt and tobacco monopolies in the Papal and Neapolitan states and by other profitable transactions. (*The Times*: 10 February 1886.)

By 1854 Torlonia had decided to withdraw from his vast commercial enterprises, give up his famous banking house and devote himself to agriculture (Brisse & De Rotrou, 1882: II, 11). He provided half the capital for the Fucino company. The first drainage plans were designed by two English engineers. The contract, drawn up by a royal lawyer 'totally ignorant of the engineering problems', was, in the opinion of Brisse and Rotrou, impossibly onerous, since any failure to comply with its smallest details entailed forfeiture of the company's entire assets.

Left in sole control, Torlonia decided, regardless of the cost, to build an outlet tunnel capable of withstanding any emergency. He dismissed the English engineers, and engaged in their place the world-famous French engineer Montricher, who had recently completed the tunnel under Marseilles harbour. The instructions he received were to proceed 'virtually with no expense spared' (idem: 16). The final cost to Torlonia was £2 000 000 sterling at a rate of £60 000 per annum.

Chief engineer Bermont and his assistants arrived in Avezzano in September 1855. It was then a town of 4500 inhabitants, with no road to Rome and one just completed to Naples, no skilled iron-workers, carpenters or masons and no one who knew anything about mining. Work was commenced at Capistrello on the west side of Monte Saviano and simultaneously, from barges, on the Fucino side.

Extensive sheds were constructed, a quarry, forges and a chapel near Capistrello and a hospital in Avezzano. On the lake-side there was an automatic railway carrying earth to the dikes, and a hundred barges were in use. By 1859 three thousand men were employed in continuous eight-hour shifts.

The danger was intense – it was necessary to keep a certain number of men on the lookout whilst the others were at work. The roof was not lost sight of for a moment, so that at the first sign of any movement in the soil the alarm might be given and the men enabled to make their escape . . . Prompt measures for the rescue and assistance of the wounded in case of need, strict obedience in the performance of each order, perfect silence, incessant vigilance and the constant presence of the leaders . . . Nor was it the case of one hour or a day even, but of weeks and months, during which those who went to work stood good chance of never returning from it. (Idem.)

There is no record of the number who died, but both this comment and an allusion in a letter from the *comune* of Luco to Torlonia suggest that not a few lost their lives in the tunnel.

The workers were not at all used to earning cash wages, and the authors describe in some detail how it took years to accustom them to receiving their money once a month instead of twice a day, as they had at the beginning. Sturdy bourgeois, the engineers count it as one of the blessings of the enterprise that 'their moral standard was sensibly raised by these habits of discipline' (idem). They admit that the wages were very low, but assure the reader that not even at the height of the disturbances accompanying Unification did 'a single man leave his work for a moment'. The authors suggest that their zeal was due to the workers' realisation that the project had given them employment and food for the last six years, and therefore they never went on strike.

Whilst there may well have been no strikes on the construction site, there was unrest in the *comune* of Luco, where, ever since the project began, the fishermen had refused to pay the tax on fish (idem). It is possible that the company had made a point of employing plenty of *luchesi* precisely in order to stifle protest in the quarter from which it was most likely — amongst fishermen threatened with the loss of their livelihood.

People in the Fucino area had already become disillusioned about promises of compensation. They had been assured of financial help when the flooding of 1846 caused extensive damage, but this had never materialised. There was no reason to suppose that they would be compensated for the loss of their fishing rights. Already voices were murmuring that since fishing was a communal right, the land beneath the lake must also be *comune* property (idem). It is not difficult to imagine the rumours and the speculations which filled the wine shops, especially in the period of Unification, when, from being subjects of the king of Naples, they became citizens of unified Italy under the king of Piedmont.

By 1862 the initial work was complete, and the first water could be allowed to pass through the outlet. Since the contract of drainage gave Torlonia all the land lying under the water, the outer confines had to be marked before any water was emitted. In late July 1862 columns were placed in each *comune* to mark the water's highest point. In August a crowd of thousands watched the opening ceremony which started a flow of water that was not to cease for another year. In September 1863 work was recommenced on lining the outlet tunnel and building the opening.

This work was completed the following year, but the outlet could not be opened on account of objections from the *comune* of Luco. The mayor and council lodged with the sub-prefect in Avezzano a claim that the markers set up in 1862 gave Torlonia more land than that laid down in the terms of the contract. A particularly high water, which reached its maximum in 1862 just when Torlonia's agents were placing the markers, had flooded land that had been cultivated by *luchesi* for 26 years, between 1834 and 1860. They claimed that this land rightly belonged to *luchesi* and not to Torlonia, who, they suggested, had deliberately delayed placing the boundary markers until the water had reached this exceptionally high level (Minutes of Extraordinary Meeting of the Commune Council, Luco, 25 July 1865).

Ordinary citizens of Luco took the law into their own hands and in the first six months of 1865 repeatedly toppled the markers into the water. This action provoked a flurry of obsequious letters to His Excellency from the councils of all the other *comuni*, assuring him of their admiration for his project, beseeching him to ignore 'the events in Luco' (Council Minutes,

Lecce, 11 May 1865) and open the tunnel. Luco's councillors tried to play down the destruction of the markers as the work of 'a few deranged citizens' (Council Minutes, 25 July 1865) but it is clear from other documents that the disturbances were more significant than that. For example, in a letter to the Government:

... it is strange and sad but unfortunately unavoidable that we call on the arm of the King's Government to enter into the controversy, almost as though the laws of Italy do not have the means to repress such wilful and violent acts. (Council Minutes, Gioia, 8 May 1865.)

Eventually the final position of the markers in each *comune* was settled by a commission of three – a representative of Torlonia, of the sub-prefect and of each council. To prevent any more trouble each marking-stone was topped with a cast-iron statue of the Madonna. It was only when they had been thus doubly sanctified that the *luchesi* desisted from pushing them over. At the end of August the tunnel was reopened and the water continued to flow until the end of April 1868. A grandiose stone superstructure with a figure of the Madonna was erected over the outlet and work on the canals and roads was begun.

How this part of the operation was carried out has received no attention from commentators. The main canal is 11 kilometres long and 15 metres wide, with a small circular canal draining into it from the lowest part of the lake, the Bacinetto. Parallel to it are 9 minor canals and 30 large ditches. Further cross-canals bring the system to a total length of 286 kilometres. These required the construction of 238 bridges, 3 canal crossings and 4 sluices. A road going all round the edge of the property was built, 52 kilometres long, then 46 numbered roads were laid out at intervals of 1 kilometre, equidistant between the canals, with a total length of 202 kilometres. The roads and canals were planted with avenues of poplar trees. I could find no record of how this work was carried out, but it must have required an enormous quantity of labour.

The population of the bordering *comuni* increased from 25 770 in 1861 to 38 170 in 1881, that is by 48 per cent in twenty years. As one writer has put it, the Fucino basin acted like a magnet on the poverty-stricken populations of Southern Italy from the commencement of the *prosciugamento* (drainage) right up to the land reform (Liberale, 1956).

Luco received a rather lower influx of new inhabitants than the Fucino area as a whole, a trend which has been consistent right up to the present day (see Table 7). It is difficult to discover the reason, but some suggestions have already been made as to why Trasacco received more immigrants than Luco in the early years after the drainage (see above, p. 22). Luco has less space for housing and a less congenial climate. In addition Luco had at that time a

Table 7 *Population and rate of increase of population 1861–1971.*

(Base: 1861 = 100)

	1861	1911	1951	1971
Luco	2784	5010	5570	4610
	100	180	200	165
Trasacco	1265	3772	5718	5311
	100	298	452	420
Fucino	25 770	48 588	64 540	66 705
Total	100	188	250	259
Provincial	253 783	337 610	346 567	293 066
Total	100	133	136	115

Source: Census 1961–71, ISTAT, Rome.

severe water shortage (see below), it had suffered considerable civil unrest and perhaps, as a fishing village, it was a more tightly-knit community, less open to newcomers than elsewhere.

The Torlonia regime 1865–1950

During 1865, as was mentioned, sections of the population of Luco protested against the drainage – most probably the fishermen who were going to lose their living. Their action was publicly repudiated by the councillors, who no doubt expected to benefit from the new land that was shortly to appear. Soon afterwards the whole population were united by a common problem, the loss of their water supply.

As soon as the lake level began to fall in 1865, it became clear that the springs which fed Luco's water supply were drying up. In 1866 the council wrote to the sub-prefect in Avezzano and to the Government, asking for a subsidy to provide a water supply. Apparently negotiations with Torlonia had failed, and a court case, expected to be a long one, had been begun to force him to comply with an undertaking in the original contract of drainage to make good all losses.

For four and a half years water had to be carried from a distance of four kilometres on the heads of the women. Only in 1871 were plans finally agreed with Torlonia, and it is not at all clear that the dispute ended then, for discussions of the problem continued until 1876 (Council Minutes, Luco, September 1866, February 1876, March 1876).

It is possible that Torlonia resented the council's actions and therefore decided not to allocate land to the most prosperous and acknowledged *signori* as he had done in other villages. Instead *appezzamenti* (25-hectare allotments) were allocated to 21 *grandi affittuari* who had not been leaders of the community. At the stroke of a pen, therefore, Torlonia created in Luco a new elite who derived their position from their ability to sublet their *appezzamenti*. However, their ascendancy was short lived. Much of the land in the *comune* of Luco became infested with marsh weed and was turned over to pasture.

In 1883 a senatorial commission of enquiry into the state of Italian agri-culture visited the Torlonia estate. In its report, known as the Iacini report, it had some harsh comments to make about Fucino. Spectacular initial yields of twenty to thirty times the seed planted had declined to between ten and fifteen times because a rotation system had not been adopted, and there were too few cattle to provide manure. The report considered that the culti-vators were exhausted by the long distances that they had to walk to work, and that rents were excessive. It recommended that Torlonia institute a *mezzadria* (sharecropping) regime, giving each family a house on the land and encouraging a proper mixed-farming system. In the event, it was only the weed-infested area, tenanted almost entirely by the *grandi affittuari* of Luco, that was repossessed and settled with *mezzadri*. Almost as quickly as they had been created, Luco's *nouveaux riches* were submerged, and the old elite revived for a short period.

As I explained, the wealth of this elite was not derived from large land holdings, either before the drainage or as tenants of the Torlonia regime. It is difficult to discover just what their sources of income were, because the last member of the last surviving *signorile* family left Luco in 1915. Older inform-ants thought that they had been state employees in various offices in Avezzano and that one had had the Post Office licence (a lucrative source of income in the nineteenth century). It was also said that in the last part of the nineteenth and early part of this century they had amassed what *fuori-Fucino* land was cultivable by taking it as security against loans, particularly for those who emigrated to the United States and never redeemed their mortgages.

After the disappearance of the last of the *signori* in 1915, the elite which gradually emerged in Luco derived its comparative wealth and status from a number of sources. A few men managed to accumulate tenancies in Fucino piece by piece, amounting in some cases to five or six hectares. One woman, Caterina D'Avrantis, a Greek who married a local potato merchant, bought twelve hectares of tenancies in the late 'twenties, and in 1950 was the largest single non-*mezzadria* tenant in Fucino (the old *grandi affittuari* having been abolished by 1920). In addition to the larger tenants there were a few func-tionaries employed in offices in Avezzano, including those of Torlonia's administration, some potato merchants and a few lawyers.

Just as in Trasacco, there was great competition amongst the former fishermen and smallholders for the sub-tenancies in Fucino. Once the land of the local *grandi affittuari* had been repossessed in the 1880s, *luchesi* had to look further afield to find land to sub-let. The problems of long distances to be covered and extreme subdivision of the land beset *luchesi* too.

Torlonia established on his estate, between Avezzano and Luco, two enter-prises which came to employ a large number of *luchesi*. A 'model' farm of 607 hectares was formed at Via Nuova out of a residue of 927 hectares which Torlonia kept under the direct control of the Administration. A second farm was established near Ortucchio. These farms produced prize horses, cattle, grain and forage crops. A foreman lived in Luco and recruited labour there. At times when work was very short, *luchesi* would march in a body to the farm and try to storm the gates and force the foreman to employ them. The contracts were short-term ones, except for a handful of specialist stockmen and foremen.

In 1913 women *braccianti* from Luco employed on the farm on a con-tract to harvest beet went on strike for higher wages. They blocked roads on the estate and prevented tenants from getting to their land. They were prosecuted for obstruction at the district court in Trasacco, but won their demand for higher wages. The court case is the only written evidence of a strike by farm workers, but it was said that they had been quite frequent, and were often instigated by women. It is possible that women had built up a par-ticular resentment against Torlonia over the water dispute, because it was they who had to carry the burden each day that it remained unsolved. The tradition was passed on from one generation to the next, for women have been involved in every subsequent action against authority in Luco (see below p. 105). In 1915, for example, women attacked soldiers who had come to requisition grain for feeding the army. A crowd of them stormed the wagons where the grain was being loaded and threw the sacks to the ground. Again a number were arrested and fined.

Whilst it is possible that similar incidents took place in other Fucino villages, the striking thing about Luco is that they are remembered and talked about still as examples of *luchese* militancy and the strength of their women.

A second source of wage employment for *luchesi* was the building and then the operation of the sugar refinery, sited, like the farm, between Avezzano and Luco (see Map 3). The factory was built by Northern artisans and local, mostly *luchesi*, labourers.

Once in full production it employed three hundred workers throughout the year, and a further five hundred contract workers for the harvest season from November to February. There was great competition for these jobs among workers from all the *comuni* in walking distance. *Luchesi* provided an average 20 per cent of the permanent workforce and a third of the seasonal labour. About half the present male population and about a fifth of the women of Luco have had some experience of working in the refinery.

The factory had a 'union' started by management, its 'workers' representatives' chosen and controlled by management. It is not at all clear what this 'union' did, for wages were negotiated by individual workers who approached the director for personal pay rises. There was considerable competition for employment; applicants are said to have had to take presents of entire *prosciutti* (dried hams) in order to get taken on. Both the tactics of management and this competition delayed the establishment of an independent union. It was not until 1947 that the Cgil gained entry, obtained an immediate 75 per cent membership among the workforce and negotiated a new contract. This contract ended the twelve-hour shifts and the arbitrary dismissals, and increased pay rates by 30 per cent. It may seem strange that the workers had not been properly unionised before 1947, especially considering the unrest in the countryside beyond the factory gates. Management policies had, however, been particularly divisive and paternalist, and this was the only factory in the area. Workers generally regarded themselves as fortunate to have been taken onto the payroll.

Radical movements and collective action 1910–21

Organisations of peasants began earlier and were more successful in Luco than elsewhere in Fucino. In 1910 a Peasant League was started and quickly gathered 400 members (Liberale, 1956). A League of Young Socialists had fifty members who were mostly the sons of small tenants and *braccianti* (ibid). In 1914, at the first elections after the introduction of universal adult male suffrage, a mayor was elected who was not a member of the old elite families. The son of a peasant, he was an advocate. His sympathies are clear from his inaugural speech:

People will not be free until they have economic, sanitary, moral, intellectual and social independence. (Council Minutes, Luco, 20 September 1914.)

Under his administration a commission was appointed in 1915 to negotiate with Torlonia for assistance with 'the rebirth of the village after the earthquake'. The main request was for the complete revision of the method of allocating tenancies. What the *luchesi* wanted referred back to some old legal actions by the *comuni* of Luco and Avezzano. These had tried to prove that Lake Fucino had been communal property and that Torlonia had usurped common rights. Not surprisingly the attempt to discuss this with Torlonia failed. The new administration elected in 1919 again supported peasant demands for changes in land tenure. The mayor, Francesco Amadoro, was a law student and a socialist.

Luco dei Marsi

The years 1919–21 became known in Italy as the *Biennio Rosso*, or the years of the 'Lost Revolution'. The long series of disturbances had begun with bread riots and anti-war demonstrations between 1915 and 1918. After the war unrest continued as land-hungry ex-combatants invaded large estates all over the country. In cities like Turin where the 'factory council' movement was strong, factories were occupied and run by the workers. Resentment developed at the high cost of living; from a base of 100 in 1913, the cost of living index rose to 365.8 in 1919 and 624.4 in 1924 (Snowden, 1972). The Giolitti government, concerned about social deprivation and afraid that a strong reaction would spark off 'the Revolution', took sporadic repressive measures (Procacci, 1973: 414).

In Luco, 'in view of the numerous conflicts that have broken out' (Council Minutes, 2 April 1921), the council wrote to the Minister of Agriculture demanding that both Torlonia's administration farms and the *grandi affit-tuari* be expropriated and 'the land distributed to associations and organis-ations of the peasants for collective exploitation' (ibid). This had no effect on the problem of land shortage, but it makes it clear that Luco's representa-tives supported the efforts of peasants to improve their conditions in a radical way. It also shows that they preferred a collective to an individualist solution.

Meanwhile, in Italy as a whole, a reactionary answer to the country's problems was coming closer. The Turin metalworkers were defeated. Land-owners and industrialists were frightened by what the socialists had achieved in factories and rural areas. Disappointed by the inconsistent response of the Giolitti government, they were turning to the Fascist Party, and giving support to its *squadristi* (strong-arm men). The petit-bourgeoisie looked to the fascists too for protection against urban unrest. Ex-officers who had resented the anti-militarist feelings that swept Italy at the end of the war, were attracted to fascism's nationalist and militarist ideology (Snowden, 1972; Procacci, 1973: 407–17; Del Carria, 1970: II, 53–18).

The opposition to fascism was divided: 'the glorious Italian Socialist Party' lost its 'maximalist' wing to the Pci in January 1921 and its 'moderate' wing to the Social Democrats in 1922. The Pope 'contributed to the final victory of fascism by withdrawing the Church's support from the Italian Popular Party and its combative leader, Don Sturzo' (Procacci, 1973: 418). In October 1921, taking advantage of a railway strike, Mussolini's *squadristi* had occupied the railways, thus controlling the main line of communication be-tween North and South. This was followed by the 'March on Rome' of *squadristi* from all over the country. Although the city, at the behest of the government, was barricaded against the arrival of the fascists, the king went over the head of his prime minister and asked Mussolini (who had only 35 deputies in Parliament) to form a government. He was given a vote of confidence by 306 deputies out of 422. The fascist regime had begun on 30 October 1921.

Resistance to fascism and German occupation

Fascism gradually penetrated every facet of life in Italy. At the local level, mayors and councils were replaced by a *podestà* appointed from above. In every *comune* the fascist party secretary acted as a direct link with party headquarters and virtually controlled local administration. Opponents of the regime were spied on, arrested and tortured in the 'dark room' which every party *sezione* in every *comune* had installed. The death penalty, abolished in 1900, was reinstated.

The Cgil, 'the last stronghold of free unionism' (Procacci, 1973: 423) was dissolved in 1925. The Vidoni pact between the unions and representatives of industrialists suppressed strikes and the formation of workers' committees. It 'more or less silenced workers' opposition' (ibid). In both industry and agriculture, in negotiations over wages and over rent, it was the owners and landlords who usually won the day. This was particularly so in Fucino. Torlonia, a personal friend of Mussolini, never had a request for a rent rise rejected by the provincial authorities.

In Luco opposition to fascism and to the Torlonia regime did not disappear, but it ceased to be open. The leadership of the Socialist Party passed from Francesco Amadoro to his brother Rocco, a peasant. After the split at the conference of Livorno the Luco socialists went over to the Pci. When persecution of communists became widespread the local party went 'underground'. Although they actually did very little against the regime, members were subject to constant harassment and occasional torture. Two tragic deaths occurred at the hands of the fascist authorities. One of these was Lenin, the son of Rocco Amadoro, arrested for singing the 'International'. He died, it is said, after three days in gaol in Avezzano. The other was Angelucci, a father of nine children, who staged a noisy one-man demonstration against the *podestà*'s unfair distribution of food and money to the poor. He too was a known communist. He was certified insane and hospitalised in L'Aquila. As it was recounted to me, his body was so destroyed by torture that, when it was returned two weeks later, it was only recognisable by the socks. Francesco Amadoro was put in preventive detention 'every time Mussolini went on a tour of Italy or foreign dignitaries visited the country'. Rocco is said to have camped out in his vineyard for almost the entire period of fascism.

These stories of the fascist years are only the most striking and well-known ones. Almost everyone in Luco has an account of petty harassment by the local *squadristi*. The importance of Lenin Amadoro and Angelucci is that everybody in the village, regardless of personal feelings towards fascism, was horrified by their deaths. That they were *luchesi* who stood up for their beliefs is something of which people of both right and left are still proud. Their martyrdom feeds into the image that *luchesi* have of themselves as anti-fascist and anti-authoritarian. They are recalled when *luchesi* want to define themselves as different from others and, if they are communists, as good comrades.

Events during the German occupation are recalled with equal pride. There was no organised Liberation Movement or Partisan army, only the Communist Party's shadowy presence. Its Red Flag was symbolically burnt when the party went 'underground', and the ashes were put in a vase on the mantel-piece of Rocco Amadoro's front room. Communists organised help for families like the Angeluccis who were in trouble, and aided Allied troops during the siege of Monte Cassino. In one incident a contingent of para-troopers was accidentally dropped on the wrong side of Monte Saviano and shot at by the Germans. The parachutists were collected at night, their wounds dressed and those who could travel were guided over the mountains. A number who were too ill were kept hidden, at great risk to *luchesi*, in cellars and behind false walls. Harbouring foreign troops normally evoked severe reprisals from the Germans. None of these clandestine activities was ever reported, which demonstrates that the whole population colluded in them.

The end of the war

In 1944, after a heavy bombardment of Avezzano, the German occupying forces withdrew from Fucino. In Luco the communists rounded up the *fascisti* and locked them in the elementary school building. In a quarrel about what should be done with them a young partisan was accidentally shot by one of his comrades. His funeral was the first formal occasion when the com-munists appeared in their red kerchiefs. The coffin, draped with a red flag, symbolised the break with the past. On the orders of the Committee for National Liberation the fascists were released without further harassment. How *fascisti* were reintegrated into the community is a problem that I was not able to unravel, and it is a subject which has not been given serious treatment except in the rather allusive style of Bertolucci's film *The Spider's Stratagem*.

The first post-war mayor of Luco, De Amicis, was not a communist but a member of the Partito Popolare (later the Dc) and had always been an out-spoken anti-fascist. He was elected by acclamation before the first nationally organised elections took place. Of the two Amadoro brothers, around whom the party had formerly coalesced, one, Rocco, had died and the other, Francesco, had moved, to practice law in Rome.

At the first elections of 1946 De Amicis was relegated to leader of the Dc opposition. The Popular Front (Pci/Psi) won a staggering 74.9 per cent of the vote for the *comune* council. In national elections for the Constituent Assembly the Popular Front was highly successful and there was an 80 per cent vote for the republic and against the monarchy. The other Fucino *comuni* also elected left-wing administrations, bringing upon them the nickname 'The Red Belt of the Abruzzo'. Table 8 shows how the vote was distributed. In none of these *comuni* was the support for the Left as strong as it was in Luco nor as consistent between local and national levels. The table also shows that by 1951 the number of Left administrations had fallen from ten out of eleven to six.

The years from 1946 to 1951 were among the most dramatic ever experienced in Fucino and the Luco Communist and Socialist Parties and their organisations of peasants and *braccianti* played a major role in the action.

Luco's Pci and the unemployed *braccianti*

The Communist Party quickly became involved in many aspects of the lives of *luchesi*. A branch of the Federbraccianti was formed, and began immediate discussions with its 400 members as to what action to take over unemployment, their major concern. A consumer cooperative was opened in the base-

Table 8 *Fucino election results 1946–1951.*

	Referendum 1946		National Elections Constituency Assembly 1946		Local 1946		Local 1951	
	Rep.*	Mon.†	Left	Others	Left	Others	Left	Others
Luco	80.7	19.3	68.5	31.5	*74.9*	25.1	*61.7*	38.3
Trasacco	48.7	51.3	46.8	53.2	*60.5*	39.5	39.2	60.8
Avezzano	36.1	63.9	52.9	47.1	48.9	51.1	27.6	72.4
Aielli	78.8	21.2	42.2	57.8	44.7	55.3	*57.6*	42.4
Celano	63.6	36.4	39.9	60.1	*50.6*	49.4	49.1	50.9
Cerchio	46.5	53.5	40.1	59.9	*60.8*	39.2	35.2	64.8
Gioia	36.3	63.7	12.4	87.6	*56.3*	43.7	43.5	56.5
Lecce	60.7	39.3	59.5	40.5	*38.5*	61.5	*53.2*	46.8
Ortucchio	39.3	60.7	30.5	69.5	37.5	62.5	*57.0*	43.0
Pescina	68.6	31.4	63.9	36.1	*69.0*	31.0	*50.5*	49.5
San Benedetto	57.2	42.8	48.6	51.4	*57.9*	42.1	*49.4*	50.6

Source: Office of the Prefect, L'Aquila.
Figures in italic indicate left administrations at the local level.
*Rep. = votes for a republic.
†Mon. = votes for maintenance of the monarchy.

ment of the Pci *sezione* building. The mayor, Ciangoli, was a father of six with only half a hectare of land. In order to provide him with a steady income and ensure that he did not have to emigrate, as had Trasacco's mayor, Di Cola, he was made manager of the cooperative. As a result the store became a daily meeting place for informal analysis of the political situation.

Adult education classes were held in the evenings in the *sezione*. Illiterates were taught to read and write, and reading groups discussed the works of Marx, Lenin and Gramsci. The Pci drama group tapped an unexpected enthusiasm for acting, and played the works of socialist writers such as Brecht and De Felippo to packed houses. The new administration made itself felt. All street names with fascist or nationalist connotations were torn down and replaced with populist and revolutionary ones. Taxes on the poor and sick were individually reviewed and often reimbursed. The salaries of the school *bidello* and the dustmen were raised. In 1948 funding was obtained to build a nursery school and twenty council flats. In the heavy snows of that year the streets and roofs were cleared by a cooperative effort of the whole population in response to an appeal by the mayor.

During this period the plight of the small tenants and landless was becoming increasingly acute. In March 1949 the *comune* council wrote to Torlonia and to the minister of agriculture pointing out that there were a thousand out of work in Luco alone (in a population of 5354). The letter warned that discontent was growing and appealed for aid with public works projects which had already been submitted for the approval of the prefect. A month later the council voted to make a start on them without awaiting permission.

In April the unemployed of Luco demonstrated outside the offices of the Torlonia Administration demanding work. In the early hours of the next morning the police arrested the mayor of Luco and four other leading members of the Pci in their homes. They were imprisoned for a month in L'Aquila, then released without charges being laid.

Between then and 1950 a strategy was worked out which would unite the landless labourers and at the same time win the support and sympathy of the tenants. The Government (as was mentioned in Chapter 3) had passed a law for the maximum employment of labour, which stipulated the percentage of their income that landlords were required to reinvest in their estates. The canals and roads of Fucino desperately needed repair, their condition was causing tenants difficulties with transport and fields were water-logged. It was proposed that the *braccianti* carry out the repairs by marching onto the estate in force whether or not Torlonia wished it. They were to carry out exactly the amount of work that the Government decree stipulated. It was hoped that this work-in, the *sciopero a rovescio*, would force Torlonia to employ and pay the *braccianti*.

At the same time the Pci was organising peasants all over the South. Land

100

invasions had taken place in Lucania, Calabria and Apulia almost continuously since 1943, led by communists and sometimes by priests. A constant theme of the invasions was that they were reclaiming common lands usurped by the bourgeoisie centuries before. In Fucino this idea harked back to past court cases against Torlonia. In Fucino it was unemployment that triggered the invasions. The work that the *braccianti* did, however, also benefited the tenants and had their support. The movement was easily fused with tenants' demands for more land and moves to invade the Administration farms. Thus, quite soon after its inception, the *sciopero a rovescio* turned into a massive popular protest against the Torlonia regime.

Only through the medium of the Pci central committee was it coordinated with other movements against large landed proprietors. Participants in Fucino do not seem to have had a vision of the struggle which encompassed areas all over Italy. Negotiations with the government were carried on separately by Fucino trade unionists, and the struggle was known by the parochial title of the *Lotta del Fucino.*[1]

The rental situation

In order to understand why tenants and *braccianti* united in this struggle, we need to know something of the existing land tenure system. Because of the difficulties of access to the Torlonia archive this account has to rely heavily on a work by Adriano Pizzutti *Le affittanze agrarie nel Fucino* (Agrarian tenancies in Fucino), produced by the Ente Fucino in 1953. Pizzutti was an employee of Torlonia and then of the Ente Fucino, a lawyer by training. His treatment is supplemented by a few small journal and newspaper articles and by oral accounts.

As far as the inhabitants of the Fucino villages were concerned, Prince Torlonia had a monopoly on all but the marginal *fuori-Fucino* land. His was a pervasive but unseen presence, for he rarely visited the Fucino estate, and when he did he never left the *palazzo* in Avezzano. He was one of the richest men in Italy. He had considerable influence both with the Vatican, where he held an honorary office, and with the government of the day. He lived in a mansion in Rome surrounded by parkland. The Fucino estate was run by a resident director and an administration of thirty based in Avezzano. Five bailiffs and thirty guards saw to it that his rights were not infringed.

Of the 14 000 hectares of land about 11 000 were let to tenants. In 1950

1 This parochialism was a feature of all the post-war land struggles in the South. Some people were hopeful that the peasant movement would lead into revolution and the triumph of socialism. It bore out rather Gramsci's prediction that without solidarity among the Southern peasantry in alliance with the advanced Northern workers there could be no revolutionary change in Italy (cf. *The modern prince*, pp. 50–1).

there were 8833 correctly registered tenants and at least another 2415 sub-tenants. The sub-tenancies were not recorded and were technically illegal. Table 9 shows the number and size of the allotments which made up the 'direct' tenancies. Most tenancies consisted of a number of scattered plots. Figure 3 shows the subdivision of three tenancies prior to the land reform. These tenants were citizens of Trasacco and were lucky in having their land reasonably nearby. They were selected by the author as representing average holdings (Pizzutti, 1953: 14). The plan demonstrates also how even the land under trees was separately let. The subdivision of the land was described by agronomists as 'pathological pulverisation'.

Subsistence crops were grown in some variety, but these took second place to the production of beet. The standard tenancy contract lasted one year, and stipulated that the rent be paid in a fixed quantity of sugar beet to be consigned to the refinery in October. The objective of Torlonia in managing the estate was to extract the maximum amount of sugar beet from it and discourage the production of subsistence crops. Therefore, although tenants could pay their rent in cash, the equivalence was not in their favour, and they tried to grow at least enough beet to pay the rent.

Pizzutti describes in considerable detail the variations in rent according to soil fertility, and the enormous changes in the prices of beet and grain during the years between 1938 and 1950. He notes that some people had a 'special concession' to pay in grain, and that those who could pay in grain were at an enormous economic advantage: a tenant paying in beet was sometimes paying *eight times* more rent than one paying in grain. Pizzutti does not however draw out the implications of this.

At the outset, the original Prince Torlonia controlled his estate and the tenants who worked it by allocating large *appezzamenti* to men on whom he could rely to control their local populations. This form of control was under-

Table 9 *Size of holdings in Fucino 1950.*

Holdings measuring	Number	% of all holdings	Area in ha	% of total area
Up to 0.50 hectares	2503	28.2	862.7	7.9
0.51−1.00 hectares	2467	27.8	1905.6	17.5
1.01−2.00 hectares	2532	28.5	3650.6	33.5
2.01−3.00 hectares	858	9.7	2069.9	19.0
3.01−4.00 hectares	263	3.0	879.5	8.0
4.01−5.00 hectares	136	1.5	617.6	5.7
Over 5.00 hectares	111	1.3	914.9	8.4
Total	8870	100.0	10 900.8	100.0

Source: Dondi, 1960.

mined by the peasant leagues, who demanded and eventually got direct tenancies for the cultivators. Without access to the archive one can only speculate about the reasons for and repercussions of the highly differentiated rents which developed during the 'twenties. It does seem likely however that they served two purposes: to prevent tenants from uniting against the system and to give those paying in grain a strong allegiance to Torlonia.

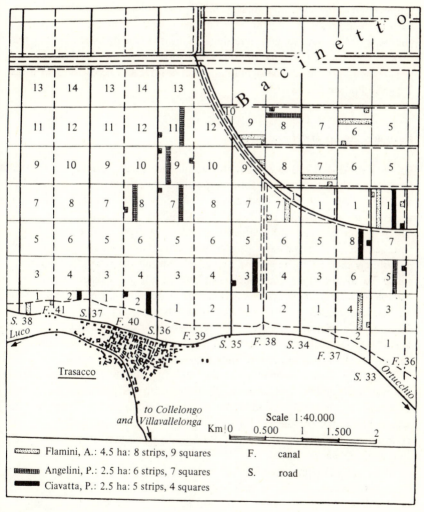

Figure 3 Examples of subdivision of tenancies (from Pizzuti, *Le affittanze agrarie nel Fucino*)

103

Luco dei Marsi

Because of high rents and a series of very poor harvests, the winter of 1947–8 saw 300 actions for debts to Torlonia pending in local courts. In January 1948 the Federation of Agricultural Trades Unions for the province of L'Aquila drew up ten demands which it invited Torlonia to discuss. One item referred to the employment of local labour to improve the condition of the roads and watercourses on the estate. The remainder asked for the reduction of rents, the withdrawal of eviction notices, cessation of the obligation to produce beet and the abolition of all 'feudal/manorial privileges' (application of the laws of trespass to people using the roads, building shelters, cutting dead wood, etc.). The negotiations were to drag on for two years amidst growing tension and agitation among the unemployed. During this period Torlonia made only minute concessions over the payment of rent arrears, and speeded up the signing of direct contracts in accordance with the Legge Gullo (see pp. 13–14).

Luco and the *Lotta del Fucino*

On 6 February 1950 the unemployed of the eleven *comuni* of Fucino, 'shovels on their backs, carts following behind, the International on their lips and their women to wave them goodbye and good luck' (Pizzutti, 1953: 95), took to the roads against the wishes of the landlord and began to repair them. Their action was carefully organised and rigorously carried out. It was founded on popular protest: people were poor, indebted and unemployed, and things seemed to be getting worse. In addition they had, in Torlonia, a single focus for their grievances. Institutions already existed which were capable of organising concerted action: the trade unions, the Pci and the Psi all had branches in Avezzano and in most other *comuni*, and all but one of the local administrations were left-wing. Even those organisations which were allied to government parties such as Uil (Social Democratic trade unions) and Cisl eventually threw in their lot with the struggle in Fucino.

The Pci in Luco had emerged as the strongest *sezione* in the Marsica after the war. Its members had been rapidly drawn into party schools, and gained experience in a variety of local organisations. The *luchesi*, 75 per cent of whom had voted for the Pci/Psi in 1946, had become a force that could be counted on to support Pci actions. So Luco became the centre from which the 'work-in' was organised.

The first marching column was selected from *luchesi*. Only later were other *sezione* brought in, when it had been proved a viable tactic. Day-to-day decisions were worked out in Luco, and transmitted to the other *comuni* by young *luchesi*. Many of these made public speeches for the first time in their lives at meetings in Trasacco, Ortucchio and so on, urging the *braccianti* to join in. According to Tarrow, Fucino was the first place in Southern Italy where women played a role in mass political action (Tarrow, 1967: 289). Indeed, it was in Luco that women's participation spontaneously emerged (see above, p. 94, for earlier demonstrations). When police were rushed to the area from Rome and drove their trucks into Luco, they were stopped by women who lay down in their path. This tactic dismayed and demoralised the police, who had never had to cope with militant women before. Women also helped the strikers by acting as lookouts to warn of police arrivals, so that it was difficult for the police to find strikers actually at work and arrest them for trespass. Amongst those arrested and tried at the court in Trasacco, *luchesi* constituted about 90 per cent of the defendants. This gives some indication of the predominance of *luchesi* in the *Lotta*.

Even heavy reinforcements of police did not prevent strikers from going out each day. By 3 March, after less than a month, the prefect had ordered the Torlonia Administration to take on two thousand workers per day. This was considerably in excess of the 9000 *workdays* which the trade unions had requested a year before.

The demonstrations did not stop, however, for the strikers now wanted to be paid for what they had already done. Eventually Torlonia sent the money to the prefect for distribution under the guise of 'poor relief'. Clearly he was not willing to accept his legal obligations to employ workers nor his responsibility to his tenants to keep the estate in a workable condition.

The *Lotta* lasted at this intensity of daily demonstrations and nightly meetings for six weeks. Within only a short time of its inception it began to involve the small and medium tenants. Even large tenants and employees of Torlonia made financial contributions to the cause. In Luco today there are only a very few people, families of large tenants at that time, who do not claim to have been actively involved. It is my impression that enthusiasm for the struggle was so intense that it would have been difficult for anyone to have remained outside it, and few could claim that it did not matter to them who owned Fucino.

The minister of agriculture visited the area a month after the beginning of the strike. In a public speech he made a veiled reference to the possibility of substituting 'small peasant farms' for the existing system of land tenure. This rumour encouraged many more tenants to take part, and the Coldiretti (Dc small farmers' union) openly urged their members to 'continue with the struggle'. In October 1950 the government announced its intention to include Fucino in a law to expropriate and redistribute large estates in various parts of Italy. The land reform took place on 1 November 1951, the day on which Torlonia's tenants became assignees of the Ente Fucino.

Luco dei Marsi

Since the land reform

According to Senator Rossi-Doria, areas like Fucino were split up into small-holdings rather than being farmed as collectives, in order to counter peasant radicalism (personal communication). A peasant with land is very different from one without land, but the government did not rely on the effects of ownership alone to change the political consciousness of the peasants. As in Trasacco, the Ente Fucino officials played an important role, demoralising the *braccianti* and discriminating against communists.

Braccianti were not given land in the reform. This forced them into a position of dependence on the Ente Fucino for work. In Trasacco the *braccianti* became disillusioned and broke with the Pci, which had accepted the Ente's ruling on land distribution. This meant that they had no organisational nor ideological base from which to combat the clientelist practices of the Ente. In Luco there were far fewer who were only *braccianti*. Those that there were had been deeply involved in the *Lotta* and very committed to the Pci. During the post-war period many had learnt to read and write in the party and felt that they had gained much from it. Therefore, when the Pci took this line in favour of a land assignment which excluded them, the *braccianti* did not repudiate their party. Their response seems to have been rather to take up the Ente's offer to help *braccianti* to emigrate. Some moved to farms of the Ente Maremma (which was then part of the Ente Fucino) and others went to South America and Australia.

Attempts to bribe people with offers of land and work were quickly foiled by the Pci in Luco. The mayor began the opposition to the Ente's tactics by refusing a bribe and then publicising it. This showed others that it was possible to resist. It created an atmosphere in which heroes exposed the corruption of the Ente while *ruffiani* (turncoats) gave in and were ostracised by their fellow villagers.

Ripaldi, or 'Sindacone' (Big Mayor) as he is affectionately known, was offered a position in the Ente, a good piece of land and an apartment in Rome if he would publicly join the Dc. He asked the officials to come to his house to discuss the details of the offer. He secretly recorded the conversation, then called a public meeting in the piazza and played the tape over the loudspeaker system.

People were so angered by this that it became impossible for anyone to accept a job with the Ente and stay in the village. Anyone who received any privilege had to be very careful to avoid suspicion. One member of the *sezione* committee did accept a position in the Ente. He was subjected to an open confrontation and then ostracised. He moved his family to Avezzano and never returned to Luco.

Of course, he was not the only one who gave in. In the elections of 1951

106

and 1953 these tactics, along with cold war propaganda, helped to win many over to the Dc. It was possible to vote Dc whilst apparently continuing to support the Pci, but not vice versa. Those who had accepted *favori* from the Ente were given special combinations of preference vote numbers to mark on their ballot papers. These enabled individual votes to be recognised. A long-term consequence of this is that people still believe that their votes can be detected.

The post-war period has seen a decline of 25 per cent in the Pci/Psi vote in Luco. In 1946 it had the support of three-quarters of the population and now barely half. This decline requires explanation.

First of all, not everyone who voted Pci/Psi in 1946 was a committed socialist or communist. The country had just emerged from fascism and the war, and to many the communists appeared like liberators promising new hope for the future. When their hopes were not fulfilled the disillusioned returned to their traditional allegiances, the Church and the party of government. Secondly, in Luco there had been a considerable loss of population from emigration. The population had declined by 13 per cent since 1951. Trasacco's population declined by only 3 per cent. The figure of 13 per cent understates the real fall in the population, for many *luchesi* working abroad have not registered their departure. Almost all migrants from Luco, I was told by informants of both parties, were communists.

To summarise this chapter, although Luco and Trasacco have superficially a very similar economic base, and are only seven kilometres apart, their historical experiences have been strikingly different. Before the drainage *luchesi* were the only villagers of Fucino who fished in the lake and sold their catch. Luco's land, at that time confined to the hilly area beyond the lake, was rather equally distributed amongst the population, so that every household had some land, and there were no large landowners. The land distribution in Trasacco and elsewhere was more unequal, so that the majority of the population were dependent on others for their livelihood.

Accounts of how the fishing was done suggest that *luchesi* cooperated in the owning and manning of boats, and that the sale of the catch gave ordinary *luchesi* contacts with the wider society that were not available to the small peasants and landless labourers in other villages.

Because they were dependent on the lake for their livelihood, it was the *luchesi* who were threatened by the drainage scheme, whilst other villagers welcomed it. The raising of the marking stones, and the fact that they marked out an area greater than that to which Torlonia was considered to be entitled, triggered the first collective actions that *luchesi* took against Torlonia. Their resentment continued through the long period of negotiations with Torlonia

107

to force him to restore their water supply, and through their successive actions to abolish the systems of sub-letting, of payment of rent in sugar beet and arbitrary increases in rent.

Luchesi, as the largest contingent in the gangs that built the drainage tunnel, were also the first to experience wage labour. Later they provided the largest part of the workforce on the Administration farm and the sugar refinery at Avezzano.

Because of those unique experiences they were not only involved in collective action in support of their own local interests, but played leadership roles in struggles affecting the whole of Fucino. It was not until the early years of this century that their oppositional attitudes and activities became formalised within an organisation (the Peasant League) drawing its inspiration from socialism. As soon as the vote was extended to all adult men, it found political expression in the election of socialist and, later, communist officials and representatives. This collective historical experience has created traditions that influence, and therefore help to explain, contemporary social relations in Luco.

8 The village and its economy

First impressions

According to the census of 1971, Luco dei Marsi has 4610 inhabitants and a
land area of 44.59 square kilometres. It is tucked under the lee of Monte
Saviano, about ten kilometres south of Avezzano. The road to it skirts the
plain of Fucino and twists round rocky outcrops that once dropped sheer
into the lake. From a fork at the entrance to the village one road goes straight
on past the town hall and through to Trasacco. The other arches up the hill to
the heart of Luco, the paved piazza, with its monument to the Fallen and its
stone benches set beneath shady trees. The arrangement of important buildings in this square is an interesting one (see Figure 4). The parish church is,
worshippers proudly tell you, built to the same design as St Peter's in Rome
— on a smaller scale. With only a single house between, the church is flanked
by the pink-washed *sezione* of the Communist Party. These buildings face
east across the piazza towards its open side. In the north-east corner is the
sezione of the Christian Democrat Party, a blue shield painted on its wall
challenging the red hammer and sickle of the Pci. The pharmacy, two bars
with canopied tables, and four gracious balconied houses complete the three
sides of the square. From the balustrade on the east side there is a spectacular
view over the lower piazza, the town hall, and an array of new roofs to
Fucino. The fertile plain stretches away to where the parallel lines of poplar
trees meet at the foot of hazy mountains on the far side. At night a necklace
of clustered lights marks the ring of villages as though they were still on the
lake shore.

Immediately round and behind the piazza old stone houses form a cluster
on the hillside. They are built close together in terraces along the narrow
streets and down the stepped alleyways which connect them. These houses
have stairs to heavy front doors, wrought-iron balconies and french windows
on the first floor and pitched roofs of curving terracotta tiles. Underneath
them are cellars hewn out of the rock, perfect for storing wine, cheese,
sausages and potatoes. Like all *abruzzesi*, *luchesi* like to eat well and pride
themselves on the dried-meat delicacies they make from hand-reared pigs.

Four or five houses have ornamental gardens with cascades of bougain-

109

villaea over the walls, but few others in the old town have even a yard. People from various parts of the town own the small number of tiny gardens which are grouped together behind the highest row of houses. The owners visit them once or twice a day to tend their pigs, chickens and vegetables.

New houses built since the land reform on what was once Fucino land are much bigger and have yards. They are neatly arranged along streets following an orderly grid plan. Alongside is an area of *casette* – earthquake relief dwellings.

The town is divided into five electoral wards. These correspond closely with the three neighbourhoods or *rioni* that pre-date the draining of the lake, the earthquake housing area and the post-land-reform houses. People give their address as *'Campane'* or *'Casette'*, and residents can distinguish anyone who lives in the *rione* from outsiders. A group of two or three middle-aged *luchesi* can together identify any married adult *luchese* and most people aged fifteen and over. They can give details of the family name, the *rione* where the person lives, their spouse's name and, very often, their political allegiance.

Wheeled vehicles can travel only along the flat east–west streets in Luco (see Map 4), and they must go slowly because of sharp bends. The streets are laid out in such a way that people, whether in cars or on foot, have many opportunities to meet during the course of a day. Whereas in Trasacco houses are dispersed and the roads wide, the proximity of housing in Luco, the narrow streets and steps make for a high degree of neighbourly interaction. To enjoy the fresh air in spring and summer, people bring chairs out of their houses and sit in the alleys. They cannot be ignored by passers-by, nor would they wish to be. No one sits alone for long, as women bring out their knitting, sewing and vegetables to prepare in company.

At certain times of the year activity in the alleys becomes intense. With no other outdoor space available, women spread the new-washed wool from their mattresses to dry on the steps. Pedestrians must pick their way carefully round it. In September tomato conserves for the whole year are boiled and bottled. Neighbouring women are to be seen hurrying to each others' cellars where the work of preparation goes on, the work-exchange group having been informally organised a day or two before. On summer nights men who can play instruments quickly gather a crowd of neighbours to join in singing and dancing.

The activities of the alleys are a feature of Luco. In Trasacco the same tasks are performed, but in the privacy of the yard. It is kin rather than neighbours who are called on to help make tomato conserve and sausages. Apart from a generally lower level of interaction between neighbours, *trasaccane* are unlikely to be aware of what is going on and therefore unable to offer spontaneous help.

The occasion to see and be seen is above all the *passeggiata* on Sunday

110

afternoon. The circumstances of the *passeggiata* in Luco facilitate encounters
between people as they do not in Trasacco. Between four and seven o'clock
every Sunday the road past the Luco town hall — also the main Avezzano—
Trasacco road — is filled with strolling groups. Traffic hazards are considerable
but this venue has many compensating advantages. There is a bar at each end
which marks the turning points and the time it takes from one to the other is
a sufficiently healthy interval between two cups of coffee. Five other bars are
passed en route where young men can lounge and observe and choose the
right moment to join in. The elderly from nearby streets bring their chairs
into the entrances to the alleys and from here they can watch and greet the
passers-by. This is a *passeggiata* where the sexes and ages mingle. Up on the
main piazza the elder statesmen stroll in greater safety and a shorter distance
between the two bars. Engrossed in serious conversation they earnestly trace
out the parallel lines in the ornamental paving.

In short, Luco is an attractive village whose cosy geography seems to
facilitate social intercourse. Another striking difference between the villages is
that Luco seems a much wealthier community than Trasacco. There are more
and better appointed bars, shops and hotels. The people's clothes and consumer durables also attest a higher general standard of living.

Luchesi explained this greater prosperity in two ways. Firstly, they said,
luchesi work harder. Secondly, they are prepared to borrow: 'Luco floats on
credit' was a common saying. The willingness to borrow in order to invest
indicates that *luchesi* had confidence in their ability to repay loans through
their own efforts. It is this combination of 'work ethic' and readiness to
invest heavily in agriculture which is said to account for the fact that *luchesi*
today own more land than residents of other *comuni.*

Agriculture and landholding

Like the other *comuni* of Fucino, Luco is an agricultural village, but the distribution of the economically active population between the three main sectors is not quite the same as that in Trasacco. Table 10 shows that more
luchesi are involved in industry (12.7 per cent of the population compared to
7.9 per cent in Trasacco) and fewer in agriculture (13.3 per cent in Luco and
17.2 per cent in Trasacco).

The census counts under each head only those whose main income is
declared to be derived from that sector. In Luco, as in Trasacco, this does not
give a true picture of actual occupations. Distortion arises both from mis-
representation to the authorities and from the fact that people have more
than one occupation. Table 11 shows the occupational distribution of men
over 21. It was derived from the census, from the register of male electors,
from a sample survey of electors and from discussions with knowledgeable

Table 10 *Distribution of active population by economic sector.*

	Trasacco		Luco	
	No.	%	No.	%
Agriculture	915	17.2	612	13.3
Industry	419	7.9	584	12.7
Other	375	7.0	274	5.9
Active population	1709	32.1	1470	31.9
Total population	5311	100.0	4610	100.0

Source: Census 1971, ISTAT, Rome.

Table 11 *Luco: distribution of occupations and land*

	1975 Males over 21			
Occupational category	Number who own land	Percentage who own land	Total in category	Percentage of total
Owner-cultivators	474	100.0	474	30.4
Workers in permanent employment	131	63.0	208	13.4
Casual labourers	104	65.4	159	10.2
Agricultural labourers	79	92.9	85	5.5
Artisans	22	21.6	102	6.5
Traders	33	45.2	73	4.7
Teachers	0	0	3	0.2
Office workers	10	38.5	26	1.7
Professionals	0	0	7	0.4
Landowners (non-cultivating)	2	100.0	2	0.1
Business owners (non-working)	5	71.4	7	0.4
Students	0	0	125	8.0
Pensioners	86	30.0	287	18.4
Herders	0	0	0	0
Total	946	60.7	1558	100.0

Source: Electoral Roll, Luco, and Census 1971, ISTAT, Rome.

informants. It attempts to show particularly the combination of landholding with other occupations. It may be compared with Table 3 for Trasacco. There is one major difference between the criteria used for the compilation of these tables. In Luco the sample survey showed that in the majority of cases, only men with four hectares or more of land did not have other income sources. In Trasacco, on the other hand, there were many farmers with only two and a half hectares of land who were bringing up families without seeking a supplementary source of income. Therefore I decided that, for the category of owner-cultivators, the lower cut-off point in Luco would be four hectares and in Trasacco two and a half hectares. Although this has the disadvantage of not comparing like with like, the relative proportions of farmers in the active population which resulted from this (30.4 per cent in Luco, 22.2 per cent in Trasacco) accorded well with the census figures.

Differences in the numbers employed in the 'Agricultural Sector' in each village suggest large variations in productivity. If we compare the amount of land cultivated with the number of people who work the land in each village it appears that *luchesi* farmers are six times more productive than their *trasaccani* counterparts. This can be explained, at least in part, by a combination of three factors. First, in Trasacco more casual labour is employed in farming. Some of this labour however is employed to work on land in other *comuni*, chiefly Luco. Secondly, *luchesi* farmers have more agricultural machinery than their Trasacco counterparts, so that Luco's farming is less labour intensive. Thirdly, because *luchesi* wives are more actively involved in agriculture, work-exchanges are much more common, and this 'unpaid' element is not recorded in the figures.

In Luco, as in Trasacco, there are two categories of land: 'Fucino' and *fuori-Fucino*. *Fuori-Fucino* land measures 3200 hectares in total, of which the *comune* owns 2564 hectares of woods and pastures. Land in private ownership amounts to 636 hectares. This is about 200 hectares less than was registered in the nineteenth century. Probably about half of it is actually being cultivated. People today only work land that can be reached by road and that is in fields large enough for a tractor. Except for a few aged eccentrics, *luchesi* are no longer prepared to walk to the fields or cultivate them with hoe and scythe.

Most families have a little vineyard *fuori-Fucino* where they produce wine for domestic consumption. A few grow grain which they rotate with forage crops, and occasionally a little beet is planted. Enough wheat is kept for making bread and pasta, and the rest is sold. For the most part this land is regarded as supplementary to the main business of cultivation in Fucino.

Fucino soil is very productive. It is planted almost exclusively with sugar beet and potatoes for the market. These crops are not usually rotated with ones which put nitrates back into the soil, nor are animals kept in sufficient numbers to provide manure. In addition potatoes and beet planted without rotation have led to the appearance of parasites, which require constant attention to eradicate them. Therefore considerable quantities of artificial fertiliser and anti-parasite preparations are used. The agronomists in the Ente Fucino express great dissatisfaction with the farmers' unwillingness to rotate crops. In the last ten years two brothers who own more land than anyone else

113

in Fucino have been experimenting with other vegetable and salad crops. Greens and lettuce have been particularly successful, and a few other farmers now produce these as a second crop in the annual cycle. Carrots have not caught on in Luco. They are a labour-intensive crop, and local labour, according to Luco farmers, is scarce. They do not want to have the worry of finding labour at the speed which is essential to this speculative enterprise. The main reasons why *luchesi* farmers stick to beet and potato production is that they are familiar with the markets for them and, through trade-union action, have some measure of control over the market through the pressure they can bring to bear on the sugar refineries to raise prices, and on the Ente Fucino to use its emergency powers to buy up the potato crop. As long as chemistry can stay ahead of the development of parasites, and the cost of artificial fertilisers and treatments do not start to eat into profits, beet and potatoes will continue to be produced without rotation.

In strong contrast with Trasacco, *luchesi* residents have been acquiring rather than selling land since the reform. Not only are there more assignees in Luco than there were in 1952, but between them they own more land. The last figures were collected in 1969. These show an increase of 79 over the 997 assignees of 1952. In 1952 *luchesi* between them owned only 11.8 per cent of Fucino, or 1571 hectares. In 1975 Ente officials estimated that *luchesi* owned or rented 28 per cent or 3700 hectares. Non-assignees who had bought in (which is illegal in Fucino) and assignees who had increased their holdings rarely reported these to the Ente. The land was acquired by *luchesi* from assignees living in the neighbouring *comuni* of Avezzano and Trasacco (see above p. 35) where people are divesting themselves of land.

Luchesi not only buy land, they invest in capital goods to increase its productivity. Some agricultural operations, such as thinning out young beet plants or weeding potatoes, can only be done by hand. Most others can be done by hand or by machine. Using a machine has the advantage of reducing the costs and uncertainties of employing labour, but the initial outlay is high, and farmers have to borrow in order to buy farm machinery. *Luchesi* farmers have realised, as *trasaccani* have not, that in order to accumulate they must increase productivity by investing in machinery. By taking out loans they can both decrease the uncertainty of getting labour at the right time and at the right price, and increase profits. 'Luco today', wrote an Ente official in 1973, 'continues to be the most mechanised in Fucino, itself among the most mechanised in Italy, ... with one tractor per eight hectares' (Gallese, 1973). Table 12 compares the growth in mechanisation in Luco and Trasacco from 1951 to 1971. In 1950 there had been only one tractor in Luco with a 22 h.p. capacity. In Trasacco there were ten tractors. By 1955 Luco farmers had as much mechanical capacity as Trasacco, and by 1961 they had outstripped their neighbours.

Table 12 *Tractor distribution.*

	Luco		Trasacco	
	No.	h.p.	No.	h.p.
1950	1	22	10	320
1955	25	879	25	827
1961	87	3965	55	2093
1971	276	10 403	170	6668

Source: Gallese, 1973.

In 1972 a huge Centenary Festival of the Madonna was held in Luco and attracted visitors from miles around. The *luchesi* held a tractor gymkhana as part of the festivities. According to the farmers, it was the most important competition of the *festa*. They had charged their brightly-coloured, if lumbering, steeds round an obstacle course in pursuit of a silver trophy.

Tractors and the many other mechanical aids (no figures are available but again more than in Trasacco)[1] are all privately owned. The Pci *sezione* bought a Russian tractor in 1960, and the Ente Fucino provided three for farmers to share. The assignees quickly tired of waiting their turn for these and started to buy their own. Brothers, *compari* and friends are more likely in Luco than they are in Trasacco to buy shares in a single machine or to buy machines which complement one another.

The feeling was much more widespread in Luco than in Trasacco that 'cooperation' was beneficial, and the sharing of machines was common and seemed to work well. But *luchesi* farmers were sceptical about the possibility of full cooperation. Two brothers, Velio and Silvio Bianchi, the biggest farmers in Fucino, held all their land and machinery in common, but the arrangement's success was thought to be due to good fortune rather than good will and perseverance.

There were two cooperatives for the production, storage and marketing of seed potatoes. The first was formed in 1966 and the second in 1970. During 1975 the *comune* initiated discussions on the formation of a cooperative to raise cattle. Livestock cooperatives are thought to be the most difficult to form and run successfully, but about fifty farmers showed their interest by attending the first meeting. Small as these initiatives are, they are unique examples of real cooperatives in Fucino. Those of the Ente Fucino are cooperatives only in name (see p. 38 above).

1 Official statistics only include machines with independent engines. Potato harvesters, beet grabs and reaper/binders are all run off tractor engines and therefore are not recorded.

Luco dei Marsi

Seed potatoes are produced only by the farmers belonging to one or other of the cooperatives, for they require special licences and techniques of handling. Normally each farmer organises his own timetable and labour force. A few farmers employ a single, permanent, salaried *bracciante*. He normally recruits the working groups, sometimes mixed, but usually all women, which do the manual labour; they are paid by the day. The most common pattern, however, is for the farmer's wife to assemble a group of women and girls. Usually they are the wives and daughters of farming families, who may or may not be related to each other. In these cases the women exchange their labour. In such groups there may also be women who are being paid, but there is no difference between exchange and paid labour in the hours they work. Labour is also employed by potato merchants, who, having purchased the potatoes in bulk from the farmers, are responsible for packing them into sacks.

Earning a living

Women provide the bulk of the manual labour force in Luco's agriculture. They are generally married, and they come from a variety of backgrounds. The majority are wives of assignees, and they usually exchange labour. Of those who work for cash, the majority are wives of men who are workers in building or industry. Cash workers are employed by the larger farmers in spring, summer and autumn, and by potato merchants in the winter.

Farming families also earn extra income by hiring out their machines, which are driven by the owners and their grown sons. A few farming wives, in addition to work exchanges, also work as agricultural labourers for payment.

Land ownership is widely distributed in Luco. Only half of those who own land are full-time farmers. The rest have employment in other sectors, while continuing to work their land. Renting is very rare. All this is very different from what has been observed in Trasacco (see pp. 76–7).

Figure miste

As in Trasacco there are people in Luco who move from one sector to another, collecting as many jobs as they can to form a viable *combinazione*. In Table 11 the separation between 'agricultural' and 'casual' labourers is an artificial one. It is intended chiefly to convey the different proportion in the amount of labour-time spent in agriculture as between Luco and Trasacco. It shows more agricultural labourers in Trasacco. In reality, in both places people do find casual labour in all sectors. However, in Luco there is more employment available with local building firms and more labourers travel to Avezzano to work on building sites. In Trasacco only about 30 per cent of all agricultural and other casual labourers own land; in Luco nearly 80 per cent. This gives *luchesi* in these categories a measure of income security and independence that their counterparts in Trasacco do not have. This relative economic independence acts as a buffer against the establishment of clientelist relations amongst casual labourers in Luco, and marks an important difference from Trasacco.

The aspiration of these people in both villages is to find permanent employment for someone in the family, for it is they who are most likely to suffer from temporary and seasonal unemployment. The very cold Apennine winters mean that all outdoor work comes to a halt. Only a very few large building firms in Avezzano can afford to pay contributions towards *Cassa Integrazione*, a fund which pays a large percentage of the salary when workers are laid off temporarily due to bad weather, decline in sales, and so on. Contractors will only contribute to this fund for skilled workers, and workers may only draw on the fund if their employer contributes to it.

Factory employment

A comparison of Tables 3 and 11 shows that there are 115 workers in permanent employment in Trasacco and 208 in Luco. Of the 208, 130 are employed in the sugar refinery, the paper mill and IMMA (a metal works), all situated in the Industrial Nucleus near Avezzano. Only 30 men from Trasacco work there. Of the women workers in the Nucleus factories 176 are *trasaccane* and 130 *luchese*. These disparities are related to the clientelistic practices of the factories that employ women and the higher level of unionisation where male workers predominate (see pp. 39—40 above).

None of the factory jobs demand highly skilled workers. Variations in pay appear to depend more on length of service than on differences in levels of skill. Both the paper mill and the sugar refinery work continuous 8-hour shifts. Night-shift workers are paid an overtime bonus.

About one-fifth of the workforce at the refinery and one-seventh of that at the mill are *luchesi*. This is high in relation to workers from other nearby towns, all of whom would like to work in these factories where wages are higher and security of employment greater than elsewhere in the Marsica.

These wages and conditions have been won through trade-union action. They are not as good as can be found in factories dominated by the Metal Workers' Union in Milan or Turin, but the Abruzzo is noted for its outdated industrial relations and low level of union militancy. The owners of the refinery, the Torlonia family, have tried various tactics to maintain personalised and paternalist management-worker relations. In 1960, for example, a new manager was appointed whose first action was to sack militant trade unionists. However, 75 per cent of the workforce was (and is) unionised and a strike forced their reinstatement. In the twelve years since it opened the paper mill has lost about ten working days per year in strikes over pay and conditions.

There are more *luchesi* on the Workers' Committees of these two factories than their numbers in the workforce would warrant. Both here and in CEME (the ITT telecommunications factory) *luchesi* constitute more than half the elected members of these committees. They are regarded by other workers as more militant and better able to state their case to management. At Valentini, a clothing factory, a strike led by women from Luco lasted four months. Eventually the owner closed the factory saying that he was almost bankrupt. A month later he re-opened and would take back only those workers who signed a document revoking their right to strike. Although this is illegal many women signed because they needed to work. *Luchesi* were not asked to return to work at all, but were offered employment as outworkers. The owner hoped, by excluding *luchesi*, to avoid a repetition of the strike. (This information was given by a social worker at the Ente Fucino who agreed with the owner that *luchesi* were too militant).

There are exceptions however; two women who worked in one of the shirt factories admitted that they had used influential contacts to get their jobs. It is possible that this was more common than prevailing attitudes in Luco would allow people to admit. However, it is also the case that not all managers are corrupt or influenced by local politicians. Many people got jobs simply because they had collected enough points to reach the top of the List of Unemployed.

Evaluating manual labour

These differences in employment patterns between Luco and Trasacco are not fully explained by clientelism and trade unionism. Attitudes towards manual labour are also a significant factor. The contrast in attitudes between Luco and Trasacco is very striking. In Luco one hears only positive statements about work: certainly manual labour is hard and exhausting but it confers not degradation but dignity on men and women to work hard. Among the most fatiguing tasks were those performed by women in the fields and potato stores. These women often said that they would do any hard work such as that and be in company rather than stay at home alone. Some women did not want their daughters to work in the potato stores, but this was not because it was degrading, they said. The stores are cold and thought to be bad for the health.

It was not a common ideal to have an office job or no work at all as it was in Trasacco. Whilst children were encouraged to continue their education, they were also expected to help out on the land and even miss school days to do so. Any graduate who claimed to be superior to farm work would have been ridiculed or punished, depending on the father's disposition. Such attitudes to hard work were not confined to labour on the land. The factories were highly esteemed as places to work. One woman told me that since she was a teenager she had dreamed of being a factory worker. At forty her dream came true. The notion of 'an honest day's work for an honest day's pay' was not the exception but the norm.

Another notable difference was that in Trasacco men with a permanent job tended to get rid of their land by sale or letting, whilst in Luco they did not. Among 'workers in permanent employment' (see Tables 3 and 11) 60 per cent in Luco owned land and only 30 per cent in Trasacco. *Luchesi* to whom I spoke about this said that they regarded their land (usually only one hectare in these cases) as an additional security against economic crises. They felt that they could always grow their daily bread if they lost their jobs.

Impiegati and *professionali*

These two categories are, in Luco, extremely small. There are only 26 office workers, nearly all of whom work for the *comune* administration. The seven 'professionals' are three doctors working in Luco and a doctor, an accountant, an engineer and a lawyer, all of whom work in Avezzano. Only the lawyer is a middle-aged man born and brought up in Luco. The other three employed in Avezzano are recent graduates. The three *medici condotti*, Luco's local general practitioners, were all born and brought up in other *comuni* of Fucino. University education for more than a tiny minority is a very recent development. In 1951 there were only four university students in the *comune*; in 1975 there were over a hundred. I cannot offer a satisfactory explanation for this slow take-up of higher education. Torlonia certainly discouraged schooling, but in spite of this Trasacco, for example, has produced many more graduates. On the other hand more *luchesi* have a minimum of education. Some political reasons for these differences will be discussed in the next chapter, for example the fact that Luco does not offer professional men the same rewards in the political sphere as they enjoy in Trasacco.

Politics and the occupational hierarchy

Politics in Luco are organised on the basis of party rather than on ties of clientelism. Two parties overshadow all the others on the political scene, the Dc and Pci, and one might expect some correlation between party and occupation: that each party draws its support from one of the two major groupings — manual and non-manual workers. My analysis of this relationship is based on interviews with a random sample of forty people drawn from the

Luco dei Marsi

comune register of families (*schede di famiglie*). The sample was cross-checked for occupational distribution against the 1971 Census. My conclusions were as follows. At the extremes of the spectrum there was a strong correlation between occupation and political allegiance. That is, professionals and teachers tend to vote Dc, *braccianti* and factory workers Pci. Amongst farmers the pattern was less distinct. Even large farmers did not all vote Dc. Party allegiance did, however, correlate with the size of holding that the person's family had rented prior to the land reform: that is, those who were large farmers *then* vote Dc *now*; those who have accumulated land from small tenancies at the time of the reform vote Pci. This finding bears out my earlier statement that the land reform looms large in the consciousness of *luchesi* today. They often explain their behaviour now, including their political behaviour, by what happened then. Small tenants joined the Pci after the war and participated early on in the movement against Torlonia. This experience shaped their political consciousness in such a way that now even those who have collected a lot of land, and earn large incomes from it, continue to support the Pci.

Not only these political experiences but also religious beliefs and family traditions mediate between occupation and political position. Devout Catholics most often vote Dc, as the protector of their Church and religion, but not all communist voters are by any means atheists. Political traditions run in families to quite a considerable extent. This suggests that family socialisation into politics is quite a strong element in party allegiance. Apart, then, from the poles of the occupational hierarchy, neither occupation nor income are reliable predictors of which party a *luchese* will support.

9 Politics in Luco

Open confrontation

Political parties have a significance in Luco that they do not have in Trasacco. The stature of the parties, their antagonism to one another, their open presence in the community, all these are sharply symbolised by their imposing *sezione* buildings which face each other diagonally across the central piazza, one flaunting the red hammer and sickle, the other the blue cross on a white shield. It also becomes apparent when public meetings are held that people are candid about their party allegiances. Attendances often reach a thousand or more. The party holding the meeting sets up a platform in front of its *sezione* and the people fill up the centre of the piazza. Those who support that party stand closest to the platform and the opposition arrange themselves behind and on the fringes. At election time, the parties quite often co-ordinate their meetings so that one set of addresses follows the other. It is then easy for the crowd to turn round to face the new speakers and be automatically in the right order and distance from the platform, with the party's supporters closest to their own speakers (see diagram of the piazza, Figure 4). Thus almost anyone in the crowd can easily be identified as Pci or Dc. In Trasacco only a tiny group of activists was willing to make their allegiances known, whilst the rest of the audience skulked on the sidelines.

This willingness to be identified politically is part of daily life in Luco. Indeed, it is far more positive than the word 'willingness' implies. *Luchesi* know one another as Communists and Christian Democrats. They will tell you, very often apropos of nothing in particular, which they are themselves. They also want to know where an outsider's political allegiances lie, and will ask straight out, early in one's first encounter. For *luchesi*, it is an important facet of personal identity, as important as one's job, spouse and number of children. This is as true of women as it is of men.

'Here we are all equal'

This constant reference to party allegiance is an immediately striking characteristic of Luco. Another is the insistence that 'Qua siamo tutti uguali' (here we

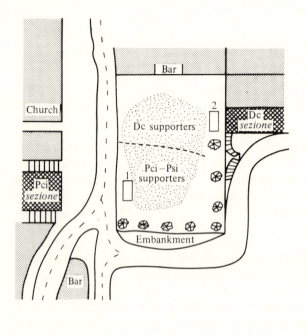

1 - Pci speaker's platform   ⊗ - trees
2 - Dc speaker's platform

Figure 4 The main piazza, Luco

are all equal). On arriving in Luco I asked repeatedly, 'Who is important around here?' I was always told, 'No one is more important than anyone else'. Often people would add, 'Now if you go just seven kilometres down the road [i.e. to Trasacco], it's another matter. There the doctor is in command, the priest is his big enemy and everyone is afraid of them.'

Of course it is not true that 'everyone is equal'. There are differences in wealth and in education and these are acknowledged. What is being denied is that these differences are significant in politics. In Luco, as in most places (see, for example, Wade, 1975; Bottomore, 1963), elective positions in voluntary associations are occupied by those with more than the minimum educational qualifications. Even in the Pci, the most important local position, that of secretary, is no longer held by a peasant with almost no land (as it was just after the war), but by a man who is secretary to the Middle School.

His predecessor was not a peasant or a worker, but a primary school teacher. This change has occurred in the Pci nationally, as it has pursued its policy of 'class alliances', but it also reflects improved standards of living and education.

However, in Luco power is not exercised by such figures as Dr Ciofani, Mignini and Don Pasquale. The influence of professional men in Luco is confined to the exercise of their professions and does not spill over into elective positions. The absence of doctors, priests and wealthy farmers from positions of political dominance in Luco could, however, have nothing to do with popular opposition to their assuming such roles, but be entirely due to each having chosen, for quite separate and personal reasons, not to participate in the political arena.

In each case there is some basis for this. The parish priest, Don Nicola, supports the Dc. He causes something of a stir whenever he refers in his sermons to 'the party favoured by the Vatican'. When he used the occasion of a large confirmation service to urge people not to allow 'the lives of these innocent children to be ruined by divorce' there were gasps of dismay in the church, and severe criticism afterwards. No one, however, has ever accused Don Nicola of using his position to 'buy' votes, as Don Pasquale of Trasacco does. Don Mario, the parish assistant, joins with the congregation in condemning Don Nicola's 'political' sermons. He abhors the 'acerbity' of political divisions in Luco. He wants to change the world, but through the hearts and minds, not through the political system.

The three *medici condotti* have similarly never tried to use their profession to make political capital. Dr Recchia is very old and lives in an isolated villa out of town. He goes hunting with an assortment of local men, including a building labourer who is a member of the Pci, and otherwise has little social contact with the village. In 1974, Dr Giancurso had only been in Luco for a year. He was not at all open about his politics, and therefore a bit of an enigma to *luchesi*. If he had any political ambition it was well concealed. Dr Di Gianfelippo was a supporter of the Psdi. He worked politically not in Luco but in Avezzano, to further the career of his brother. He said that Luco was no good for him as a politician because you have to be either Pci or Dc and he was opposed to both.

These three doctors and the two priests have in common that none of them are *luchesi* born and bred. It may be that they cannot acquire political influence in Luco, not because *luchesi* reject professional men as politicians, but because they are outsiders. It is not inconceivable that the obverse of community solidarity and strong party allegiances is that outsiders are excluded from playing a political role in the community.

On the other hand, there are 'insiders' who could have used their positions, their wealth or their reputations as Ciofani and Mignini have done. Mignini's opposite number in Luco, Di Rosa, is the local secretary of the Psdi. He is a passionate amateur archaeologist and is secretary of a club which he started that has six members. Clearly he is not in the same business as Mignini. The Psdi rarely gets more than 3 per cent of the vote, which confirms that he did not use his influential position to win votes for his party. Another likely contender for a political career seemed to be Silvio Bianchi. He and his brother have the most land and are the wealthiest farmers in Fucino. Married but childless, Silvio is thought to have plenty of money to spare. He has a reputation for generosity and many people are indebted to him for personal loans. Silvio is a Christian Democrat, but he has not used his money to win electoral support. He gives loans according to criteria quite other than political ones. The largest loan that I knew about was for £2000 to a well-known Pci activist to help him build a house. Neither in that or any other case was there a suggestion of a political *quid pro quo*. Silvio was elected as a Dc councillor in 1970, but he resigned after only a few months. He is a more dedicated farmer than he was a politician. Council business was, he said, taking him away from what he really wanted to do, which was to develop his farm.

In Luco, therefore, neither outsiders nor insiders who occupy the same positions from which men in Trasacco have built up 'vote banks' have in fact done so. In the cases so far outlined, personal choice seems to account for this. However, *luchesi* themselves insist that no clientelist politician can make any headway. First of all, nobody is allowed to claim greater eligibility for an elective position because of his education or status. At a meeting of the Associazione Sportiva (the football club) to elect new officials, somebody shouted out that the *sindaci* should be *'coloro che hanno studiato'* (those who had studied).[1] This was met by a chorus of 'rubbish!' and 'what for?'. The mover of this proposal remained silent and the assembly proceeded to elect a tailor, a draughtsman, a farmer and a factory worker. In the same vein, I was told of two people who had been forced to resign from the seed-potato cooperatives for 'acting superior because they had more land'. Secondly, I was told the *luchesi* will not stand for clientelist practices.

An aspiring political boss

The only recent attempt to build up a clientelist following in Luco was made by Biagino Venditti. His story reveals the difficulties in the path of an ambitious politician. Biagino had a number of power bases. He was an officer in the Guardia Forestale (Forestry Corps), responsible for the tree nursery near Avezzano. In order to be accepted in the Corps young men need to have a period of experience in the nursery. Biagino could help would-be recruits to

1 Every voluntary association must have four *sindaci* who are not members of the committee, but to whom the minutes and accounts are available on request.

124

get this experience. Secondly, his position in the Guardia Forestale gave him an ex-officio seat on the consortium or governing body of the Industrial Nucleus. It was said that this gave him some influence over who was and was not employed in the factories of the Nucleus. Indeed, the consortium on which he sat was dissolved in early 1974, without explanation but amidst rumours of corruption that were not officially denied.

In 1970, when Luco still had a system of proportional representation for the *comune* council, Biagino formed an electoral list independent of any party label. The only other person of note on the list was Cesare Organtini, a registrar of the court in Avezzano. Organtini's two brothers were important men in Luco, one being the bank manager and the other the largest supplier of building materials. All three Organtini brothers had long been members of the Dc. Biagino had once been a member of the Psi. His application to join the Dc a few years before had been turned down.

In 1974 the village was still full of stories of how Biagino had visited people who had recently been offered employment in the Industrial Nucleus factories. Apparently he claimed to have been instrumental in their good fortune and that a vote for him would be an acceptable repayment. One old communist recounted how he had 'thrown Biagino out of the house' when he had offered to get his son into the Guardia Forestale. People said that they had felt insulted by these approaches. In spite of his list's connections and his own 'influence', only Biagino and Organtini were elected, with 387 or 14 per cent of the vote (Pci/Psi: 1469, 52 per cent; Dc: 968, 34 per cent).

The only way in which Biagino could go on from there was to defeat the Pci in the local elections and become a member of the ruling *giunta*, or to seek power at a higher electoral level. For either of these objectives he had to have the backing of the Dc. He had already been turned down for party membership, but he hoped to force their hand by getting a personal reputation for efficient administration. The means that he chose to secure this were to run a prestigious village festival and to become president of the largest and most popular voluntary association, the football club.

In 1971 he 'emerged' as chairman of a large committee of people who were interested in organising a centenary festival of the apparition of the Madonna to a villager in 1872. The *festa* far exceeded in size and quality of entertainment anything normally offered by such a village. Through connections with the Vatican, Biagino arranged for a detachment of the Vatican Guard Band to parade at the opening ceremony. The 'historic centre' was illuminated by talented professionals. The most famous pop singer of the day gave a concert, and appeared in all the newspapers with Biagino's arm round her.

He also invited Natali and Gaspari to speak in the course of the celebrations since the national elections were imminent. But this did not, as he must have hoped, endear him to the Christian Democrats, for their electorate is critical of Don Nicola's political sermons and of the Vatican's interference in politics, and likewise disapproved of the admixture of politics to their 'religious' *festa.* The *festa* is a 'community' affair, it was said: communists had contributed to its success, both privately in donations and officially through the local council; it was bad taste and bad faith to use the *festa* as a platform for Dc electioneering. The *festa* did, however, establish Biagino's reputation as an organiser.

When he made a bid for presidency of the Associazione Sportiva the opposition were unable to resist him. In the seasons of 1973–4 the Angizia, as the Luco football team is called, was promoted to the next division. At the 1974 Annual General Meeting, where a new committee was due to be elected, a number of Biagino's friends made speeches about how the club would need a lot more money to compete in the higher division. Biagino then announced that he could provide the money: he had sixty men, each prepared to contribute 100 000 lire (£70) if he were made president. This took the meeting completely by surprise. The socialist deputy-mayor, who was in the chair, attacked the move, which became known as the *Golpe* (a reference to the Colonels' coup in Chile), as undemocratic because it precluded from office those too poor to contribute 100 000 lire.

The meeting went on till 1.0 a.m. and was adjourned to the next evening. The opposition could not propose any alternative to Biagino's method of raising the money, which everyone had come to believe was necessary. After midnight the following evening, when everyone was exhausted, Biagino and his friends were elected to the committee.

Biagino's first year in office was disastrous. The coach, a fruit vendor called Loreto, was dismissed. He had trained the team for years and had brought it promotion. He was an active member of the Pci. It was rumoured that strongly anti-communist elements on Biagino's committee had pressed for his dismissal. Later in the year, two professional coaches and many defeats later, Biagino asked Loreto back, apparently without consulting his committee. The committee meeting at which this decision was revealed ended in uproar.

At the AGM in 1975, the committee still had another year to run in office. However, Biagino was forced to resign because of the poor showing of the team, the huge expenditure on professional coaches and footballers and, above all, the rumours of dissension in the committee. In order to return as president Biagino had to make a deal with the Pci.

This finally dashed any hopes that Biagino had of joining the Dc. The handling of the Associazione Sportiva was only the last of a series of blunders which Biagino had made. The Dc *sezione* know their members well and know that *luchesi* do not like people who try to buy their votes nor those 'who throw their weight about'. Everybody used to say 'of course Biagino wants to be mayor, that's why he is desperate to be president of the Sportiva'. That alone was enough to make people distrust him. *Luchesi* have this much in common with other Southerners: they do not trust people who are out for office.

How to be a politician in Luco

The way men get office in Luco is the same as the way they win respect in other parts of their lives: by hard work and consistency. The leaders of both parties in Luco have been loyal members for a long time, and have worked their way slowly to the top. Just after the war, of course, people came quickly to leadership positions, but all had given evidence of their reliability. Ciangoli, the first mayor, had been a close associate of Rocco Amadoro, the 'underground' Pci leader. 'Sindacone' the next, had fought with the partisans in Yugoslavia. Rigazzi, the leader of the Dc from 1946 to 1973, had been an officer in the Italian army in Greece, and his father had been a local councillor. The present Pci secretary, and those who will succeed him, have been brought up in communist families and in the Fgci (young-communist league). No one who had ever changed parties had any influence or held an elected position. Whilst I was in Luco, one man, Angelo Bianchi, was trying desperately to rise within the Dc. He had been an *assessore* (member of the *giunta*) in the communist administration of 1965–70. At the end of his term he resigned, on the grounds that the communists were being unnecessarily parsimonious with the local budget. They did this, he said, so that they could blame the lack of amenities on the Dc, who controlled the allocation of funds to local authorities. Though never a member of the Pci, he was strongly associated with it. The Pci said they had refused to renew Angelo's candidature because he had practised favouritism to his friends and relatives whilst in office, a fact which they did not wish to publicise. Angelo tried very hard to make a contribution to the Dc. He was always to be seen in earnest conversation with the younger Dc activists. He gave vociferous applause to public speakers, and was ready to engage in verbal destruction of communists at the slightest provocation. Nevertheless, although he was allowed membership, his support was not rewarded by election to the Dc committee. The reason that I was given for his failure to achieve a position in the Dc was that he is a *ruffiano*. *Ruffianismo* is a cardinal sin in Luco.

In Italian, the word *ruffiano* or *ruffiana* means, strictly, a pimp or go-between. By extension it can denote a worker who reports on his workmates to the boss, or a girl who sleeps with the boss to get promotion. So, in general, it carries the notion of betrayal for personal advancement. In Luco it is used in all these senses, but most often it means someone who is *politically* disloyal: he takes out a party card to get a job, or accepts a *favore* in exchange for a vote. This means that he must have *changed party*, for it is assumed in Luco that everyone has a firm political position from which nothing ought to subvert him. Thus a person who gets a new job and also changes parties will, inevitably, be labelled *ruffiano*. So closely is party change associated with the suspicion of personal gain that even when change occurs from sincere conviction, it will be called *ruffianismo*. A *ruffiano* is ostracised for years. The only fight I ever saw was between a member of the Pci and a man who had left it to join the Dc nine years before. This attitude to *ruffianismo* may also be the reason why Dr Di Gianfelippo is politically active (though not a candidate) in Avezzano but not in Luco. He and his brothers were communist partisans at the end of the war and are now anti-communist Social Democrats. Whenever a man's reliability is under discussion his political record is recalled. *Ruffiani* are not and can never be reliable. *Coerenza* (consistency) is therefore an essential requirement for aspiring political leaders, and so is hard work. It does not really matter whether the work has been in the fields or the factory or the party organisation, but it must be evident. *Coerenza* and hard work are values of general salience in Luco. In politics they define what political activities are legitimate.

Luco is not, however, isolated from the political forms which dominate other *comuni*. Within the Dc there have always been people who argue that the methods which it uses to fight the Pci in Luco are ineffective. These are the methods of open and democratic opposition, public speeches, posters, attacks on the actions of the council locally and on communism nationally and internationally. The 'young Turks', as they are called, point to the success of clientelist methods in other localities, and try to introduce them in Luco. Reputedly, their activities have most often taken a material form: giving away bags of rice in the 'fifties and transistor radios in the 'seventies. I never heard of the kind of transactions that took place in Trasacco: promises of jobs, transfers, credit, help, and so on, in exchange for votes. In the 1975 elections, by some means or other, two young men had obtained from 150 people promises that they would vote for a particular set of preference votes. These two were Dc activists. They had promised these preferences to two men standing at the provincial and regional levels. The 150 *luchesi* who had agreed to vote these preferences were Dc supporters. When the vote count was over, the two emerged complaining bitterly of the *brutte figure* (sorry figures) they were going to cut with their superiors, and cursing the *mentalità luchese* (the way that *luchesi* think and behave) since they had got a total of only 20 preferences!

Election results

So far I have argued from observational data that politics in Luco are conducted in a different way from Trasacco, and that what is normal behaviour in Trasacco is regarded in Luco as *ruffianismo* and contrary to the *mentalità luchese*. I have shown that there is antagonism to people who try to build a political career on their professions or personal dominance of non-party-political organisations.

At this point I would like to introduce the evidence of electoral results in support of these arguments. (To facilitate comparison a *selection* of results from 1946 to 1975 appears as Tables 13 and 14. Figure 5 is a bar graph showing visually the proportion of the vote for each party in each of the villages.) Several significant points emerge from these elections: firstly, the stability of the vote in Luco and the fluctuations in the vote in Trasacco; secondly, the higher turnout in national elections than in *comune* elections in Luco, and the opposite in Trasacco, taking into account variations in the electorate;[2] thirdly, the proliferation of minor parties in Trasacco and the concentration of political conflict between the Dc and Pci in Luco. In addition, the number of preference votes cast in each *comune* is very different and is evidence of the type of political conflict that is being engaged in.

In Trasacco I asked people how they explained such 'peaks' as that for the Msi in 1958 in elections for the Camera, of the Pci for the Senate in 1968 and for the province in 1975. *Trasaccani* said it was because popular local people had stood: Dalla Montà in 1958, D'Amato in 1968 and Taricone in 1975. The figures seem to support this explanation. When a party receives an unusually large vote at one electoral level, this is not reflected in a similarly large vote at other levels, even when electors fill in their voting schedules during a single visit to the polling booth. When, in 1958, the Msi received nearly 45 per cent of the vote for the Camera election, the percentage taken by the Msi for the Senate was in no way comparable. People who voted Msi for the Camera were clearly not voting for the party at all, but for Dalla Montà. Had they supported the party they would have voted for an Msi senator too. In 1975 the Dc took 1404 votes for the region and only 556 for the province, a net loss of 848 votes. These went partly to the Pri, some to the Msi and 343 more to the Pci candidate, Taricone, who was elected. This does not mean that people were dissatisfied with the Dc as a party, but that they preferred the alternative candidate.

One must ask why there are no such fluctuations in the vote in Luco. An obvious answer might be that it has no 'favourite sons', but this is not the case. Santirocco, a *luchese*, is the most famous politician Fucino has ever produced. He is now leader of the Pci in Abruzzo, and a national deputy. He has genuine cross-party respect and affection in Luco. Yet when he stood at the

2 The electorate for the Senate is restricted to those over 25. In 1975 the electorate for *comune*, province and region was expanded by the inclusion of 18-year-olds.

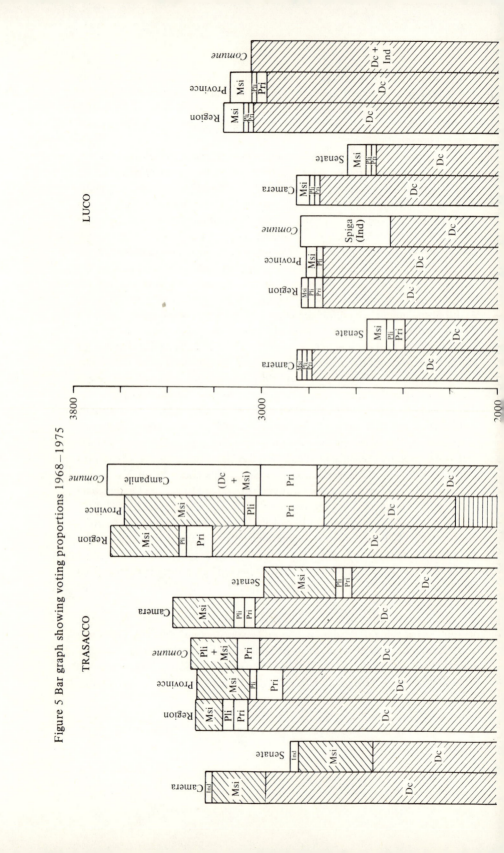

Figure 5 Bar graph showing voting proportions 1968–1975

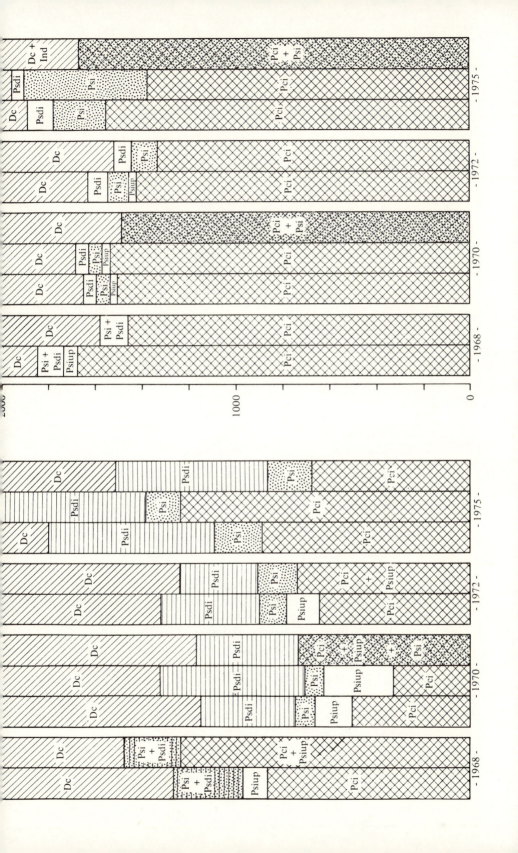

Luco dei Marsi

Table 13 *Luco – Selection of election results.*

	Constituent Assembly 1946	Comune 1946	Camera Deputati 1948	Comune 1951	Camera Deputati 1953	Comune 1956	Camera Deputati 1958	Comune 1961	Camera Deputati 1963
Pci							1419		1530
							46.7		52.5
Psiup									
Psi							302		165
							9.9		5.6
Pci +	1772	1721	1929	1653	1720	1774		1530	
Psi	68.5	75.9	65.2	61.7	57.2	60.3	(56.6)	59.1	(58.1)
Pdsi					26		82		180
					0.9		2.7		6.1
Dc	578	576	904	1024	1127	1166	1004	1056	936
	22.4	24.1	30.5	38.3	37.5	39.7	33.0	40.9	32.1
Pri	95				3		24		4
	3.7				0.1		0.1		0.1
Pli					10		21		14
					0.3		0.7		0.8
Msi			34		68		164		80
			1.1		2.3		5.4		2.7
Pci + Psi + Pdsi									
Msi + Dc									
Msi + Dc + Pdsi									
Others	186		115		50		23		
	5.4		3.2		2.6		0.8		
Total	2631	2297	2982	2677	3004	2940	3039	2586	2909

Source: Ufficio Elettorale, L'Aquila
*denotes alliance with Psdi
( ) denote combined percentage of Left parties

provincial and regional levels he attracted no more *luchesi* votes for the Pci than when he had not stood. Another *luchese* respected by people of all parties is Rigazzi of the Dc. He often stood at the provincial level, but never significantly increased the Dc vote.

There is, however, one exception to this general stability – the socialist vote at the provincial level in 1975. The socialist candidate for the constituency of Luco, Trasacco and San Benedetto was a *luchese*, Beppino Di Giamberardino. He held the office of deputy-mayor, but for five years, in the absence of Giannino Venditti (the Pci secretary, excluded from the council and mayoralty by a technicality), Di Giamberardino had acted as mayor of Luco. He is extremely competent, but as a socialist he could not have been promoted to the position of mayor.[3] Two-thirds of the extra votes that he collected (180 out of 302) came from people who voted Pci at the regional level. To many *luchesi* the Pci and Psi are almost indistinguishable: they pre-

---

3 The man who was nominally mayor was a medical student in Rome, and rarely even visited the *comune* during his term of office.

Comune 1965	Camera Deputati 1968	Senate 1968	Regional Council 1970	Provincial Council 1970	Comune 1970	Camera Deputati 1972	Senate	Regional Council 1975	Provincial Council 1975	Comune 1975
485	853	1241	504	336		639	740	902	1245	675
15.7	26.7	42.9	15.3	10.3		18.9	24.6	25.1	34.5	18.4
207	116		145	295		148				
6.7	3.6		4.4	9.0		4.3				
139	286*	223*	80	74		107	186	215	140	189
4.6	8.9	7.7	2.4	2.2		3.1	6.2	5.9	3.9	5.2
(27.0)	(39.2)	(50.6)	(21.7)	(21.5)	735					
					22.3	(26.3)	(30.8)	(31.0)	(38.4)	(23.6)
292			406	620	440	439	350	694	814	645
9.5			12.4	19.0	13.3	12.9	11.6	19.3	22.5	17.6
1610	1711	1061	1900	1577	1834	1701	1376	1404	556	1251
52.2	53.4	36.7	58.0	48.5	55.6	50.3	45.9	39.1	15.4	34.1
		32	53	67	103	20	41	104	289	225
		1.1	1.6	2.1	3.3	0.5	1.3	2.8	8.4	6.2
	19	21	29	28		22	30	43	24	
	0.6	0.7	0.8	0.8		0.6	1.0	1.1	0.8	
350	199	311	156	256	184	231	273	277	525	
11.3	6.2	10.7	4.7	8.1	5.5	6.8	9.1	6.3	14.5	
	17									
3083	3201	2889	3273	3253	3296	3307	2996	3639	3593	3669

sent a unified list for the *comune* elections, and almost always agree on local issues. Activists of both parties urge their members to attend each other's meetings. Di Giamberardino is a trade unionist of the Alleanza Contadina, which is dominated by the Pci. It is rumoured that he is a 'plant' in the Psi, to attract the votes of 'socialists' who cannot bear actually to vote communist. In short, Di Giamberardino passes, in all but his electoral label, for a communist. Indeed, confusion about his political identity led to a large number of spoiled papers as people cast a list vote for the Pci and a personal preference vote for Di Giamberardino. It must be emphasised that, unlike Taricone in Trasacco, he did not win the votes of a notable proportion of Christian Democrats.

Fluctuations in the vote in Trasacco therefore seem to be accounted for by 'personalism' — large numbers of personal votes are given to popular individuals which are not reflected in votes for their parties at other electoral levels. The only similar case in Luco arose from a confusion over the 'real' political identity of the candidate.

The second difference between Luco and Trasacco which can be inferred

Luco dei Marsi

Table 14 *Trasacco – Selection of election results*

	Constituent Assembly 1946	Comune 1946	Camera Deputati 1948	Comune 1951	Camera Deputati 1953	Comune 1956	Camera Deputati 1958	Comune 1959	Comune 1960	Camera Deputati 1963
Pci							474			644
							14.6			23.3
Psiup										
Psi							354			225
							10.9			8.1
Pci + Psi	1191	1163	965	1067	953	936	(25.5)			(31.4)
	46.8	47.4	32.4	39.2	32.9	32.2				
Psdi					227		136			42
					7.8		4.2			1.5
Dc	1112	971	1692		1263	1160	784	1273		1635
	43.7	39.5	56.8		43.6	39.9	24.1	41.6		59.3
Pri							3			
Pli					27		4			25
					0.9					0.9
Msi			80		334		1451			181
			2.7		11.6		44.7			6.5
Pci + Psi + Psdi						167		1784	1575	
						5.7		58.4	61.2	
Msi + Dc									1001	
									38.8	
Msi + Dc + Psdi				1658		644				
				60.8		22.2				
Other	256	323	285		91		41			5
	8.5	13.1	8.1		3.2		1.3			
Total	2559	2457	3022	2725	2895	2907	3247	3057	2576	2757

Source: Ufficio Elettorale. L'Aquila
*denotes alliance with Psdi
( ) denote combined percentage of Left parties

from election results is in the level of 'turnout'. More people in Trasacco vote in *comune* elections than in other elections. This confirms the picture we already have of Trasacco politics as a conflict between individuals rather than parties. The chief arena of competition is the local level. It is in local elections that activists work hardest to get out their supporters, because it is here that they themselves have a chance of being elected.

In Luco there is more interest in *le politiche* (national elections). More emigrants return for national elections than for regional, provincial and communal ones. Only in 1970 was the *comune* vote high. This was the year in which Biagino Venditti and Cesare Organtini ran a 'clientelist'-style campaign. They did manage to raise the turnout level, mostly, it is said, of the poorer voters. It would be a distortion to imply that nobody in Luco changes votes from one election to another: the results are not identical. However, there are not enough vote changers in Luco to cause violent fluctuations. I only once came across a couple who said they were 'thinking about' whom to vote for at the next elections; for most people the question did not arise. One group of communist voters who had built houses on a road out of town where there was no water supply threatened to vote Dc in 1975 if they did not get their

Comune 1965	Camera Deputati 1968	Senate 1968	Regional Council 1970	Provincial Council 1970	Comune 1970	Camera Deputati 1972	Senate	Regional Council 1975	Provincial Council 1975	Comune 1975
485	853	1241	504	336		639	740	902	1245	675
15.7	26.7	42.9	15.3	10.3		18.9	24.6	25.1	34.5	18.4
207	116		145	295		148				
6.7	3.6		4.4	9.0		4.3				
139	286*	223*	80	74		107	186	215	140	189
4.6	8.9	7.7	2.4	2.2		3.1	6.2	5.9	3.9	5.2
(27.0)	(39.2)	(50.6)	(21.7)	(21.5)	735					
					22.3	(26.3)	(30.8)	(31.0)	(38.4)	(23.6)
292			406	620	440	439	350	694	814	645
9.5			12.4	19.0	13.3	12.9	11.6	19.3	22.5	17.6
1610	1711	1061	1900	1577	1834	1701	1376	1404	556	1251
52.2	53.4	36.7	58.0	48.5	55.6	50.3	45.9	39.1	15.4	34.1
		32	53	67	103	20	41	104	289	225
		1.1	1.6	2.1	3.3	0.5	1.3	2.8	8.4	6.2
	19	21	29	28		22	30	43	24	
	0.6	0.7	0.8	0.8		0.6	1.0	1.1	0.8	
350	199	311	156	256	184	231	273	277	525	
11.3	6.2	10.7	4.7	8.1	5.5	6.8	9.1	6.3	14.5	
	17									
3083	3201	2889	3273	3253	3296	3307	2996	3639	3593	3669

water. In the event none of them could actually bring themselves to vote for 'the enemy'.

The third point of difference between Luco and Trasacco is the relative strength of minor parties in Trasacco and their almost complete absence in Luco. In Luco the Psdi normally takes less than 3 per cent of the vote, and the Republican, Liberal and Neo-Fascist shares are derisory. In Trasacco the Psdi is quite substantial and Pri and Msi have both had momentary flowerings at the expense of the Dc when local notables stood or disaffected clientelist politicians wreaked revenge on their colleagues by transferring their personal vote banks to these parties.

Finally there is the problem of preference votes. Preference votes are votes which electors can give individually to a restricted number of candidates within the party list which they have marked with a cross. A large number of preference votes may enable a candidate to rise above the position in which he has been placed by the party. In other words, in *comune* elections if a party wins 12 seats over-all and X is thirteenth on the party list, if he gets more preferences than Y who is twelfth, X will become a councillor and Y will not.

135

Hence the total number of preferences cast in any community is a good measure of clientelism, since in a clientelist constituency it is preferences, not list votes, that are fought over. The clientelist politician asks his clients to vote first and foremost for him, and only secondarily for his party. In the 1975 local elections 7129 preference votes were cast in Trasacco, an average of two per voter. The total in Luco was 217 in an electorate of 3041. For the regional elections there were fewer preference votes in Trasacco (which again indicates less intensity than at *comune* elections). On the other hand, preference votes at this level rose in Luco. Even the Pci promotes a certain combination of preferences in regional elections in order to ensure the election of local representatives. About 40 per cent of the electorate in Luco cast preference votes for regional candidates. However, this is still significantly lower than in Trasacco, where there was more than one preference per voter. Clearly this preference voting denotes 'personalism'; but why else is preference voting so important for the clientelist politician?

Where resource allocation takes place

Being a councillor is not an onerous role in either Trasacco or Luco. In both cases the council is simply a rubber-stamping body for decisions which have been taken outside. Yet, curiously, in Luco the parties have difficulty in finding twenty people willing to stand for each electoral list, whilst in Trasacco there is immense competition to become a councillor.

The majority system of sixteen seats to the winning party and four to the loser has enhanced the rubber-stamping quality of the Luco council. But this was already the case before this system applied to Luco. Because of the extremely open nature of the political process in Luco, the constant discussion of politics and the accessibility of politicians to the electorate, councillors rarely come to the debating chamber without a good idea of what the prevailing attitudes amongst the electorate are towards a particular policy. Within the Pci, which is where decisions about the spending of council money are ultimately made, discussions are carried on informally in many contexts in an unceasing effort to arrive at a consensus about priorities. Non-members can also make their preferences known in similarly informal ways.

Consensus is not always possible however. Heated debates between Pci and Dc take place in the council chamber, but since their outcome is already known, the opposition is more rhetorical than real. Even within the Pci, policy decisions sometimes enrage members. In 1975, for example, the Pci was determined to go through with a corporate Town Plan which would designate growth areas and housing densities. This naturally affected the value of properties within the growth areas, and those excluded felt hard done by. To avoid accusations of favouritism, the plan was drawn up by a town planning consultant in Rome, but many communists were very annoyed, and said so.

In Trasacco decisions are also taken outside the council chamber, but in this case the venues are closed ones, such as the *circolo* and private dinner parties. It is not a matter of seeking a consensus in the electorate but of striking bargains, forming alliances and sorting out relative advantages. The administration fails, as we have pointed out earlier, when these alliances and agreements, which are arrived at in private, break down in public.

There is another reason why council meetings are not that important. The taxes which can be locally raised are very small. The major share of any council's budget is allocated to it by the regional council. The administration puts in bids for the money it needs to carry out its policies, but the allocation is made by balancing the demands and pressures and the politics of others. There are differences in the ways that the *giunte* of Luco and Trasacco go about getting money for their administrative functions. In Luco when there is a crisis, as there was in 1975 when the water supply broke down, an all-party delegation visits the regional *assessore* for public works and pleads for his assistance. The mayor frequently attends personally at the regional offices to plead for money for public works projects.

In Trasacco the minimum budgetary allocation is not increased through these formal channels. It is done by personal contacts of an 'informal' nature between local councillors, regional councillors and national politicians. This is why there is so much competition for places on the electoral lists in Trasacco and why preference votes are so important. Elections establish for each *politicante* the amount of support he can muster personally and which he can deliver up the line to his superior co-factionists. It is his position on the local hierarchy that will determine how much will be channelled through him from the national and regional budgets for local projects.

It is the absence of these channels of *favori* that so frustrates some 'young Turks' in the Luco Dc. They cannot deliver the goods in terms of votes and preferences and they therefore cannot get their hands on the wherewithal to oil the wheels of clientelism. So insignificant is the Luco Dc *sezione* that it took them a whole year to persuade the provincial branch to send an observer to validate their *sezione* elections. The 'young Turks' can see no hope of winning the battle with the Pci on its terms, which are ideological and pragmatic ones ('the Pci runs a more efficient *comune*'). It is unlikely though that they would win, in Luco, on clientelist terms.

Administration

A Pci-run *comune* such as Luco faces certain constraints in carrying out its policies. Every item of the budget and of expenditure is checked by the prefect, who is the representative of the central government in the province. In spite of the difficulty of getting approval when the *comune* is not run by a government party, Luco has amenities which are unique in Fucino. It alone has a crèche, a clinic and a children's playground. Its water supply functions all the year round and the bye-laws to prevent 'the accumulation of noisome substances in the built-up area' are effective. The 'historic centre' has been protected from ugly modernisation and the urban plan, strictly applied, has prevented the haphazard development that makes most Fucino *comuni* sprawling and characterless.

The administration also leaves much to be desired, however. Tractors are allowed to drive through the main streets, rousing the populace at 4.0 a.m. and making the roads slippery with mud. Concessions are made to farmers because the council cannot afford to offend them. More seriously, the new crèche and clinic could not be built in the village centre where they would have been accessible to all because, it was rumoured, 'Sindacone has sold off the council land there cheaply to his friends'.

It has been suggested that when communists control local administrations they gain access to resources which can be used to feed a patronage system identical to that which any Dc *comune* runs. Tarrow cites the words of 'a high level union official':

The Pci in the South is a party of clienteles. This is true in the sense that they seek power through advancing the interests of their followers on the local level and within the party system. The Party in the South partakes of the backwardness of the society. (Tarrow, 1967: 240.)

Macciocchi, writing to Althusser about her electoral campaign, remarks that

Many local and provincial councillors and deputies end up being a sort of parliamentary–administrative bureaucracy, destined to get as much out of the existing social order as they can on the practical level. (Macciocchi, 1969: 27.)

It is true that party activists, including councillors and trade unionists, spend some of their time helping with forms for pensions, assistance, social security and so on. It is also the case that amongst *comune* employees communists outnumber Christian Democrats. However, if a clientele system were being operated, one would expect that *all* would be communists. This is not the case. The Borough Surveyor is a Christian Democrat and none of the other professional appointees (such as *medici condotti*) are Pci supporters.[4] Amongst the lower-paid employees too, some are Christian Democrats.

4 Even the Pci in Trasacco has adopted 'universalistic' criteria in these matters. The Pci-led administration of 1960–5 appointed Dr Ciofani to his present position of *medico condotto*.

Given that most low-paid workers vote communist, this is the kind of distribution one would expect if universalistic selection criteria were being employed.

One of the main appeals which the Pci makes to the Italian electorate is that they are offering something different: clean government and social change that will favour the under-privileged. The notion that they had to set a good example and be a showcase for communism was present to all the Pci and Psi councillors. Their tactics to win popular support were to do things for whole groups of people and not for isolated individuals, and also to keep their budget balanced.

My reading of the budget figures (which may not be accurate due to ignorance of Italian accounting methods) is that the Luco balance was closed in 1973 with a surplus of 20 million lire (about £14 000). Trasacco closed with a deficit of 41 million lire (about £29 000). A study of larger *comuni* concluded that the Pci administrations tend to be financially more conservative than Dc ones (Fried, 1971). Luco and Trasacco confirm this finding. When we compare the items of expenditure, however, we find that there is less waste in Luco (for example, money is not spent on tarring roads unnecessarily), and that money has been spent on social amenities of benefit to the whole community.

The council is also concerned with the minutiae of people's lives, but it tries to deal with these problems for groups rather than individuals. One person came to the *comune* to complain that his pension had not arrived at the Post Office. Rather than sort this out as a personal favour, the deputy-mayor phoned the Post Office and ascertained that all the industrial workers' pensions were delayed. A telegram was dispatched and the pensions arrived four hours later. This may seem the most rational course to have followed, but a clientelist politician would have treated each case separately in order to enhance his political influence.

A similar response met the farmer who, in the spring of 1975, complained to the *comune* that the Ente Fucino cooperative was paying out less than a third of what it owed them on the previous year's potato crop. The deputy-mayor called in the Pci leadership and a demonstration was organised. After an occupation of the Ente Fucino offices by five hundred farmers from Luco, the full amount was promised within three days.

These were practical actions. Others have a supportive significance that is purely symbolic. Since the early 'fifties the Luco council has passed motions and written letters condemning international events like the Cold War and the interference of the United States in Chile. In local affairs there have been debates in support of strikers and letters to government bodies appealing for more employment. These are a great irritation to the Dc opposition. For the ruling party they help to keep the public informed and to activate the Pci's

139

slogan 'the people to the administration and the administration to the people', which was coined in 1946.

Open politics

Within an hour of arriving in Luco, I was asked what my politics were. I was later to discover that this forthright political curiosity was characteristic of *luchesi*. Indeed, it is a component of the *mentalità luchese*. Virtually everyone is both a partisan and a participant in political debate. The saying 'we are all equal here' most clearly illustrates the political consciousness of *luchesi*.

By turning to a 'patron' for help, the *trasaccano* demonstrates that he is 'aware' of 'politics', but he himself is only the object of the political process, not someone who influences it.

The contrast between the open and closed nature of politics is reflected in the way that policy decisions are arrived at in the two villages. In both, the council chamber, the formal locus of policy making, is, in reality, seldom more than the arena for rhetorical combat. In Trasacco, policy is arrived at by 'patrons' bargaining in private. In Luco, public discussion characterises policy making. Although in the final analysis it is the activists of the Pci who have the power to dictate policy, in practice the whole population has access to the discussion and there is a clear striving for consensus. Christian Democrats are involved in this process, but both parties are at pains to point out that they never 'collaborate'.

The political consciousness of *luchesi* extends to an awareness of the environment in which their village is situated. They are proud that their political procedures are relatively democratic, and they contrast disparagingly the patron-controlled *comuni* around them.

In Luco, the priests, doctors and other professionals who practise there are all 'outsiders'. For this reason, even had they wished to, they might be handicapped in establishing themselves as patrons. Biagino is an example of an 'insider' who did try to build a political career from a bureaucratic base, using clientelist techniques. Ostensibly Biagino's downfall was due to the declining performance of the football team. However, it was made clear to me by members of all parties, that a ground-swell of reaction had long been building up at his offences against the *mentalità luchese*.

The *luchesi* are alive to the threat that Biagino posed, they realise that it is not only from outside the Pci that clientelist politicians emerge. They have the example of Lecce, twenty-one kilometres away, where Dr Spallone, once private physician to Togliatti, controls the *comune* in an even more pervasive way than Ciofani does in Trasacco.

10 Social relations

In Trasacco social organisation, political practice and the values that both underpin and grow out of these, are materially and historically rooted in scarce employment and restricted access to the means of subsistence. Personal relationships as well as corporate organisations are penetrated by clientelist political practices; and, furthermore, the language of 'affective' relationships, as used in relations of political dominance, serves to legitimise clientelist politics.

In Luco resources are no less scarce and unevenly distributed, as they are in the South generally. However, clientelist politics have not pervaded the social fabric. Moreover, the tensions arising from the dialectic of social relations are perceived, articulated and resolved differently in the two communities.

Three levels of social organisation claim the allegiance of *luchesi* – personal ties, the political parties and the community. Conflicts arise constantly between these personal, political and communal loyalties. Public discussion centres on these issues and how they ought to be resolved, as well as on matters of public policy.

Formal associations

The one type of club which Luco and Trasacco have in common is concerned with football. In both places football is the most popular single activity. In Trasacco it is elitist: the team is made up of professional players, few of whom come from Trasacco, and it is run autocratically by Dr Ciofani. The football team reflects the closed nature of associational life in Trasacco. By contrast, the Luco club is very much enmeshed in the community. It engages the interest and participation of both Communists and Christian Democrats, as players, spectators, elected officials and members of the Associazione Sportiva.

For many years it functioned successfully as a 'community' club outside the sphere of party politics. This happened not because the leading figures were apolitical but because they observed an unwritten agreement to exclude 'politics' from the day-to-day running of the club. Indeed, both political parties could claim to have influence in the club but neither could realistically claim to dominate it. The president, Beppino Rigazzi, was leader of the Dc opposition in the local council and secretary of the Luco Dc *sezione*. The team's trainer was Loreto 'Zoccolante', a Pci activist. Both were men who commanded cross-party respect. In the words of a local journalist of the extreme Left:

Rigazzi is a most honest person. He has always carried on his politics based on honesty, even if many times he has been wrong. Precisely because he is honest he never exploited the weak points of the Pci: when it would have been easy to make a 'demagogic opposition' he never did so. If he opposed something it was always for the good of the village, never for the interests of his party. He is extremely honest, admired even by the communists. Judging by the opinions he expresses, he is a man to the right of the Dc, but, as an administrator, he could belong to any party. If you set him to administer anything at all, you can be sure that his own interests would not matter, only those of the collectivity.

Loreto 'Zoccolante', the trainer, was an itinerant fruit and vegetable vendor. He was both respected and popular, for he carried his political ideology into his business: he worked longer hours and charged less for his goods than any other shopkeeper. He brought his politics to the game as well, wearing a red tie and carrying a copy of *L'Unità* sticking out conspicuously from his pocket at every match and particularly when photographs were taken. Relations between the two men were compounded of mutual esteem for their respective skills and an equal desire to produce good football.

Rigazzi's resignation on grounds of ill health coincided with the team's promotion into the premier division of the provincial league. Before the Luco amateurs under Loreto had a chance to prove themselves, Biagino's inspired *Golpe* (coup) took place (see above p. 126).

Some of the opposition to Biagino came from the suspicion that he wanted to use the club to further his political ambitions. In addition, some members of the new committee were known for their extreme anti-communist views. These misgivings were confirmed when Loreto and some of the local players were dismissed and replaced by highly-paid professionals. After a dismal season, with relegation inevitable, Biagino invited Loreto back. At this the anti-communists on the committee threatened to resign. In the course of this long Annual General Meeting in June 1975, an agreement was reached whereby Biagino made an alliance with the communists, for the purposes of the Associazione Sportiva.

Supporters wanted to see good football and a successful local team. They did not want to be constantly confronted by quarrels and recriminations which they saw as having led to bad decisions, low team morale, relegation. It was felt that the intrusion of party politics had caused the trouble.

It was also argued that Biagino had brought a completely new and unwelcome atmosphere to the club. Under Rigazzi and Loreto the emphasis had been on its community and amateur character. The senior team consisted of local boys who had come up through the youth teams formed on Loreto's initiative. Therefore a large number of *luchesi* actually had friends and relatives in the different teams. Biagino had changed all this by dismissing Loreto and some of the local players (also, it was said, communists) and taking on professionals who had no parochial loyalties or connections. Biagino seemed to be interested only in the performance of the senior team which would reflect to his credit. The neglect of the youth teams revealed that it was political ambition and not community football that motivated him.

In spite of all this opposition Biagino manoeuvred in such a way that no motion of censure was put at the Annual General Meeting in June 1975. The meeting adjourned with no solution and no resignations. Biagino, knowing that his prestige had suffered badly, was desperate to stay in office until the team's fortunes improved and he could claim success. Mounting pressure however was moving inexorably towards a demand for his resignation at the meeting a week later. With consummate opportunism, Biagino approached the Pci, offering the resignation of his whole committee a year early if they would support his continued presidency. The Pci exacted a high price for this support. The new committee of twenty-five had thirteen of their nominees and Loreto had a free hand in team selection.

This may look like a Pci take-over, but in fact the Pci had deliberately not nominated only communists. Their declared aim was to re-establish the *status quo ante*. The day after the elections the local paper published an account of the results under the headline *'Compromesso storico nell'Angizia'* (Historic compromise in the Luco Football Club) — a reference to the 'historic compromise' between Pci and Dc then being discussed at the national level. Indeed, it was a 'political' compromise, but its purpose was to ensure that party politics were thenceforth excluded from 'community' football.

The football team involved many *luchesi* and symbolised their 'community'. Growing sectarianism coupled with the team's relegation powerfully mobilised public opinion. A rather smaller group of men, about eighty in all, were interested in hunting as a sport. Questions of political allegiance also arose amongst them and ended in their division into two clubs. In contrast with the football club, these events caused scarcely a ripple in the village at large.

For some time all the hunters in Luco had been members of a hunting club in Avezzano. In 1975 it was decided to open a branch of the same association (Federcaccia) in Luco. This would save journeys to Avezzano and give greater local control over restocking and shooting. In the course of negotiations with the parent body, it was discovered that Federcaccia was part of a national leisure organisation affiliated to the Dc. The Pci members called a meeting to discuss what action to take. The discussion became heated when two opposed views emerged. One group argued that they could not stay in a club which furthered the interests of *i padroni* (the bosses). Others pressed for a different view: that they had all been members of Federcaccia for some time; that they would never persuade the Dc hunters to join the Pci-allied organisation, ENAL-Caccia; that they had everything to lose and nothing to gain from forming a separate club. These 'communitarians' argued that the best thing for the hunters of Luco, as a whole, would be to stay in one club, Federcaccia, and all pull together. Politics, they affirmed, were not relevant to good hunting. Neither the name of the national organisation nor its affiliations mattered. Those who could not stomach being associated, however indirectly, with the Dc, left to form a branch of ENAL-Caccia.

Another association, the Società Operaia per Mutuo Soccorso (Workers' Society for Mutual Aid), had interesting antecedents, though by 1975 its activities were reduced to an annual outing for members and Christmas charity. It had been founded in 1906 to insure members against sickness, unemployment and funeral expenses. It had had three categories of member: the 'ordinary', the 'well-deserving' and the 'honorary'. The three categories contributed different amounts in dues. 'Ordinary' and 'well-deserving' members could claim sickness and unemployment benefits. 'Honorary' members ran the club, collecting dues and making decisions about the disbursement of funds. Funeral rites varied in sumptuousness according to the member's category: 'ordinary' members could not expect fellow members to attend their funerals as a group in their robes. The bridge between 'ordinary' and 'well-deserving' membership was a literacy test, perhaps intended by the sturdy and self-sufficient 'honorary' members to encourage the poor to raise themselves from a state of ignorance.

In 1975 the Società Operaia had 130 members, mostly clerks and artisans, and an annual income of £1000 from the rental of its hall to the cinema operator. It used the money to provide gifts for elderly members at Christmas and to pay the coach operators and restaurants on the annual outing for members and their families.

As far back as 1906, though this was six years before universal suffrage, the Society's founders were aware of the dangers of political dissension: the constitution precludes 'any discussions on political matters' (a clause which confirms what has been said about the degree of politicisation in Luco at this time). In 1975 the president, a tailor and a socialist, said that whilst the committee included members of both Pci and Dc, no president had ever been a communist 'because the Society tries to be apolitical and communists make everything political'.

A similar line had been taken in the two seed-potato cooperatives. The original one was founded in 1966. It began operations in 1969 with a contribution of 900 000 lire (£630) from each member towards the construction of a modern potato store. The government matched the total of 50 000 000 lire raised by members with a grant of 25 000 000 and a loan of a further 25 000 000 at 2 per cent interest. By 1974 plans were being discussed to extend the store, and another cooperative had been in existence for three years.

The founder members of both cooperatives had been as much aware of political dissension as their forefathers of the Società Operaia in 1906. Both constitutions specifically ruled out political discussion in meetings. The membership of both cooperatives was politically mixed, though all were well-to-do farmers. The rule was extremely strictly adhered to at meetings. The considerable financial investment kept any political disagreements under control. It was not enjoyment of a sport but their livelihoods which the entry of politics could have undermined.

Members said that they did not think politics mattered in the cooperative, and that they would not have worked any better if all the members had been of one party. What mattered was a commitment to make the cooperative work.

Trade unions

Chapter 6 showed how *trasaccani* belong to trade unions but are sceptical of the motives of their representatives. In Luco most farmers are members of the appropriate union — the Coldiretti (Dc) or the Alleanza Contadina (Pci/Psi). The Alleanza holds a weekly 'clinic' in Luco where farmers go with their problems, and they also attend on other days at the branch in Avezzano. I never heard *luchesi* being cynical about their motives. The Luco deputy-mayor was one of four full-time employees of the Alleanza in Avezzano, and he was a popular and respected man.

Nearly all industrial workers in Luco belong to the Cgil. They play a role on the factory committees out of proportion to their numbers. A particularly outstanding trade unionist from Luco was Scolastica Angelucci (daughter of the martyr to fascism), mother of six and a Pci activist. She was the most militant of the women in the CEME (ITT) factory. She had initiated unionisation, and had transformed industrial relations in the factory. She was highly respected by the workers, not least because she took up all complaints against management and made sure they were answered. She wrung from management the grudging admission that she was an intelligent and articulate negotiator. After five years on the employment list, and with six children and an unemployed husband, Scolastica qualified for a job at CEME. Knowing of her reputation, management decided to reject her after a month's probation. She refused to accept the decision, won her case on appeal and was taken on permanently.

The only Cisl member I knew of in Luco (there were probably more, but membership is recorded by factory, not place of residence) was also a union militant and a shop steward in his factory, the Ente Fucino sugar refinery.

Luchesi, therefore, in contrast to *trasaccani*, participate with some enthusiasm in their unions, and many are local leaders. Union activities involve workers from many villages. They are concerned to unite workers against *i padroni* (the bosses) — managers of the factories and functionaries of the Ente Fucino. The 'class enemy' of union members is not in the Luco community at all, but somewhere outside it, in the place of work or in a government department or even the United States (where ITT has its head office).

On some issues, economic interests overcome the political divide between members of the different unions. An example of this was when the farmers of Luco occupied the Ente Fucino offices in Avezzano in 1975. The motorcade from Luco to Avezzano was led by Pino Venditti of the Pci and Beppino Di Giamberardino of the Psi and Alleanza Contadina. The Coldiretti organiser took no part in the action. Because Di Giamberardino was deputy-mayor, and the troubled farmers had come to see him at the *comune*, it was possible to call the demonstration 'a protest by the farmers of Luco'. Farmers of all parties went along, even though they could see who the leaders were. They could also see, however, the advantages of an 'all-party' protest organised in a communitarian rather than sectarian way, and, as in the past, Dc farmers happily followed the Pci lead. Union loyalties do not, as a rule, clash with community loyalties.

The conflict between union and family, however, is one which has beset unionism from its early beginnings. How does one continue to strike when the family is starving? Even today in Italy, the strike fund is not adequate in many industries. The problem is particularly acute amongst women. Some of them are single parents or single breadwinners. Others are simply not interested in strikes for higher pay (let alone improved conditions like crèches) because they are single girls, living at home with minimal expenses and needing money only for their own clothes, amusements and building up a *corredo* (trousseau). There were signs though that militancy increased with length of experience in a factory environment amongst all workers, but particularly women. It may mean that the question of family v. union will be posed more seriously in future.

Clubs for the young

Many Italian towns have, in addition to the political parties themselves and

branches of their affiliated trade unions, branches of other affiliated organisations such as Azione Cattolica (Catholic Action, often a springboard into Dc
leadership positions), Acli (left-wing Dc leisure organisation), Comitati Civili
(Civil Committees — right-wing Dc organisation), Udi (Communist Women)
and so on. In Luco the Fgci (Communist Youth) is such an organisation. Its
'rival' for the allegiance of the young was the church choir, run by Don Mario.
The choir's activities extended from singing and rehearsals to social gatherings,
pilgrimages and welfare.

The Fgci was the youth arm of the Pci. The first task of young members
was to sell *L'Unità* house-to-house on Sundays, and this continued until their
promotion to full membership of the Pci when they came of age. The Fgci
serviced public meetings of the Pci by preparing pamphlets, posters, the platform and loudspeakers. Its president and secretary in 1974 were very energetic young engineering students, Pino Venditti and Giuseppe Angelucci
(nephew of the fascist martyr). They organised social gatherings, mountain
walks and political discussions. They also went in groups to talk in villages
where there was no Pci. In 1974–5 they provided the main labour force for
the redecoration of the Pci *sezione*.

The Fgci had trouble in recruiting girls. Even communist mothers were
concerned that their daughters might set tongues wagging and spoil their
marriage chances if they were seen associating with boys 'unchaperoned' in
the Fgci activities.

The Dc also had a youth wing, but it did not have either the same number
of members or the continuous presence in the community that the Fgci had.
The youth wing had a member on the Dc *sezione* committee, and most of its
activities were the result of requests from that committee to carry out pre-
electoral publicity functions. The question of debate with them was never
raised in the Fgci: they were dismissed as both bigoted and ignorant. The Dc
youth were themselves reluctant to engage in political discussion with Fgci
members, whom they regarded as 'too well prepared'.

A number of attempts were made by the Fgci to organise joint activities
with 'Don Mario's group'. In particular the Fgci were keen to have a debate
on divorce. One girl who actually belonged to both groups acted as a go-
between, but nothing materialised. It was possible for this girl, Alessandra, to
be in both groups because Don Mario's was ostensibly non-political and had
neither constitution nor membership lists. Its members came from families
with strong Catholic traditions, however, and therefore it had, if not a pro-Dc,
certainly an anti-communist bias. Its members were mostly of that age which
is not expected to have yet made a political commitment. A few young
people in Don Mario's group did go on to join the Fgci, but rather more
ended up with the Dc.

Socialisation into party politics

It is not at all surprising that Dc youngsters should feel themselves at a disadvantage against Fgci opponents. Many of the latter have been raised in families where discussions of potato prices, items on the TV news, local gossip, are all related to an interpretation of the world in terms of owners and producers, exploiters and exploited, multi-nationals and one-man businesses. Tiny children are often taught *'Avant'il popolo'* ('Forward the People') as their first nursery rhyme.

The Pci has a wealth of popular songs and stories of heroic comrades which engage and delight the young. The hymns and Bible stories of the Church are taught in school and catechism classes, but they do not lead on inevitably to support for the Dc. Indeed, many children learn both, but those who are exposed to both go on sooner or later to support the Pci.

The majority of children are not overtly political at school, though a minority (always Pci-oriented) are. It is not until they leave school and take up work that many start to participate in political discourse and take up a committed position. Most follow family traditions. Of those who did not, none have been from communist families. Young people from Dc families who join the Pci usually have close friends in the Pci, or join Cgil rather than Cisl when they start work. It is from these movements of the young that the Pci hopes to increase its support.

In Luco most children grow up loyal to family traditions; in Trasacco, very few. Children are socialised rather into safeguarding their employment prospects. For this they are made aware of the power configuration in the village which might influence those prospects. Even those young people who go outside to university and are drawn into left-wing movements tend to conform when they come home to the village.

Party politics and personal ties

In Trasacco ties of kinship and friendship are politically significant in two distinct ways. First, people themselves said that they would vote for kinsmen (and this extended also to *compari*). Secondly, political activists used the language of kinship and friendship both to claim votes and to mask relations of clientage. Ordinary voters usually acknowledged the obligation to vote for kinsmen and to repay *favori* with political support. In speaking of the relationship of indebtedness they also used the idiom of friendship.

In Luco a number of families were politically divided. The most prominent of these were the Moscas. Angelo was one of five children; he alone was a communist. He had changed politics whilst an emigrant in South America as a very young man. Aged 50 in 1975, he had been a *comune* councillor for ten years. When asked whether she voted for him, his sister-in-law replied:

No. For him there is respect. If he was in need of something, if he were ill, my husband would tell me to take him food, to help, so that one day if we needed it . . . But everyone has his own beliefs. Maybe one would avoid talking politics because he is communist, but the respect remains. And when the question of voting arises, we vote for our party.

My landlady was quite angry when, after a year and a half in Luco, I put it to her that some of the people on the Christian Democrat election list might have been selected because they had large kinship networks. Looking at me very sternly, she replied, 'Here that doesn't come into it. Kinship is one thing, politics another. The people on the democratic [i.e. Dc] list have always been those with "democratic" ideas.'

These examples are deliberately chosen from Christian Democrats since one might expect them to be equivocal about the separation of kinship and politics. In other places the meshing of the two spheres benefits the Dc. For communists the idea of kinship influencing politics means backwardness and clientelism. In Luco Christian Democrats were just as adamant as communists, however, that these spheres should not impinge on one another. I never heard the opposite view expressed. Indeed, *luchesi* used this as an example of the profound differences between themselves and *trasaccani*. Like the saying 'We are all equal here, but in Trasacco the priest and doctor command', it confirmed *luchesi* in their sense of superiority to *trasaccani*.

Kinship, in other words, was not allowed to influence politics, in the sense of how people voted. The obverse of this was that party politics or conflicting political allegiance were not allowed to impinge on personal ties. This too was regarded as a 'progressive' view, in comparison with those of twenty-five years ago.

In the years following the end of fascism, political commitments to the newly-legalised parties were made. These commitments polarised the *luchesi* and many existing relationships were affected. Family relations had been sundered by political divisions between brothers, neighbours had not greeted one another, different bars had become associated with each party and fights had been frequent until about 1954.

My impression was that neighbours now relate to one another irrespective of party, borrowing household necessities, working together in the *vicoli*, making their conserves and so on. Bars no longer had any particular political associations. Physical fighting was rare, though one I did witness, which I mentioned earlier, was caused by one man referring to another as a *ruffiano*. The latter had left the Pci nine years before to join the Dc, and his critic was a communist. Nor were references to politics censored out of conversations between political opponents in order to keep the peace. There were people who were 'not on speaking terms', but even when they were politically opposed, the reason was often quite different.

Talking politics

In Trasacco Dr Ciofani and Don Pasquale head the small Dc elites who control political life. No one outside these elites has access to the decision-making process. It could be argued that a similar clique operates in Luco, except that here it is the Pci. Indeed the Pci do control the local authority, and the local party does itself have leaders. Policy decisions are taken by this small group of activists. But as was noted earlier, it is not an oligarchy. Leaders do not, as a rule, take policy decisions until an attempt has been made to reach consensus. They do this by encouraging the open political discussion for which the *luchesi* are famous.

Men discuss current issues in the bars and piazza and women in the fields and the *vicoli*. Conversations between men and women about politics outside the family take place on social occasions like the *passeggiata*, and luncheons to celebrate weddings, first communions and so on. Women are not reticent in voicing their opinions in male company. This contrasts strongly with Trasacco, where women are much more confined by traditional expectations about their role.

In Luco men pace up and down the piazza talking about politics and farming. To do so is to put oneself in the public eye. Asking whether someone was politically active or not I was told, 'Well, not really — he does not go to the piazza'. There are men who go to the bars in the piazza to play cards and watch TV, but do not walk up and down the piazza. They are not engaged in political discussion. The division between those who do walk and those who do not is not a matter of class or occupation — men of all kinds can be found there. Being 'in the piazza' signifies a desire to engage in political discourse and to make one's views known to those who are involved in policy decisions.

Each group is most commonly composed of men of similar political views, but this is by no means an absolute rule. When Pci and Dc stroll together, verbal attacks may be savage, but the atmosphere is amiable, with each sally emphasised by a slap on the back, or a particularly complex point accompanied by an arm slung round the opponent's shoulder. Political activists whom I questioned closely on this point said that they enjoyed debate with political adversaries.[1] This 'open partisanship' did not, however, prevent them from making disparaging remarks behind one another's backs.

Politics was a popular subject of conversation in women's working groups

1 This is in line with Tarrow's finding that Italian activists are what he calls 'open partisans' (Tarrow, 1973). Almond and Verba found that left-wingers, not only the elite but voters too, liked to debate with opponents (Almond & Verba, 1963: 115–16).

in the fields. One of them observed to me, 'The men have the piazza to talk politics, the fields are our piazza'. Working groups were more commonly composed of women of similar political views than otherwise. This may have arisen for different reasons among work-exchange groups and wage-labour groups. The women in work-exchange groups are often kin or close friends. Often the lines of kinship and friendship go together with similar views. The stable wage-labour groups may have been nearly all communists simply because *braccianti* tend to vote communist. There may also have been a deliberate policy designed to ensure solidarity vis-à-vis the employers. In one long-standing group there was a single staunch Dc woman, Maria. Her group argued constantly about politics, but also showed no inclination to exclude her. She, as the wife of a Pci activist, is used to political dispute. She also helped out in her daughter and son-in-law's bar, taking every opportunity to enter into political discourse with customers. Women who worked in shops and bars were often extremely forthright about their political views. A few, however, felt that they ought not to express partisan views in front of their customers, and one Dc butcher was, according to his wife, constantly upbraiding her for talking politics (she was a communist) in the shop.

I have alluded in the course of this discussion to two 'mixed marriages'. The Dc butcher who tried to restrain his Pci wife was an uncommon case. In most mixed marriages the husbands were Pci and the wives Dc. I was unable to discover how many such marriages there were, but in those that I knew the women were not overshadowed by their husbands. Nor was it my impression that these marriages had special problems. Young men who were courting girls of a different party were always quite sure that they would win them over, but my impression was that this did not always happen. People whom I questioned about the political allegiance of their children assured me that if their children joined another party it would not divide the family, as long as their ideas were arrived at sincerely and in a considered way.

Even if conflicts between party and personal loyalties had been severe in the past, they are no longer very pronounced. This may be because the old animosities have faded and today the lines of friendship are more likely to correspond with those of political allegiance. In part too there is no conflict because opposing views can be accommodated within the norms of everyday social encounters. When political argument is relished, it rarely brings the protagonists to blows.

However, amongst young activists of the Pci, the lines of confrontation are sharply drawn. During a day out on a mountain walk, a group of young communists, which included new recruits and old hands, played a number of games. Some of them were games of forfeits — excuses for kissing, slaps and marriage proposals. Others were about political commitment.

In one of these, *'Tizio'* (any player) was sent out of earshot while the others each suggested an adjective to describe *'Tizio'*s' defects. In the second round they thought up words of praise. When *'Tizio'* returned the list of adjectives was read out to him and he had to guess who had proposed each one. Even the criticisms were taken in a good spirit, but what gave most pleasure was to be called by Pino Venditti, the leader, *coerente* (consistent) or *preparato* (well prepared). Both words have a particular force for communists. They denoted that *'Tizio'* (or *'Tizia'*) was accepted by the group as a worthy political ally.

In a second game people were being tested for their *coerenza* in selecting friends. *Tizio* and *Caio* were friends. *Tizio* went out of earshot whilst the others asked *Caio* about his views on friendship. When *Tizio* returned he was asked the same questions. Their answers were compared, ostensibly to see if the two were compatible as friends. However, the questions articulated very clearly the norms of this group. For example, 'Could you have a friend who is a Christian Democrat?', 'or a fascist?', 'Do friends need to be equally committed and involved politically?'. After the game, discussion turned to *Tizio*'s girl-friend, who was a member of Don Mario's group. The others asked him how they got on politically. They pointed out that if he was going to go on being an activist, he would need a girl-friend who supported him, not one who disagreed and would try to stop him. *Tizio* assured everyone that she was 'slowly coming over to our ideas'.

The priests and politics

Luchesi condemn the *trasaccani* for their *soggezione* subordination) to Don Pasquale, the parish priest. Communists, of course, heartily disapprove of the intrusion of the Vatican and of local priests in politics. *Luchesi* − including churchgoers and Christian Democrats − unite in criticising Don Nicola, their parish priest, when he delivers a political sermon. He does this only very rarely, when it is forced on him by a papal directive.

Whilst I was in Luco he spoke only once at Mass on a 'political' issue − that of divorce. The occasion for this sermon was a First Communion service. Don Nicola expressed the hope that those in the congregation would help to ensure that the misery of broken homes would never be inflicted on the little children gathered before him. As he said this the congregation gasped, and murmurs drowned the next minute of his sermon. Afterwards knots of people in the piazza discussed this unwarranted intrusion of politics into a service of particular significance for the young. Some communists suggested that Don Nicola had deliberately delayed the First Communions to the Sunday just before the Referendum on Divorce, in order to make the maximum impact. Many parents objected vociferously to the nuns at the Catholic crèche giving the children notes to bring home couched in similar terms to those of Don

Nicola's sermon. These objections were made by practising Catholics and Christian Democrats as well as the more regular opponents of the Church.

Don Nicola is not a locally born man. He is reported to be rich, but uses neither his money nor his influence as parish priest for political purposes. He has been in the village for thirty years or more. In the early 'fifties he refused to marry or baptise the children of the most militant Pci activists (most of whom were quite happy with this decision. Apparently they were compelled by family pressure to ask for such weddings and baptisms when they themselves wanted civil nuptials and no baptisms). This policy did not last very long, and though he was criticised (chiefly for his avarice) Don Nicola kept out of party politics.

The parish assistant, Don Mario, came from San Benedetto. He was an extraordinarily energetic man of thirty. One of eight children, he always went home once a week to his family, and he helped them at harvest. He taught religion in both primary and middle schools and devoted a lot of time to his choir group. He was studying medicine in order to become a medical missionary, and already had two degrees in theology and philosophy. He was intelligent and well read, and held fairly 'progressive' views, which were reflected in his clothing: black or grey polo-neck, leather jacket and no dog-collar or soutane. Young communists such as Pino Venditti felt that if only they could talk to him for long enough, he would become a 'Marxist priest'. Don Mario, however, was at pains to avoid any encounter, although he always expressed great interest in 'an exchange of ideas'. He had, after three years in the village, won wide respect. He made it a practice to visit and talk to any family about to celebrate a wedding, baptism or First Communion. Communists reported that he never tried to talk politics, or put any pressure on them concerning the 'incompatibility' of their politics and their faith. Both priests thus appear to have largely respected the 'ethos' of Luco, in maintaining the separation of religion and politics.

Communism and Catholicism

The people who are known by the generic term 'communist' in Luco can be divided into three groups: the activists, the members and the voters. In 1975 there were 1539 Pci voters in the regional election and the party claimed 669 members. Only the inner core of activists and a few old members who are well read in Marxism can be described as atheists. Amongst ordinary members and voters their Catholic faith and political ideology co-existed in varying degrees of intensity.

Very few communists, either voters or members, were regular attenders in church. Most were anti-clerical, and would declare that their faith was a personal matter. They could not, they said, see any reason for the mediation of a priest. Such people would attend weddings, baptisms, First Communions and funerals, and try to remember to go to Mass on at least one of the obligatory festivals. Only the few who were convinced materialists would go so far as to refuse to darken the doors of the church. Rigid materialist interpretations of communist ideology were not proselytised. It is my impression that this is in line with standard Pci practice in Italy. In general the Church is subjected to severe criticism, but the faith is immune from attack. In Luco, as elsewhere, the advent of the 'Catholics for Socialism' movement was welcomed as a possible ally against Christian Democracy.

The *'Mentalità Luchese'*

Luco, or 'little Moscow' as it is locally known, has the reputation of being 'communist', militant and modern. Although this is true in comparison with a village like Trasacco, Luco, as the *luchesi* frequently point out, is not at all a 'commune' in the socialist sense. To be sure, there are two seed-potato cooperatives, the Bianchi brothers have pooled their land, and machinery is often owned in partnership by two or more men who are not necessarily kinsmen. Cooperation on any large scale, however, is completely absent. *Luchesi* regard this as regrettable, but observe candidly that they are *'troppo egoisti'* to cooperate. Primary responsibilities are to the family. The financial risks that they fear would be necessary are too great for them to pool land or run a cattle stall collectively, although both ideas have been mooted and discussed several times.

Where *trasaccani* and *luchesi* differ radically, however, is in their attitudes to land, to work in general, and manual work in particular, and to what is morally correct political behaviour. In addition, *luchesi* make a link between political beliefs and personal behaviour which is morally opposed to the average *trasaccano*'s sense of political obligation to kinsmen and those who have rendered him *favori*.

As was mentioned before, *luchesi* are busy buying land as fast as it comes on the market. Very few assignees, even those with only one hectare, have relinquished their holdings. By 1965 the number of *recognised* assignees had risen by 7 per cent to 992. In addition, many original assignees have acquired more land to increase their holdings, which now extend over 28 per cent of the whole basin, making Luco the *comune* with the largest single interest in Fucino.

Farmers are very proud of their holdings. Although some are reluctant to reveal just how much land they have, and will evade direct questions on the subject, they enjoy taking visitors to look at their fields and admire their crops. They discuss at length the merits of different varieties of potato, single-germ beet seed, types of fertiliser and how to eradicate pests. This is

very different from the attitude of *trasaccani* and that of Southerners generally. The Ente officials regard *luchesi* as good husbandmen and usually ask
farmers amongst them to undertake experiments.

Commonly the whole family is involved in the cultivation of its land.
Wives usually organise the tasks which are done by women: they recruit any
paid labour, and arrange work exchanges with relatives, neighbours and
friends. Children are expected to help after school and in the holidays, and
even students studying for the prestigious professions are not excused from
lending a hand. This contrasts strongly with Trasacco, where students are
prevented from helping because they are symbols of family prestige. *Luchesi*
families try to educate their children to the limits of their financial resources
and the capacity of the child, but they tend to be very sceptical about
employment opportunities outside, and therefore encourage children to be
capable of farming. In each farming family one child at least is singled out as
heir to the land. He is often self-selecting, being the son with least academic
potential. One boy, however, who wanted to farm was exceptionally bright,
and was going to study agricultural economics in the North before taking over
the running of the farm.

The decisions of returned migrants to Luco are also rather different from
those of *trasaccani*. A number of men in Luco had returned in the last five or
ten years from distant countries like Australia and Latin America. Some of
these had opened bars in both Luco and Avezzano. A few had, however,
managed to buy land in Fucino by using the name of existing assignees and
making arrangements by private treaty. They were working the land themselves, and none of them had yet spent money on new housing.

Of course, prestige is attached to the professions in Luco, especially to
medicine. Of those who were studying, however, half were girls on teaching
courses. Of the boys, 20 out of 125 were doing engineering (none in
Trasacco). There was no evidence of the typically Southern great divide (see
above, p. 43), neither in parents' aspirations nor in the ambitions of children
themselves. Middle-school children in both villages were asked what they considered to be the best occupation for men. Roughly similar proportions gave
high status to teachers, doctors, architects and engineers. However, *trasaccani*
children held state functionaries (23.8 per cent compared with 18.2 per cent
in Luco) in high regard, as also spectacular pursuits such as pop-singing and
football-playing (32.4 per cent to 20.4 per cent). More children in Luco
placed farmers (10.7 per cent to 5.0 per cent) and skilled manual workers
(22.2 per cent to 11.3 per cent) at the top of their occupational hierarchy.
Furthermore, Luco's farmers and factory workers have sufficient sense of
their own dignity to be able to deride office workers as being lazy and parasitic. One of the components which contributes to the formation of a man
who is worthy of respect is 'one who has something to show for his life –

who has increased his patrimony by hard work'. This was said by a man thinking about the kind of person with whom he would be willing to form a cooperative. The theme of increasing one's capital by hard (manual) work was a constant one in discussions of a man's worth.

Another component of worth or respect was *coerenza*, a concept touched on earlier (see above, pp. 128 and 152). Men or women who are *coerenti* conduct their lives in accordance with their beliefs, whether political or religious. An oft-cited example was that of Loreto 'Zoccolante', the trainer of the football team. He carried his socialist beliefs into the context of his work by charging low prices, and into football by teaching all the small boys who wanted to come. His training included sportsmanship and comradeliness as well as technique. He had brought up three sons who were regarded as fine examples of *luchesi* youth: generous and thoughtful for others.

If the reputation for *coerenza* is the most valued quality in Luco, that of *ruffianismo*, its obverse, is the most despised. As we have seen, it is most commonly associated with those who have changed their political allegiance. Once a man is designated a *ruffiano*, it is said that he carries the reputation of being inconsistent, disloyal and untrustworthy, for the rest of his life.

It is quite impossible for a *ruffiano* to make any headway in public life, I was told (see the case of Angelo Bianchi, who resigned from a Pci administration but was unable to succeed in the Dc, p. 127). The vital estimation of *coerenza* is achieved by consistent behaviour in political and social relations and through effort in one's occupation. Both socialism and Catholicism (see references to Guizzardi, pp. 72–3) are seen, in different ways, to enjoin hard work on their adherents. A *luchese* is not tested against his marital record, as is common elsewhere (see Davis, 1969a). Out of five mayors of Luco since the war, one, 'Sindacone', was a bachelor, and another, Santirocco, lived with a married woman during his ten years in office (and until they were able to marry in 1973 when divorce became possible). Nor is wealth regarded as a necessary condition for proving oneself capable of public responsibility. An obvious example is that of Ciangoli, mayor from 1946 to 1951, who was so poor that the party had to find him a job to enable him to carry out his mayoral functions. None of Luco's mayors have had more than an average amount of land or income.

It is not wealth, but the way people handle their money that is admired in Luco. *Luchesi*, it is said, do not put the money that they make in the bank, but invest it: 'They have worked hard for it, and then they make sure it works hard for them', as one woman graphically put it. *Luchesi* contrast themselves favourably with *trasaccani* on this score. In Trasacco, they say, people have sold their land to build ostentatious houses. What they do not realise is that 'la terra fa le case, ma le case non fanno la terra' (land produces houses, but houses do not produce land). A sensible man therefore accumulates as much land as he can manage on his own, or he gets a job and works hard for more money. He does not build a new house but renovates his old one so that it is clean and has a decent kitchen and bathroom. Ideally, when his children are grown and contribute to the family income he starts to think about building so that by the time the first son gets married and needs a house, the family have built a new house and can give an apartment in it, or the old house, to the married couple.

Housing statistics suggest that *luchesi* have followed their precept about land and houses, while *trasaccani* have not. In 1971, 54 per cent of the occupied houses in Trasacco had been built since the war, half of them in the period immediately following the land reform (1950–60). The other half had been built since 1960. In Luco only 12 per cent of the housing has been built since the war. Furthermore, although Luco's housing stock is generally older than Trasacco's (51.6 per cent of houses in Luco were built before 1919; only 35.3 per cent of houses in Trasacco are so old [Census 1971, ISTAT]), it is only since 1971 that new houses have begun to be constructed on any large scale in Luco. Most *luchesi* who had new houses had thus waited twenty years to consolidate the gains of the land reform before embarking on the expenditure of house building (houses cost between £10 000 and £15 000 in 1975). Most new houses had been built by farmers. In a few cases factory and building workers had managed to build, but only by doing a good deal of the construction themselves. These men and women who worked on their own houses were held up as fine examples of the *mentalità luchese*.

Finally, there is an attribute which only communists aspire to, but to which even Christian Democrats concede a grudging respect: that of being *politicamente preparato*. This is a complex idea and cannot be directly rendered into English. The most *preparato* of *luchesi* is an old man, a *contadino*, Tommaso Petricca. He is over sixty and farms one hectare of land in Fucino and two on flat land *fuori-Fucino*. He has a small, unmodernised house lacking even hot water. He is married, with four grown children. Petricca went to school for only two years, but attended the Luco night school and a college for party organisers. He is widely read in Marx, Lenin and Gramsci. He takes both *L'Unità* and the party's intellectual weekly, *La Rinascita*. From 1946 to 1954 (when it was disbanded as a separate organisation in the Marsica) he headed the Federbraccianti. In 1974 he was included in the five-man emergency executive of the Luco Pci *sezione*, which was designed to rebuild its morale and organisational strength.

Petricca is esteemed within the party as a model of a good socialist, generous, warm, loyal and willing to give up both time and money to the party. Above all, in Pci circles he is held in high regard for his ability to analyse political situations and make clear judgements based on the classic texts, modified by his own experience. He is *un compagno molto preparato* (a well-prepared comrade).

Both inside and outside the party, Petricca is seen as embodying the *mentalità luchese*: politically reliable, hard working, frugal and *coerente*. At his funeral, a civic one no doubt, where the coffin will be draped with a red flag, there will be many mourners who do not share his politics, but admire him as a fine *luchese*.

It is not only Petricca himself, but also his family who command respect. His wife was a communist before they met and has supported his personal and financial contribution to the party. The son has emigrated to Germany where he is a leading immigrant trade unionist. Two of the daughters are married to Alfasud shop-stewards in Naples. They all return regularly to visit their parents and form a family group, if they can, on the May Day parade. The youngest daughter emigrated and worked with her husband in Germany; on their return, he found a job as an electrician and they set about building their own house. It took them two years, working in the evenings and at weekends. She dug foundations, laid bricks, mixed mortar, in short, everything which her husband did. People both admired and were intrigued by her industry in this particular enterprise, which was a new departure for a *luchese* woman.

The notion that a woman could work as hard as that was by no means uncommon. Women expect and appear to be willing to work every bit as hard as their husbands to ensure the security and well-being of the family. This is accompanied by greater participation of women in social occasions and, in particular, in political discussion.

In a single utterance, one *luchese*, Luigi, summed up the characteristics of open political partisanship, itself an essential feature of the *mentalità luchese*. Luigi came to call on a family that I was visiting in Trasacco. He already knew me from Luco, and, after greeting the family, he said to me:

I am a communist. Do you know what he [the father, a *bracciante*] is? He's probably one too, though you'd never guess it. In Luco we are proud of what we are. In Trasacco, no. They sit quiet because they are afraid of the doctor and the priest. We are not. In Luco we are all equal and no one defers to anyone. There are people in Luco who have suffered for their convictions. People who exchange their vote for a personal *favore*? We don't think that's right. If someone does me a material *favore*, I am prepared to repay it, but only in material ways. Let us be clear, one's heart is not for sale.

This young man was just an ordinary voter for the Pci. The sentiments he expressed are not at all unusual in Luco and could equally well have been stated by a Christian Democrat.

The three cardinal points Luigi touched on are, firstly, 'we are proud of what we are', by which he meant, 'which political party we support'; whereas *trasaccani* 'sit quiet': they try to keep their political views, if they have any, to themselves. Secondly, he said that 'material *favori*' must be repaid in 'material terms', and not by selling one's vote. Finally, whilst in Trasacco 'they are afraid of the doctor and the priest', in Luco 'we are all equal, no one defers to anyone'. In Luco such beliefs are dominant in interpreting and passing moral judgement on the political, economic and social order.

The 'political village'

Two interwoven themes have been taken up in this chapter. The first is that Luco is an 'open' place, both socially and politically; a place with a strong sense of egalitarianism. *Luchesi* believe that they can participate in the political discussions which inform the policy decisions governing the running of their *comune*. When this right is threatened by the actions of the politically ambitious, they have been seen to close ranks in reasserting 'open partisanship' and to reinstate community control. As a concomitant of this, the qualities of hard work, frugality, *coerenza*, political loyalty and integrity, which constitute the *mentalità luchese*, are seen as being of benefit to the *community* as well as to the individual.

Luco, like Trasacco, is fundamentally an agricultural *comune*: working the land is directly and indirectly the main source of subsistence. It is in their attitudes both to land and labour and to the political process, that the *luchesi* and *trasaccani* most clearly illustrate their different values. Rather than disdaining the land, the *luchesi* grasp the opportunities it offers with both hands. They are not alienated from the object of their labour as the *trasaccani* are, but are proud of their farms and enjoy their work. This commitment to the land is evidenced by the level of investment and the dedication of the farmers. As a lawyer from Milan (who knew both villages well) put it: 'The *luchesi* farm with their brains, the *trasaccani* send their brains to university'.

Unlike the *trasaccani*, the *luchesi* farmers reinvest their surplus product, either back into agriculture or into other sectors. This is commonly perceived, not just by farmers, as being both an individual and a communitarian activity: it creates work for others in the community as well as increasing the individual patrimony.

The validation of farmwork in Luco is paralleled by a respect for productive labour of any kind and scorn for the man or woman who does nothing. Whereas in Trasacco the ability to consume leisure in a conspicuous manner is sought after and attracts a measure of esteem, in Luco the rich layabout is as despised as the poor good-for-nothing. Neither can rise to positions of influence in Luco.

When it comes to decision making for the community as a whole, discussion of policy is wide-ranging, and involves many people. Although not

159

everybody does so, there is a sense that anyone who wishes can have his views taken into account in the survey of opinion which guides the policy-makers.

What gives a person's opinion weight in Luco is not his occupation nor his wealth nor the 'votes he can command'. *Luchesi* are judged by the different criteria of *coerenza*, frugality and hard work. It is by these qualities that *luchesi* characterise themselves and differentiate themselves from others.

These valued qualities do not add up to 'socialism', but their congruity with socialism is obvious. *Luchesi* are not, as is frequently stated, 'all communists here', in any total sense. Many of them are not even communist voters, and of those who are few have a real grasp of what being a 'communist' might entail. What *they* mean when they say they are communists, I think, encompasses a number of related ideas. Firstly, they value qualities which are within everyone's grasp, and so they think of themselves as in some sense equal. Secondly, they feel 'equal' because they avoid relations of deference and dominance in their social and working lives. Thirdly, they believe that *luchesi* do not succeed individually at the expense of others. Finally, they feel that their politics are 'open' politics. They mean this in two senses, that people's political sympathies are known, and that 'politics' is open to all.

These ideas take many forms, are expressed in many ways and are often inconsistent with observed practice. The central idea, however, that Luco is a politically open and community-minded village, is incontestable.

PART IV

11 Conclusion

The limits to patron–clientelism

Studies of Southern Italy are dominated by discussions of clientelism, a form which has also been discovered and analysed in the context of other developing countries. Some writers have seen clientelism (or 'patron–clientage') as an 'integrative' mechanism, facilitating the process of modernisation. As countries develop, or modernise, it is argued, their central institutions penetrate the peripheries which, for topographical and historical reasons, have remained relatively isolated. Patron–clientelism serves to link peripheral areas and peoples into the central institutions. This is the approach of Boissevain (1966), Powell (1970), Weingrod (1968 and 1974) and Wolf (1966). They use words like 'mediator', 'broker' and 'middleman' rather than 'patron', to distinguish the modern form from the traditional patron–clientelism of which it is a development. The 'traditional' form is seen as, in essence, a relation between peasants and their landlords. Through the landlord/patron the peasant gained access to land, protection and what he needed from the 'outside world'. In exchange the landlord gained labour and political support. The change from the traditional to the modern form occurs when the national political system penetrates the periphery and party politicians replace the landlords in providing the link between the peasant and the 'outside world' (cf. Weingrod, 1968; Silverman, 1967). Thus 'modern' clientelism is seen as a form which promotes development, and which is also a concomitant of it.

Challenging this approach, several writers take a different view. Lemarchand and Legge (1972) and Zuckerman (1974), for example, argue that patron–clientelism does not promote modernisation but acts as a brake on development towards the modern forms of representative democracy, and the rational distribution of goods and services. If patron–clientelism continues to predominate, they argue, its particularist and personalistic values continue to take precedence over universalistic ones. In order to function properly, 'modern' institutions require that criteria of merit are used in the selection of personnel and the distribution of resources. In a 'modern' democracy, it is implied, every citizen is able to influence the government through the ballot box. Neither of these processes can begin to be effective if access to jobs, resources and the government is mediated through 'patrons', 'brokers' and 'middlemen'.

Whether patron–clientelism promotes or inhibits modernisation is one point of contention between students of the subject. Another is whether some of the characteristics of patron–clientelism, such as 'reciprocity' or 'emotional affect' crucially distinguish it from a naked power relation or alternatively mystify and disguise the power which derives from its being a relationship of class domination.

Patron–clientelism in traditional societies is very often empirically associated with affective ties such as co-godparenthood and with linguistic elisions like *padre–padrone*: father–boss/patron. These forms have dominated the analyses of some researchers, even when, as in the first of the following examples, they are looking at 'modernising polities'. Lemarchand and Legge argue that patron–clientelism is characterised 'above all' by affectivity (1972). Pitt-Rivers makes the relationship analogous to friendship, albeit, he admits, 'lopsided' (1954: 40). Kenny takes the view that its origins lie in the 'desire of the disadvantaged to seek out primary personal relationships' (1961).

There are, however, intimations, even in this literature, that 'affect' and 'reciprocity' are 'illusions' which serve to conceal from the client its real basis. Wolf, for example, writing generally about patron–clientelism, observes that 'in the political process . . . the element of power emerges which is otherwise masked by reciprocities' (Wolf, 1966). However, even Wolf shows that he is using the language of the 'mask' and has let slip his grasp on the underlying structure, when he argues that clients have a 'leverage' because they can threaten to withdraw support and give it to a competing patron.

Closer examination reveals this notion of 'leverage' as yet another illusion. Clients do not have a 'real' choice (that of opting out of clientelist relations) but a choice between one patron and another. Even then their 'leverage' is weak, because clients are many and patrons who can offer them anything are few. A client has to compete for the attention of a patron. He weakens rather than strengthens his position by leaving one patron for another. As a 'new' client, he has to join the end of a queue of supplicants. He has no 'leverage' on the new patron unless he has something more than the others to offer him. A patron distributes rewards, not to the most needy, but to those who can do most for him.

More importantly, however, the client's leverage is weak because the 'rewards' are often the very essentials of subsistence[1] — jobs, access to land,

---

1 Words such as 'rewards' and 'tokens' which are sometimes used in this type of analysis, serve also to conceal from the reader the real content of what is being exchanged.

credit, medical treatment, legal assistance — as well as those which enhance the quality of life — education, connections to electricity and water supplies, 'holidays for deprived children'. Traditional patrons exercised control over who got what, and so do modern ones, even when they are called 'middlemen', 'brokers' or 'mediators', words which imply a facilitating function rather than a controlling one. Traditional patrons, by owning the only productive resource, controlled access to it. Modern patrons exercise control by their positions in the professions and institutions like banks and government departments, and through their political links with employers and government servants. In other words, patron—clientelism is always a relation between those who have and those who do not; between those with power and those without it.

In all the analyses of patron—clientelism so far discussed, both the language which many authors use ('lopsided friendship', 'affect', 'tokens', 'rewards', 'mediators', 'brokers', etc.) and the functionalism which informs them ('integrative mechanism', 'closing gaps', etc.) suggest that they have explored the empirical forms, but have not recognised that underlying its forms it is: 'a relationship between different and opposed classes ... [and] works, in functional terms, for the maintenance of the status quo' (Li Causi, 1975).

I have been considering in this discussion both 'traditional' and 'modern' patrons. In Trasacco patron—clientelism is of the 'modern' type and has many similarities with the forms described elsewhere. The client has a sense of moral obligation to repay *favori* with his political support. He perceives this as a reciprocal exchange. The relationship between patrons and clients is sometimes cemented with the tie of *comparaggio*: a form which is culturally freighted with norms of mutual obligation. *Trasaccani* commonly attempt to get *favori* by promising to vote and recruit support for one or other of the political leaders. The most important politicians exercise control over employment opportunities. In these situations, where employment or other resources are being sought, bureaucratic norms are not operating.

However, though largely absent, the norms of universalism, rationality and anonymity are not always entirely absent, neither in modernising societies in general, as Lemarchand and Legge point out, nor in the specific case we are dealing with here.

There is the growing differentiation of the social, economic and political spheres, the expansion of bureaucratic structures, the emphasis on welfare values and secularisation — all reflective of a response to social mobilisation. [But] in its actual operation the system constantly tends to swing back into the clientelistic mould of its predecessor. The result is a hybrid situation in which clientelism resuscitates itself in the traditionalistic interstices of modernising polities. (Lemarchand & Legge, 1972.)

Indeed some areas that affect the lives of *trasaccani* have been freed from

Conclusion

clientelist control. Pensions do eventually reach those entitled to them without the intervention of 'mediators', even though this may happen after long and apparently unwarranted delays. Factory managements which are determined to resist the efforts of local patrons to influence who is employed and promoted, or which are forced to do so by militant trade unions, do pursue policies based on 'merit'. This could be described as 'uneven development'. In Lemarchand and Legge's analysis, however, its cause has surely become confused in the complexity of their language: what kind of a 'thing' is clientelism, for example, that it can 'resuscitate itself'?

The reification lends to the process a specious air of neutrality and inevitability. Nor does evidence from Luco and Trasacco support their view that clientelism continues or revives because of 'a lag in social change at the mass level'. To be sure, the 'masses' play a part in the relation, but at least two other factors are involved.

Barnes and Sani are aware of one of these, namely, the actions of politicians. They argue that the unevenness of change in the political sector of Southern Italy depends on the 'practices of elite politics . . . especially when these practices are institutionalised in roles and processes dominated by successful politicians' (Barnes & Sani, 1974). Far from mass politics 'lagging behind', Barnes and Sani suggest, they are 'probably ahead of elites' in abandoning older practices (i.e. clientelism). It is the elites who maintain or even bring back clientelistic forms of economic and political participation 'in the interstices' when circumstances allow it 'because they have little to gain from taking the lead in changing the system' (Barnes & Sani, 1974).

Barnes and Sani make their point in circumspect fashion. From the Abruzzo evidence I would argue that elites *only* gain from maintaining the system as it is. Indeed, their status, power and often their affluence crucially depend on it.

The system benefits both the professional elite and the career politician. If clientelism is endemic in a system, reaching to the highest levels of government, bureaucrats and professionals can become very rich and powerful by being elected to political office. Trasacco's functionaries, doctors and priests had much more power in the local community than Luco's doctors and priests (and were also feared as those in Luco were not) who neither had nor sought party-political backing. Conversely, a professional or bureaucratic niche is almost a prerequisite for pursuing a career as a clientelist politician, for it enables one to grant and withhold goods and services. Dr Ciofani's position as medical practitioner certainly played a part (but only one part − a considerable amount of his power came from his political contacts and other roles in the community) in his obtaining votes from people who expected to need his professional care and *raccomandazioni*. Don Pasquale could use the

164

religious needs of his parishioners (for the sacraments, for example) and benefits controlled by the clergy (such as church-financed holidays for children) as a lever to extract votes for the Dc. Mignini became a powerful figure only after his appointment to the Employment Office. In Luco Biagino Venditti tried to recruit support by using his seat on the Control Commission of the Industrial Nucleus and his job in the Forestry Corps.

However, the practices and desires of 'political elites' cannot alone create clientelism. Clientelism can only exist under certain material conditions: that 'benefits', particularly employment, are scarce and can be controlled by individuals or elite groups. Clientelism cannot flourish where resources are abundant and employers are chasing workers. Local patrons therefore do not obstruct the creation of employment, for without any jobs they would have nothing new to distribute. They do need, however, to control what employment does exist. Thus it is scarcity, coupled with control, that provides the material basis of clientelism. It is also vital that the belief be maintained that factory managers and bureaucrats cannot be approached directly, but have to be reached by means of influential contacts. Therefore it is not only material control that is needed, but control over information.

If we return to the assertion that clientelism is an 'integrative mechanism', I would argue that far from performing the function of *closing* the 'gaps' between the local community and the 'wider society' as Wolf (1966), Silverman (1967) and others have all argued, patrons need to make sure that they alone pass across the 'gap' and can prevent clients from making direct contact with employers and bureaucrats. In Trasacco there were many resources which were actually controlled by local patrons, like jobs for women in the factories, positions in the hospital in Avezzano, benefits controlled by the Church. Even though not all benefits are controlled by them, the belief is widespread that little can be achieved without at least the *raccomandazioni* and, more potently, the direct intervention of the powerful.

All this has profound repercussions on the political process. By fostering divisions between clients, it inhibits the formation of alliances or class-based organisations, for clients are in constant competition with each other for the attention of the 'patrons' and for what resources are available. As we saw in Trasacco, even when such alliances are formed and mass action occurs to take control of resources for the deprived, as happened during the *Lotta del Fucino*, it is still possible for political elites to reinstate clientelistic processes. The comparison between Luco and Trasacco, however, demonstrates that this can only occur under certain conditions. These are: if elites have sufficiently large state resources to distribute, if the population is needy and if left-wing parties lack the organisational strength in the locality to counter the fears of individuals that they will be left out.

Conclusion

Avant'il Popolo!

Luco is a close neighbour of Trasacco, which could be described as a 'classically' clientelist village. It occupies the same ecological niche and is, like Trasacco, part of a region dominated by clientelist forms. The case of Luco clearly suggests that clientelism is a less pervasive and enduring phenomenon than is often suggested. There are, however, some objections which might be raised to the interpretation that Luco is 'really' different. It might be argued that what *luchesi* say about *trasaccani* and the apparent differences in their political processes are simply a variant on the well-known theme of *campanilismo* (parochialism).

After a period of fieldwork in Luco, and looking for a known 'clientelist' village, I almost rejected Trasacco for comparative study, so convinced was I by the arguments of colleagues that *campanilismo* would explain the *luchesi*'s description of Trasacco as a stronghold of the abhorred clientelism. Any doubts as to the existence of clientelism in Trasacco were completely dispelled in a period of living there. On my return to Luco, I was determined to unearth the clientelism that I was now sure lurked under the cover of hostility to it. Instead I witnessed the blows dealt to the political ambitions of Biagino Venditti, who had violated the ethics of the *mentalità luchese*.

The differences between Luco and Trasacco were thus proven to exist, not only as expressions at the level of values, but at the level of action. That it is not action *per se*, but collective action that distinguishes the two villages was evidenced by two events which also followed hard on my return to Luco. One was a mass demonstration by *luchesi* in protest at the Ente Fucino's dilatory behaviour over the disruption of Luco's water supply. The other was the occupation of Ente Fucino offices by *luchesi* farmers in support of their demand to be paid for potatoes consigned to the Ente the previous winter.

The farmers of Luco took collective action. Others did not, although they were approached to join in. It is all the more surprising that Luco's farmers did so since they are the wealthiest in Fucino and have established lines of credit. They were, therefore, in a stronger position to await payment than other Fucino farmers. Demonstrations in support of collective demands are common in Italy and their occurrence is frequently reported in the press and on TV. It cannot be argued therefore that other Fucino farmers were either less needy or less conscious of the possibility (or indeed the efficacy) of demonstrating. It was left to the farmers of Luco to demonstrate to protect their interests and, in the process, those of the other farmers. The farmers of other *comuni* stood about saying 'When are those communists in Luco going to do something about it?'. They have come to expect *luchesi* to take action in such matters.

It was not surprising that the farmers of Luco took the lead on this

166

occasion; collective action has a long history in Luco. Since the draining of the lake a hundred years ago, each generation of *luchesi* has witnessed resistance when livelihood or living conditions were threatened. It it this history of collective action which I wish to stress in analysing the present political process in Luco.

In 1865, when all the other *comuni* were urging Torlonia to open the sluices of the new tunnel, *luchesi* stood alone in resisting the drainage work which was to deprive many of them of an important part of their livelihood. This was followed by the struggle for a water supply. Between 1866 and 1870 women had to carry water long distances when, with the lowering of the water table, their springs dried up. In both cases the person responsible was clearly identifiable as 'Torlonia'. When *mezzadri* were introduced in 1886 they were given land at the expense of *luchesi*. Again it was 'Torlonia' who did this. From 1903 onwards, when the Luco Peasant League fought for direct tenancies, their aim was to eliminate intermediate tenants, but the demand was addressed to 'Torlonia'. The women's strike for higher wages in 1913 was also an attack on 'Torlonia's' interests in keeping wages on the Administration farm low. The women's resistance to grain requisition in 1915 was directed against a more diffuse target, the government. However, 'Torlonia' was once again their adversary throughout the 'twenties and 'thirties. They continued to resist paying rent in beet, and they went on strike each time the rent was raised.

Each collective action became part of the shared history of *luchesi*. Each success reinforced the sense that changes could be made or resisted if enough people took part. With each failure more people came to perceive 'Torlonia' as responsible for their trials; he was no benevolent benefactor who had done the world a service by draining Lake Fucino, but a capitalist landowner determined to extract his profits regardless of the well-being of those who depended on him for their subsistence.

Although the figure of 'Torlonia' dominated the lives of all the people of Fucino, awareness of and reaction to *la miseria* of the Torlonia regime is not only chronicled in the archive of Luco, as it is not elsewhere, but also lives on in its oral traditions. There are a number of reasons which explain why this should be so.

Before the advent of 'Torlonia', the means of material existence had been more equally shared amongst the inhabitants than elsewhere. Unlike Trasacco, there were no big landowners living in the village, no one on whom they were dependent or to whom they had to defer in order to gain access to land or fishing. For generations their world had been wider than 'the idiocy of rural life', because the market for their fish was in Rome, giving them connections in all the intervening towns and in the metropolis itself. From 1854 onwards, as the largest single group employed in the tunnel construction, *luchesi* were drawn into a profoundly different set of economic relations, with engineers, overseers and with one another, as workers on a large-scale, capitalist enterprise. This proletarianisation continued in the employment of *luchesi* on the Administration farm and the sugar refinery, both, of course, owned by 'Torlonia'. Caught in these changing economic circumstances *luchesi* struggled together for material and collective goods — fish, water, fair wages and reasonable rents. In each case 'Torlonia' could be identified as their 'oppressor'. When threatened with their loss, *luchesi* took collective action.

The earliest of these struggles took place long before the advent of explicit socialist ideas in Italy, and certainly before socialism was heard of in the Marsica. The earliest forms of socialist organisations in Italy were the Peasant Leagues of the present-day 'red' rural areas of Tuscany and Emilia Romagna and the Camere del Lavoro of the Northern industrial cities. Ideas and organisation were disseminated to remoter areas of Italy by railway workers, itinerant labourers, returned emigrants and political militants. The Rome—Avezzano railway line was completed in 1888; Northern workers spent from 1897 to 1902 building the sugar refinery in company with local labourers. Emigrants returned from areas of the United States where anarchist and communist Italians were active. Finally, Trapanese, a socialist trade unionist from Orvieto, came to Fucino in 1895 and after some years founded the first Camera del Lavoro in Avezzano and the first Peasant League in Luco in 1903.

Trapanese probably chose Luco because it had, by this time, a reputation for unity and collective action. However, *luchesi* had so far reacted collectively without formal organisation, and they had no coherent set of ideas to inform and give continuity between struggles. The arrival of Trapanese brought together this 'proto-socialist' practice with the socialist ideology and organisation of the Peasant Leagues. Luco became and remained the stronghold of socialism in the Marsica.

Luco was the first *comune* in Fucino to elect a mayor who was a member of the Socialist Party, though it had had a mayor of socialist sympathies as early as 1914. This socialist administration lasted only three years before its replacement by a fascist *podestà*, a man from outside the village.

During the fascist period it was again Luco which provided the leadership for the protests in Fucino against rent rises, probably because only in Luco was there a core of communist leaders around whom resistance could coalesce. Communists could survive relatively unharmed during the repressive years of fascism and the German occupation because they were embedded in a community which supported them and did not betray them to the authorities. The martyrs of the fascist era were not rejected as fanatics: their tenacity was respected and their deaths were mourned by the whole village.

After the fall of fascism and the liberation from German occupation, unrest in the Fucino area increased, as it did elsewhere. Just as Luco had provided the focus for the development of Peasant Leagues in Fucino fifty years before, so it was the focus of the *Lotta del Fucino*. It could provide the support for the Pci and the leadership that was necessary for a successful initiative.

However, although this community solidarity in Luco was a significant factor in the *Lotta del Fucino*, it seems unlikely that post-war developments would have taken quite the form that they did, in the absence of links with the organisational structure, experience and ideology of the Pci. The leadership of the *Lotta del Fucino* came from Luco, but the strategy of the 'work-in', the arguments put forward against the Torlonia regime, the pressure for expropriation were worked out and refined in night schools, in the party College for Cadres, and at meetings with the trade unions, the Federazione and officials from the Central Committee in Avezzano.

Significant too for the eventual outcome of the *Lotta* was the fact that Fucino was only one locality amongst many where land occupations, coordinated and led by the Communist Party, were taking place. The widespread unrest severely stretched the forces of law and order and forced the government into an early capitulation to the peasant organisations.

People in all the Fucino *comuni* participated in the *Lotta*; some were members of the Pci, others supported the struggle without joining the party. Once the minister of agriculture had visited the area and hinted at the possibility of expropriation, the Coldiretti (Dc small farmers' organisation), capitalising on the mobilisation of the peasants, threw its weight behind the campaign and issued leaflets urging its members to continue the struggle. So although the *Lotta* was communist-led, it had broad cross-party support, particularly as a successful outcome became more likely.

In the first elections following the land reform, support for the Pci declined, due at least in part to the persuasive activities of Ente Fucino officials. The 1951 elections also took place at the height of the Cold War, and were accompanied by massive and compelling propaganda.

Even in Luco the communist vote declined from the 75 per cent of 1948, but it never fell sufficiently for the Left to lose control of the administration. One reason for this is that the Pci administration had always proved itself better at running the village than those of other *comuni*. But the steady vote for the Pci in Luco is not confined to the local level, so clearly it is more than a vote for efficient local government.

This section on Luco started with questions about hostility to clientelist politics and collective action and has evolved into questions about the stability of the Pci vote. This is no accident, for the two issues are connected.

The Pci has come, in Luco, to represent a bulwark against the type of politics which *luchesi* see all around them, and which they abhor. Clientelism represents for *luchesi* all that they got rid of when they ended the Torlonia era by 'throwing him out of Fucino': exploitation, *soggezione*, inequality and corruption.

Socialism and the *mentalità luchese*

The confrontation of the people of Luco with 'Torlonia' had had, even before 1919 when the first socialist administration was elected, a long history. In the compelling words of Wolf (who is making a general point), experience of the past

lives on in the present and continues to determine its shape and meaning. Everywhere this historical experience bears the stigmata of trauma and strife, of interference and rupture with the past, as well as the boon of continuity, of successful adaptation and adjustment – engrams of events not easily erased and often only latent in the cultural memory until some greater event serves to draw them forth again. (Wolf, 1969: 276.)[2]

Interference and rupture with the past *luchesi* had suffered more severely than others in Fucino: originally relatively independent cultivators and fishermen, they were forced into capitalist relations with 'Torlonia' as workers and tenants. This profound economic change affected the lives of many *luchesi* whose subsequent relations with 'Torlonia' were established as relatively immediate and direct. In other *comuni*, the change in the ownership and organisation of the means of production which was wrought by the drainage was mediated by the local gentry. Those who had been large landowners *fuori-Fucino*, and the landlords and employers of the inhabitants, became the *grandi affittuari* in Fucino, and continued to be their 'landlords'. The traditional paternalism of this relationship blurred the confrontation with 'Torlonia' and helps to explain why socialist organisations never put down such deep roots in other *comuni*.

In Luco socialist ideas met with a concrete reality that was easily interpreted in terms of those ideas. The experience of working in large numbers on the tunnel, in the factory and on the farm fitted closely with notions of monopoly capital and exploitation; similarly the compulsion to grow beet and the single source of banking credit. Differential rents were also clearly designed to 'divide and rule'. Socialism informed them that, in choosing collective action, not only was it the correct strategy for overcoming their *miseria*, but they were also morally in the right.

In such a situation socialist ideas make sense of the world for workers and

2 Although Wolf depicts very clearly the role of communist parties in his six case studies of peasant wars, and in five of these the superseding governments were communist in some form or other, he does not draw out in his conclusion the importance of the party in providing the organisational and ideological links without which no peasant uprising is likely to succeed.

tenants, and they also have certain advantages over the organising themes of the ideologies of elites. An interpretation of their trials in terms of the exigencies of capital and of themselves as an exploited class can remove from subordinate classes the sense of arbitrariness which they often feel at the changes and shifts in their fortunes. In addition, as Parkin points out, 'Attachment to the ideals of socialism can provide men with a sense of personal dignity and moral worth which is denied them by the dominant value system.' (Parkin, 1972: 97.) It is this last which is so striking about Luco. The dignity of work is an almost tangible value there. Whilst the idea is part of socialist ideology, it probably pre-dates socialism in Luco, and is certainly not confined to communists today. The dialectic of historical experience and the ideas which have illuminated that experience have made of Luco a place apart, totally unlike its neighbours.

All the evidence suggests that clientelism is most unlikely to find a foothold there and that even 'personalism' plays little part in the political process. This is why I take issue with Tarrow, who has explained the electoral majority of the Pci in Luco as due to its being 'the birth place of the regional communist federation secretary [Santirocco]' (Tarrow, 1967: 194). Tarrow is not unaware of the importance of historical experience, as his book shows and as the following comment reveals: 'What you describe is typical of a comune where the Pci has been in power for thirty years.' (Tarrow: personal communication.)

This observation draws attention to important questions. To what extent is Luco a unique case? Are there other 'Lucos' in the South? Do we have an idea of Southern politics as predominantly clientelist only because all those *comuni* so far studied happen to have been 'patron—clientelist' places?

In order to emphasise the comparative nature of this study, the political processes of Luco and Trasacco have been relatively polarised and isolated from their national political environment. There is a general tendency among 'Italianists' to divide the country in two, associating 'open partisanship' with the Centre—North and clientelism with the South. However, the two forms co-exist everywhere. Which form is dominant will depend, I would argue, on the historical specificity of the locality or region. Vicenza (Rumor's constituency) is only one of the many known 'clientelist places' in the North (cf. Zuckerman, 1974). Logically, therefore, one would expect to find that Luco is not the only non-clientelist place in the South. Furthermore, the example of Lecce is evidence enough that other 'Lucos' (non-clientelist places) cannot be discovered by picking out *comuni* with Pci administrations, but only by further empirical research employing a similar methodology.

This research has demonstrated the value of an historical approach in uncovering local political processes. Along these lines, researchers should examine patterns of land tenure and the distribution of access to sources of subsistence, and how these have changed since the abolition of feudalism. Any radical changes should be given particular attention, to discover whether they were accompanied by social unrest and what part was played by the gentry. Voting patterns are important indicators: where there is a long history of a Pci majority, of socialist administration prior to fascism and of correspondence between the proportion of the vote given to the Pci at local, regional and national elections, we should expect to find other similarities with Luco. There might be a similar configuration of attitudes towards political allegiance, clientelist politicians, *coerenza*, employment strategies and manual work. Community solidarity might be expressed in terms of those values.

Afterword

Having examined clientelism in the field and thinking about it whilst writing it up, I wonder whether this research has any practical application in hastening its demise. It is a parasitic form which feeds on the fears of those subject to it. I use the words 'fears' and 'subject' in a considered way: just as clearly as the dignity of labour has an almost tangible quality in Luco, so does fear in Trasacco. For the patrons, fear among the clients is a major lever of their power.

Patron—clientage is rooted materially in the economic sphere and ideologically in the sphere of popular consciousness, and the two are mutually reinforcing. The most obvious, although an 'economistic', way to eliminate clientelism, would be to stimulate the Southern Italian economy and so provide full employment and a rising living standard for everyone. This would require radically different policies at the national level which are likely to be initiated only under a different government.

However, the Luco case has shown that even without abundant resources and full employment, clientelism can be resisted. Perhaps ways can be found to initiate forms of collectivism that will begin the process of changing popular consciousness. I have shown that where there is a history of common material interests being collectively pursued and defended, there is a tendency towards 'open partisanship' and resistance to clientelism.

It is here that a start can be made, for even within the existing limits of government policy there is support available for schemes which have the potential to accelerate the erosion of clientelism. The Cassa per il Mezzogiorno already has a fund for promoting cooperative enterprises. Agricultural and other forms of cooperation could provide the material basis that might secure both the subsistence needs and the collective interest that are necessary for breaking the hold of clientelist forms.

What I have described is not instant transformation but a process by which a particular consciousness is developed: a consciousness which is not amenable

Conclusion

to the institution of clientelist forms. The formation of cooperatives could
only mark the beginning of such a process. What will emerge from this process is not likely to take a 'socialist' or 'communist' form, but rather the
'proto-socialist, collective individualism' that characterises Luco.

Whether or not the cooperative initiative is generalised on any large scale
will depend entirely on the willingness of the government to tackle seriously
the problem of clientelism. The Christian Democrat Party, which dominates
the present government, has often stressed the desirability of change in its
own practice. This is unlikely to happen as long as the most powerful politicians in the party depend precisely on the maintenance of clientelist forms.

GLOSSARY OF CHARACTERS

L = resident in Luco
T = resident in Trasacco

L Amadoro, Francesco		mayor 1919–22
L	Rocco	leader, Pci, 1922–41
L	Lenin	son of Rocco, died 1932
L Angelucci, Piero		communist, died 1938
L	Scolastica	daughter of Piero
		Factory Council, CEME
L	Giuseppe	student, engineering
		Pci activist
L Bianchi, Silvio		
L	Velio	largest farmers in Fucino
L Ciangoli		*bracciante*, coop manager
		mayor 1946–51
T Ciofani, Dr		*medico condotto*
		leader of Natali faction
		provincial councillor 1970–5
T Courier, Teofilo		*bidello*, middle school
		trade unionist, Uil
		leader, Psdi *sezione*
T Dalla Montà, Dr		*medico condotto*
		candidate, Camera dei Deputati, 1958, Msi
T D'Amato, Aristotele		teacher, primary school
		secretary, Pci *sezione*
T	Beppina	sister of Aristotele
		mother of Michele Morisi
L De Amicis		*contadino*
		mayor 1944–6
T Del Boccio		mayor 1974–5
T Di Cola, Beppino		mayor 1946–50

174

Glossary of characters

L Di Giamberardino, Beppino		trade unionist, Alleanza Contadina
		deputy mayor, 1970–5
		activist, Psi
L Di Rosa		employment officer
L Don Mario		parish priest's assistant
L Don Nicola		parish priest
T Don Pasquale		parish priest
		leader of Gaspari faction
Gaspari		leader of Dorotei faction, Abruzzo
		member, Camera dei Deputati
T Ippoliti, Beppino		teacher, middle school
		secretary, Dc *sezione*
	Francesco	mayor, 1956–9
T Mignini		employment officer
		mayor 1970–5
T Morisi, Michele		nephew of Aristotele D'Amato
		graduate in economics and commerce
L Mosca, Angelo		*contadino*
		Pci *accessore* 1965–
Natali		leader of *Fanfaniani* faction, Abruzzo
		member, Camera dei Deputati
L Organtini, Pietro		merchant, building materials
L	Franco	bank manager, Banca del Fucino, Luco
L	Cesare	registrar, Law Courts, Avezzano
		councillor, 'Independent' 1970–5
L Petricca, Tommaso		*contadino*
		leader, Federbraccianti 1946–54
T Quaglieri, Dr		resident in Trasacco, employed in hospital in Pescina
		leader of dissident *Gaspariani* within the Dc
L Rigazzi, Beppino		teacher, primary school
		secretary, Dc *sezione* 1946–73
		president football club ?–1974
L Ripaldi 'Sindacone'		*contadino*
		mayor 1951–61
L Santirocco, Luigi		cadre, Pci regional secretary
		mayor 1961–1970
Spallone, Dr		Lecce, formerly physician to Togliatti, general secretary of Pci ?–1956
T Taricone, Sergio		trade unionist, Alleanza Contadina
		regional councillor 1975–

175

Glossary of characters

Trapanese, E.		early trade unionist from Central Italy
L Venditti, Biagino		officer, Guardia Forestale
		president football club 1974—6
L	Giannino	secretary, middle school
		secretary, Pci *sezione*
		mayor 1975—
L	Pino	student, engineering
		leader, Fgci
L 'Zoccolante', Loreto		fruit and vegetable seller
		trainer, football club
		activist, Pci

GLOSSARY

affittuario (grande) — tenant (large i.e. of 25 ha)
amico, amicizia — friend, friendship
appezzamenti — 25-ha sections of Fucino land
arretrato — backward
assessore — member of the *giunta* in charge of a sector of public activity, e.g.
    edilizia (building)

bidello — school, college, university porter, doorman, caretaker
bracciante — (agricultural) labourer usually landless

Camera dei Deputati — Chamber of Deputies
campana (campanile) — bell (bell-tower), symbol often chosen by 'localist'
    groups
campanilismo — parochialism, pride in own village
casetta — small house
Cassa per il Mezzogiorno — Fund for the South
catasto — land register
clientela (ismo) — clientele (ism)
coerenza — correspondence between ideas and actions, generally used to
    denote political 'coherence'
comare — co-godmother
compagno — comrade
comparaggio — co-godparenthood
compare — co-godfather
comune — local administration unit (coll. village)
contadino — peasant, now also farmer

diplomato — person with a diploma
Don — title originally for noble, then of general respect, now confined to
    priests in Fucino area

egoista — self-centred
ente — board, corporation

177

Glossary

Ente di Riforma – Land Reform Board

fascisti – members of Fascist Party
fatica – work which induces exhaustion
fattore – factor, organiser of agricultural work
favore (scambio di) – (political exchange of) favour
federazione – organisational level of political party that groups together a
    number of *sezioni*, usually corresponds with provincial boundaries, but
    not in L'Aquila where there are two *federazioni*
figura (bella) – good impression
    (brutta) – shameful figure
    mista – man who does many types of work
fuori-Fucino – land *outside* the area covered by the Land Reform, or the
    property of Torlonia or the lake prior to drainage

giunta – executive committee of local or regional council
graduatoria – promotion scale

libretto – medical card granting entitlement to insurance
Lotta del Fucino – Struggle for Fucino

medico condotto – general practitioner appointed and paid in part by local
    council
mentalità – mentality, outlook
mezzadria – system of share-farming
mezzadro – share-farmer
mezzogiorno, Mezzogiorno – midday, Southern Italy

nullatenente – have-nothing

parente – relation, relative, kinsman
passeggiata – stroll
podestà – mayor appointed by Fascist Party
politicante – member of political elite, political activist
polverizzazione – fragmentation of landholdings
povera gente – poor unfortunates
preparato – knowledgeable, well-prepared, well-read
pretura – the lowest level of the judicial system
prosciugamento – drainage (of Lake Fucino)
prosciutto – spiced and dried leg of pork

raccomandazione – recommendation (letter of)

Glossary

rione – quarter, ward

ruffiano(a) – pimp, go-between, toady – in Luco one who is a political turn-
coat

sacrificio – work entailing sacrifice, exhaustion

Senato – Senate

sezione – local division of political party

sguardare – to look askance at

signore – Mister, (historically) noble member of the upper class

sindaco – mayor or auditor

università – (historically) local council prior to 1861

uso civico – common right

vergogna – shame

vicolo – alleyways (with steps in Luco)

BIBLIOGRAPHY

Acquaviva, S.S. & Santuccio, M., *Social structure in Italy*, trans. Colin Hamer, Martin Robertson, London (1976).

Agostinoni, E., *Il Fucino*, Arti Grafiche, Bergamo (1908).

Alavi, Hamza, 'Peasant classes and primordial loyalties', *Journal of Peasant Studies*, vol. 1, no. 1 (1973), pp. 23–62.

Alavi, Hamza, 'The politics of dependence: a village in West Punjab', *South Asian Review*, vol. 4, no. 2 (1971), pp. 111–28.

Allum, P.A., 'The Neapolitan politicians: a collective portrait', *Politics and Society*, vol. 2 (1972), pp. 377–406.

Almond, G.A. & Verba, S., *The civic culture: political attitudes and democracy in five nations*, Princeton University Press, Princeton (1963).

Arpea, Mario, 'La Marsica e il comprensorio del Fucino', *Nuovo Mezzogiorno*, 5–6 (1958), pp. 19–26.

Banfield, E.C., *The moral basis of a backward society*, Free Press, New York (1958).

Barnes, S.H. & Sani, G., 'Mediterranean political culture and Italian politics: an interpretation', *British Journal of Politics*, vol. 4 (1974), pp. 289–303.

Blok, A., 'South Italian agro-towns', *Comparative studies in society and history*, vol. 11 (1969), pp. 121–35.

Boissevain, J., *Friends of friends: networks, manipulators and coalitions*, Basil Blackwell, Oxford (1974).

Boissevain, J., 'Patronage in Sicily', *Man*, vol. 1, no. 1 (1966).

Bottomore, T.B., 'Social stratification in voluntary organisations', in D.C.V. Glass (ed.), *Social mobility in Britain*, Routledge and Kegan Paul, London (1963).

Brisse, A. & De Rotrou, L., *Il prosciugamento del Lago Fucino*, Typografia Polyglot, Rome (1882).

Brögger, J., *Montevarese: a study of peasant society and culture in Southern Italy*, Universitetsforlaget, Oslo 1 (1971).

Cancian, Frank, 'The Southern Italian peasant: world view and political behaviour', *Anthropological Quarterly*, 34 (1961), pp. 1–18.

Cappanari, S.C. & Moss, L.W. 'Estate and class in a South Italian hill village', *American Anthropologist*, 64 (1962), pp. 287–300.

Cappanari, S.C. & Moss, L.W., 'Patterns of kinship, comparaggio and community in a South Italian village', *Anthropological Quarterly* (1960), pp. 28–9.

Cassin, E., *San Nicandro: histoire d'une conversion*, Librarie Plon, Paris (1957).

180

Bibliography

Colapietra, R., 'La Riforma nel Fucino', *Nord e Sud*, vol. 3 (1957), pp. 78–108.

Colclough, N.T., *Land, politics and power in a Southern Italian village*, unpublished Ph.D. thesis, University of London (1969).

Connolly, W.E., 'On "Interests" in politics', *Politics and Society*, vol. 2, no. 2 (1972), pp. 459–77.

Covello, L., *The social background of the Italo-American schoolchild*, Brill, Leiden (1967).

Cronin, C., *The sting of change*, University of Chicago Press, Chicago (1970).

Davis, J., 'Honour and politics in Pisticci', *The Curle Prize Essay* (1969a).

Davis, J., *Land and family in Pisticci*, L.S.E. Monographs, London (1973).

Davis, J., 'Morals and backwardness', *Comparative studies in society and history*, vol. 12 (1970), pp. 340–53.

Davis, J., *Peoples of the Mediterranean*, Routledge & Kegan Paul, London (1977).

Davis, J., 'Town and country', *Anthropological Quarterly*, vol. 42 (1969b), pp. 171–85.

De Felippis, S., *Il Fucino e il suo prosciugamento*, Tipografia S. Lapi, Città di Castello (1893).

Del Carria, R., *Proletari senza rivoluzione*, 2 vols., Edizione Oriente, Milan (1970).

Di Pietro, Don A., *Agglomerazioni delle popolazioni attuali della diocesi dei Marsi*, Tipografia Magagnini, Avezzano (1869).

Dondi, G., *La riforma nel Fucino*, Tipografia il Agricoltura, Avezzano (1960).

Franchetti, R., *Mezzogiorno e colonie*, La Nuova Italia, Rome (first published 1874, reissued 1950).

Franklin, S.H., 'Social structure and land reform in Southern Italy', *Sociological Review*, 9 (1961), pp. 323–49.

Fried, Robert, 'Communism, urban budgets and the two Italies', *Journal of Politics*, 33 (1971), pp. 1008–51.

Gallese, G., no title, mimeo, Ente Fucino (1973).

Galli, G. & Prandi, A., *Patterns of political participation in Italy*, Yale University Press, New Haven, Ct (1970).

Galt, A.H., 'Rethinking patron–client relationships: the real system and the official system in Southern Italy', *Anthropological Quarterly*, 47 (1974), pp. 182–202.

Giustiniani, R., *Dizionario geografico–ragionato del Regno di Napoli*, Tipografia Manfredi, Naples (1802).

Gower-Chapman, C., *Milocca: a Sicilian village*, Allen & Unwin, London (1973).

Gramsci, A., *The modern prince and other writings*, New World Paperbacks, International Publishers, New York (1957).

Gramsci, A., *Selections from the prison notebooks*, ed. and trans. Q. Hoare & G. Nowell-Smith, Lawrence & Wishart, London (1971).

Graziano, Luigi, 'A conceptual framework for the study of clientelism', *Western Societies Program Occasional Papers No. 2*, Cornell University mimeo (1975).

Gudeman, S., 'The Compadrazgo as a reflection of the natural and spiritual person', *The Curle Prize Essay* (1971).

Guizzardi, G., 'The "rural civilization" – structure of an "ideology for consent" ', *Social Compass*, vol. 23 (1976), pp. 19–56.

181

Bibliography

Hobsbawm, E.J., *Primitive Rebels*, Norton, New York (1959).

Iacini, N., *Inchiesta agraria del Senato*, Tipografia Dello Stato Italiano, Rome (1884).

Iatosti, B., *Storia di Avezzano*, Tipografia Magagnini, Avezzano (1876).

Kenny, M., 'Patterns of patronage in Spain', *Anthopological Quarterly*, 33 (1960), pp. 14–23.

Kenny, M., *A Spanish Tapestry*, Cohen & West, London (1961).

Landsberger, H.A., 'The problem of peasant wars', *Comparative studies in society and history*, vol. 15 (1973), pp. 378–88.

La Palombara, J., 'Italy: fragmentation isolation alienation' in Pye & Verba (eds.), *Political culture and political development*, Princeton University Press, Princeton (1965).

Lear, Edward, *Illustrated excursions in Italy*, vol. I, Maclean, London (1846).

Lemarchand, R. & Legge, K., 'Political clientelism and development: a preliminary analysis', *Comparative politics*, 4 (1972), pp. 149–78.

Liberale, R., 'Profilo di fatti e figure del movimento contadino nel Fucino', *Movimento operaio*, vol. 12 (1956), pp. 446–60.

Li Causi, L., 'Anthropology and ideology: the case of "Patronage" in Mediterranean societies', *Critique of Anthropology*, vol. 4/5 (1975), pp. 90–109.

Littlewood, P., 'Strings and kingdoms: the activities of a political mediator in Southern Italy', *Archives Européennes de Sociologie*, 15 (1974), pp. 33–51.

Lopreato, J., *Peasants no more*, Chandler, New York (1967).

Lopreato, J., 'Social stratification and mobility in a South Italian town', *American Sociological Review*, vol. 26 (1961), pp. 585–96.

Macciocchi, A-M., *Lettere dall'interno del Pci a Louis Althusser*, Feltrinelli, Milan (1969).

McDonald, J.S., 'Agricultural organisation, migration and labour militancy in rural Italy', *Economic History Review*, vol. 16 (1963–4) pp. 61–75.

McDonald, J.S., 'Italy's rural social structure and emigration', *Occidente*, 12 (1956), pp. 432–57.

McDonald, J.S. & L., 'Institutional economics and rural development: two Italian types', *Human Organisation*, vol. 23 (1964), pp. 113–18.

Mack Smith, D., *Italy: a modern history*, University of Michigan Press, Ann Arbor (1959).

Mancini, C., *Il Fucino agrologicamente considerato*, Tipografia S. Lapi, Città di Castello (1890).

Mancini, C., *Il principato del Fucino al Concorso Agrario Aquilano*, Tipografia S. Lapi, Città di Castello (1889).

Maraspini, A.L., *The study of an Italian village*, Mouton, The Hague (1968).

Marcone, N., *Il lago dei Marsi e suoi dintorni*, Tipografia Sociale, Rome (1886).

Martin, F., *Un voto del consiglio provinciale*, Tipografia dell'Opinione, Avezzano (1882).

Miegge, M., 'La politica di riforma agraria nella Marsica', *Quaderni Rossi*, 6/7 (1966) pp. 42–71.

Moore, Barrington Jr., *The social origins of dictatorship and democracy*, Penguin, Harmondsworth (1973).

Moss, L.W. & Cappanari, S.C., 'Estate and class in a South Italian hill village', *American Anthropologist*, 64 (1962), pp. 287–300.

Bibliography

Newby, H., 'The deferential dialectic', *Comparative studies in society and history*, vol. 17 (1975), pp. 139–64.

Pagini, G., *Avezzano e la sua storia*, Abbazia di Casamari, Sulmona (1968).

Parkin, F., *Class inequality and political order*, Paladin Books, St Albans (1972).

Pitkin, D.S., *Land tenure and family organisation in an Italian village*, unpublished D.Phil. thesis, Harvard University (1964).

Pitkin, D.S., 'Mediterranean Europe', *Anthropological Quarterly*, vol. 36 (1963), pp. 120–9.

Pitt-Rivers, J., *The people of the Sierra*, Weidenfeld & Nicolson, London (1954).

Pizzorno, A., 'Amoral familism and historical marginality', *International Review of Community Development*, vol. 15 (1966), pp. 55–66.

Pizzuti, A., *Le affittanze agrarie nel Fucino prima della riforma fondiaria*, Quaderni della Maremma, Avezzano (1953).

Powell, J.S., 'Peasant society and clientelist politics', *American Political Science Review*, vol. 63 (1970), pp. 411–25.

Procacci, G., *History of the Italian people*, Penguin, Harmondsworth (1973).

Rinascita, La, 'Torlonia e Fucino', vol. 1 (1944), pp. 14–25.

Rossi-Doria, M., 'Land tenure system and class in Southern Italy', *American Historical Review*, vol. 64 (1958), pp. 46–53.

Russo, G., *Baroni e contadini*, Laterza, Bari (1955).

Sartori, G., 'European political parties: the case of polarised pluralism', in J. La Palombara & M. Weiner (eds.), *Political parties and political development*, Princeton University Press, Princeton (1966).

Sartori, G., 'Politics, ideology and belief systems', *American Political Science Review*, 63 (1969), pp. 398–411.

Schneider, P.T., 'Coalition formation and colonialism in Western Sicily', *Archives Européennes de Sociologie*, vol. 13 (1972), pp. 255–67.

Scott, T., 'Exploitation in rural class relations: a victim's perspective', *Comparative Politics*, vol. 29 (1975), pp. 489–532.

Serpieri, A., 'La riforma agraria in Italia', *Economia Internazionale*, 7 (1954), pp. 720–42.

Seton-Watson, C., *Italy from liberalism to fascism 1870–1925*, Methuen, London (1967).

Silone, I., *Fontamara*, Editrice Farò, Rome (1946).

Silverman, S.F., 'The community–nation mediator in traditional Central Italy', in Potter, Diaz & Foster (eds.), *Peasant Society: A Reader*, Little, Brown & Co., Boston (1967).

Silverman, S.F., 'The Italian land reform: some problems in the development of a cultural tradition', *Anthropological Quarterly*, vol. 44 (1971), pp. 66–77.

Silverman, S.F., 'Social structure and values in Italy: amoral familism reconsidered', *American Anthropologist*, vol. 70 (1968), pp. 1–19.

Silverman, S.F., *The three bells of civilisation*, Columbia University Press, New York (1975).

Sivini, G. (ed.), *Partiti e partecipazione politica in Italia*, Giuffre, Milan (1968).

Snowden, F.M., 'On the social origins of agrarian fascism in Italy', *Archives Européennes de Sociologie*, 13 (1972), pp. 368–95.

Bibliography

Stehle, H., 'The Italian experiment and the communists', *The world today*, vol. 3 (1977), pp. 7—16.

Surace, S., *Ideology, economic change and the working class: the case of Italy*, University of California Press, Berkeley (1966).

Tarrow, S., 'Communist activism at the grass roots: party involvement and public activity at the local level', *American Council of Learned Societies*, mimeo (1973).

Tarrow, S., 'Integration at the periphery: partisanship and political exchange among French and Italian local elites', Cornel University, mimeo (n.d.).

Tarrow, S., *Peasant communism in Southern Italy*, Yale University Press, New Haven (1967).

Tarrow, S., 'The political economy of stagnation: communism in Southern Italy 1960—70', *Journal of Politics*, 34 (1972), pp. 93—123.

Vidimari, R., *Il Fucino, Torlonia e i contadini*, Coldiretti, mimeo (n.d.).

Villari, L., *Italian life in town and country*, Newnes, London (1902).

Wade, R.H., 'The base of a "centrifugal democracy": party allegiance in rural Central Italy', in J. Boissevain & J. Friedl (eds.), *Beyond the community: social process in Europe*, Ministererie van Onderwijs en Wetenschappen, The Hague (1975).

Weingrod, A., 'Patronage and power', *Centre for Mediterranean Studies*, seminar mimeo (1974).

Weingrod, A., 'Patrons, patronage and political parties', *Comparative studies in society and history*, vol. 10 (1968), pp. 377—400.

Weingrod, A. & Morin, E., 'Post-peasants: the character of contemporary Sardinian society', *Comparative studies in society and history*, vol. 13 (1971), pp. 301—24.

Wolf, E.R., 'Kinship, friendship and patron—client relations in complex societies', in M. Banton (ed.), *The Social Anthropology of Complex Societies*, ASA 4, Tavistock Publications (1966).

Wolf, E.R., *Peasant wars of the twentieth century*, Harper & Row, New York (1969).

Zanatta, A., *Il sistema scolastico Italiano*, Il Mulino, Bologna (1971).

Zuckerman, A., 'Clientelist politics in Italy', *Centre for Mediterranean Studies*, seminar mimeo (1974).

INDEX

Abruzzo, 1, 5, 17, 21; Dc factions in, 45–6; emigration from 64; history of, 17, 67
Accettura, 6, 30, 47, 58, 61
Acquaviva, S.S. & Santuccio, M. (1976), 60
activists: in Luco, 138, 140, 151–2, 153; in Trasacco, 48–9, 58; *see also politicante*; politicians; 'Young Turks'
administration, *see comune* administration
Administration, of Torlonia Estate, 11, 12, 13, 27, 101, 105; farms, 14, 22, 101, 168
administrator, of Torlonia estate, 11
affittuario, grande, see grandi affittuari
agricultural machinery: hiring of, 116; investment in, 36, 113, 114–15; sharing of, 78, 115
agricultural methods: in Luco, 112–16 *passim*; in Trasacco, 74–5
agriculture: dependence of South on, 74; in Luco, **112–16**; in Trasacco, **33–6**, 74 ff; proportion of active population engaged in, 74, 111; *see also* agricultural machinery, investment in; land
Albatros (shirt factory), 39, 40
Alleanza Contadina, 57, 133, 145
alliances: electoral, 26; parliamentary, 27; political, 61; political, between individuals, 5
Almond, G.A. & Verba, S., 58; (1963), 53, 150 n.
Althusser, L., *see* Macciocchi
Amadoro, Francesco, 95, 97, 98
Amadoro, Lenin, 97
Amadoro, Rocco, 97, 98, 127
amenities, civic: in Luco, 138; in Trasacco, 60
amicizia, 54, 68
amministrative, le, 44
Anb (Associazione Nazionale Bieticoltori), 15
Angelucci, Giuseppe, 147

Angelucci, Piero, 97
Angelucci, Scolastica, 145–6
animals, farm: attitudes to, 35; insufficient numbers of, in Fucino, 113
anti-clericalism, 72, 74
apartments, investment in, 77
appezzamenti, 22, 102; distribution of, in Luco, 93; distribution of, in Trasacco, 21–2; division of Fucino into, 11; subdivision of, 22; *see also grandi affittuari*; *mezzadria*
Apulia, transhumance to, 9, 19, 64
assessore, 137
assignees, 105; and Ente Fucino officials, 28; holdings of, 31; in Luco, numbers of, 114; in Trasacco, numbers of, 77; purchases by, 114–54; restrictions on holdings of, 35; sales by, 35, 77
associations, voluntary/formal, 122, 124 n.; as vote banks, 81; conditions for, 67; in Luco, **141–5** *passim*; in Trasacco, **63–7** *passim*; paucity of in South Italy, 63; *see also* cooperatives
Associazione Sportiva: Biagino Venditti's presidency of, 126–7, 142–3; in Luco, 124, 126, 127, 141–3; in Trasacco, 65, 81, 141
Avezzano, 12, 90, 97, 106, 124, 145, 146; bombardment of, 98; communications with Rome and Naples, 87; employment office, 39; hospital, 56, 89; Industrial Nucleus, 39–40; party and union branches, 104; sugar refinery, 12
Azione Cattolica: in Luco, 147; in Trasacco, 66

Banfield, E.C., 7, 53, 63, 69; (1958), 53, 61, 72, 75
banking, in monopoly of Torlonia, 12
Barnes, S.H. & Sani, G. (1974), 43, 164
beet, 15, 34; *see also* sugar beet
Benedictines, 83
Berardo, Conte, 17

185

Index

Bertolucci, 98
Bianchi, Angelo, 127, 156
Bianchi, brothers, 115, 124
bidello (*i*), 40, 55, 100
Biennio Rosso, 96
Blok, A. (1969), 39
Boissevain, J. (1966), 161
Bologna, 78
Bottomore, T.B. (1963), 122
bracciante (*i*), 23, 52, 80; and the Ente
Fucino, 25–6; and the land reform, 14,
106; and the *Lotta del Fucino*, 25; and
the Pci, 106, 151; and the *sciopero a
rovescio*, 14; conditions of, 24, 27, 40;
emigration of, 106; vulnerability of, to
clientelism, 24, 26
Brecht, 100
bribery, 106, 128
Brisse, A. & De Rotrou, L. (1882), 87, 88
Brögger, J. (1971), 61
budget, *comune*: control of, by prefect,
137–8; of Luco and Trasacco compared, 139; of Trasacco, 60
building, 38, 41–2; employment in, 38,
116
building regulations, 60–1
Burgundians, 17, 19

Calimera, 6, 60, 61
campanilismo, 166
canals: and irrigation, 35; construction of,
9, 91; deterioration of, 13, 100; repair
of, 14, 25; restriction on use of, 13
Cancian, F. (1961), 63, 74, 76
Cappanari, S.C. & Moss, L.W., *see* Moss &
Cappanari
career aspirations: in Luco, 155; in
Trasacco, 76
carrots: for export, in Trasacco, 35–6;
neglected, in Luco, 114
Cassa Integrazione, 117
Cassa per il Mezzogiorno, 38, 61, 65, 172
catasto, 20
Catholicism: and communism, **153–4**;
and the rural electorate, **72–3**
Catholics, 152–3; and the socialist movement, 74, 154
cattle, 34, 35
Cbf (Coltivatori di Bietola Federati), 15,
66
CEME (ITT), 51, 145; and clientelism,
39; unionisation at, 40, 118, 145
census (1971), 15, 23, 31, 120; returns, 31
Cgil (Confederazione Generale Italiana del
Lavoro), 40, 66, 95, 97, 145; dissolution

of, 97; in CEME, 40; in sugar refinery,
40, 95
Christian Democrat Party, *see* Dc
Christian Socialist Movement, 74, 154
Church, Catholic: and divorce, 152; and
politics, 69, 107, 153; as landowner,
19; political ideology of, 72–4, 81
Ciangoli, 100, 127
Ciofani, Dr, 46f, 62, 64, 65, 77, 82, 123,
150; and cattle stall, 35; breach with
Mignini, 49; fear of, 56, 81; influence
of in Dc, 50–2, 56; kinsmen of, 52;
political power of, 66f, 164; runs football club, 141
circolo, 29, 64, 137; Circolo Febonio, 65;
membership of, 42; political decision-
making in, 137
Cisl (Confederazione Italiana Sindacati
Lavoratori), 40, 146; and the Ente
Fucino, 26, 40; and the *Lotta del
Fucino*, 104
class: 6; alliances, 2, 6, 123; and status, in
Trasacco, 33; differences and friendship, 68; loyalty, 146; solidarity, 28;
stratification, 63, struggle, 5
Claudius, Emperor, 8, 17, 88
clergy, and politics, 71–2
clientele networks, 137; attempt to build,
in Luco, 124 ff; operation of, **50–4**;
weakening of, in Trasacco, 164 ff
clientelism, 2, **4–5**, 6, 58, 63, **161–70**,
171, 172–3; and administrative
inefficiency, 62; and *braccianti*, 24;
and fear, 55, 56, 62, 81; and job market, 15, 24, **39–41**; and kinship, 70;
and power of elite, 164–5, 173; and
Southern Italy, 5, 161; and underdevel-
opment, 6; attacked by Pci, 58; attitudes to, in Luco, 5, 6, 49, 70, 124,
169; benefits of, to elite, 164; elimination of, 172; in the Pci, 56f; resusci-
tation of, 163; resistance to, 172
clients, 81; alleged leverage of, 162; competition amongst, 5, 165
clubs: in Southern Italy, 64; in Trasacco,
64–7, 81; youth, in Luco, 146–7; *see
also circolo*
coerenza, 128, 152, 156, 159, 160
Colapietra, R. (1957), 14
Colclough, N.T., 58; (1969), 29, 30, 42,
47, 53, 58, 61, 68, 69, 70, 75
Coldiretti, 73, 145, 146; and the *Lotta
del Fucino*, 105, 169
collective action, 64, 95–7, 104–5, 108,
166–8, 170; ownership, of land, 2, 96

186

Index

Index

Tourism, Ministry of, 65
town-dwelling, 30−1, 75
town planning, 30, 136−7
trade unions, trade unionists, 1, 13; action, 117; and clientelism, 39, 40, 55, 81, 164; and points system for employment, 40; attitudes to, in Trasacco, 66; behaviour of, 66; in Abruzzo, 117; in Luco, **145−6**; weakness of, 40; *see also* individual unions and factories
Trapanese, Ernesto, 168
tunnel, Fucino, 8, **88** ff, 167−8; cost of, 89
'turnout' in elections, 133−4

Uil (Unione Italiana dei Lavoratori), 55, 104
Ulterior Abruzzo, 19
under-employment, 15
unemployed: action by, 100 f, 104; list of, 118, 145; *see also graduatoria*; points (system)
unemployment, 13, 15, **40−1**, 100; action by *comune* of Luco, 100; action by Government, 100; *braccianti* and, **40−1**; effects of, 13, 41; poor level of benefits, 40 f; seasonal, 15, 40
Unification (of Italy), 90
unionisation, higher among male workers, 117−18
università, 19−20
university: entrance to, 41; faculty preferences in, 43; graduates, employment of, **41−2**; prestige of, 42; salaries of, 41
usi civici, 8, 19, 33; *see also* common rights

Valentini clothing factory, 118
values and attitudes, 172; of *luchesi* and *trasaccani*, **154−9**; of *trasaccani*, **74−82**; to animal husbandry, 35; to clientelism, 5, 6, 49, 124; to land, 154−8; to manual labour in Luco, **118−19**
Vatican: Guard Band, 125; interference of in politics, 71, 126, 152
Venditti, Biagino, **124−7**, 140, 166; as president of Football Club, 126, 142; attempts to obtain political position, **124−7**; 'clientelist' electoral campaign of, 134; use of official posts to recruit support, 165
Venditti, Giannino, 132
Venditti, Pino, 146, 147, 153

Via Valeria, 8
Vidoni pact, 97
vines, 8, 34
violence, outbreaks of, between *braccianti* and small tenants, 25
voluntary associations, *see* associations
vote: decline in Pci/Psi, 26, 99, 107; fluctuations in the, 129, 133
vote banks, 51, 61, 124; and job distribution networks, 51; and kinship, 50; and personal influence, 50−4 *passim*; transfer of, 48, 49, 56
voters: and kinship obligations, 70; and party loyalty in Luco, **129−34**, 169; and *politicanti* in Trasacco, **54−6**; behaviour of, 54−5, 119−20; bribes to, 106, 128; threats of, 134; threats to, 62
votes, 50; preference, 50, 53 n., 54, 57, 107, 133; spoilt, 133; switching of, 61
voting: evidence on, 53; *favori*-based, 52, 53; ideological, 51; kin-based, 51−2, 61, 62; patterns, 172

Wade, R.H. (1975), 122
wages, 89, 97, 117
wards, electoral, in Luco, 110
water-supply, of Luco, 92, 107−8, 137
wealth: attitude to, of *luchesi*, 156−7; sources of, 93
Weingrod, A., 55; (1968), 61, 161; (1974), 161
wheat, 34
wine, 113
Wolf, E.R. (1966), 161, 165; (1969), 170, 170 n.
women, 158; and anti-clericalism, 72; and Dc, 72; and inheritance, 80; and water supply, 92; and work-exchanges, 110; attitudes of men to, **80−1**; chastity of and its control by men, 30−1, 39, 75, 79−80; in employment in Trasacco, 38−9; in factories (and clientelism), 39−40, 119, 145; in farm work, 80, 116, 118; in mass action, 105, 165; in political debate, 150, 151; militancy among, 94, 105
wood cutting, 19, 33, 34
work: attitudes to, 74, 75 f, 118 ff, 154; factory, 119; manual, **118−19**; of *luchesi* compared with *trasaccani*, 118−19, 155 f
'work-in', 14, 104; see also *sciopero a rovescio*

194

CAMBRIDGE STUDIES IN SOCIAL ANTHROPOLOGY

General Editor: Jack Goody

196

*Also published as a paperback

E4